Finding SONG in SORROW

BY NECHAMA DINA WASSERMAN LABER

FINDING SONG IN SORROW:
My Journey from Loss to Legacy and Light

ISBN: 978-0-578-55652-9
First Edition - August 2019 / Menachem Av 5779

Copyright © 2019 by Nechama Dina Wasserman Laber

All rights reserved. No part of this book may be reproduced in any form without written permission from the copyright holder.

Published by JGU Press. www.JewishGirlsUnite.com
Printed in the USA.

Design & Layout by Carasmatic Design
www.CarasmaticDesign.com

Cover photo by Rivkah Laber

Table of Contents

Author's Note	8
1. Childhood Memories of Love and Loss	10
2. Singing in Sorrow	40
3. Legacy: A Truly Long Life	76
4. The Power of Thoughts	92
5. Shine Your Inner Light	116
6. Embrace the Inner Child	130
7. From Roses to Pearls	148
8. G-d Comfort Me	164
9. One More Light	184
10. Hidden Blessings	212
11. Lighthouse on the Hill	236
Epilogue: Weaving the Tapestry	268
Acknowledgments	291
Glossary	295

DEDICATION

It is my honor to dedicate this work of healing to my dear friend of over 20 years, Nechama Laber.

You gave me the amazing opportunity to be a part of your healing and spiritual journey. Your vision and outreach gives strength to girls and women faced with many challenges and losses, and allows them to grow without feeling like they have no voice.

At a young age I lost my father too and I wish I had the teachings of Torah and spirituality to guide me, like this book will bring to others in need.

My friend Nechama, you touch the hearts and souls of many and you exclude no one.

You have a Neshama right from Hashem, may you go from strength to strength!

Blessings and Love,
Micki Massry

DEDICATION

To my precious children, Chaya Mushka, Chana, Azriel Yitzchok, Shaina, Raizel, Rivkah, Menachem Mendel, Yehudah Leib, Shneur Zalman, Baruch Mordechai, Yosef Chaim and grandchildren, Azriel Yitzchok and Aharon. I love each and every one of you and I wrote this book for you so you will understand how your Zaidy Wasserman is still a part of our lives. Even though you never met him, he continues to give us the strength to rise above the challenges to transform pain into purpose, sorrow into song, and darkness into light.

And to all Jewish daughters around the world: I wrote this book for you so you will know that your soul is more powerful than any sadness, loss or pain. May you grow into proud, healthy, joyful, and confident Jewish mothers and leaders. Remember: Each of you is a beacon of light for your family and community.

Author's Note

This is my story of loss, legacy, and light, which has taken over 30 years. It has been growing within me like a baby's transformation from conception to birth. I breathed through the pain of the contractions to birth my story and share it with you so you can understand others facing loss and the power of creating a legacy for our loved ones.

Having repressed my emotions since I was a young girl, they had become so deeply buried in my heart that I was not conscious of how they influenced my daily life. It was only with G-d's help and the love and support of mentors that I was able to acknowledge and validate the pain to discover a path to solace and healing. It was a path that led me through beautiful places and dark tunnels, a path that unleashed a new light. In the process of venturing beyond my comfort zone, I asked myself, "Do I want to deal with these intense emotions rising to the surface?" I feared that my sad story would define me. But I came to understand that as long as I ignored and avoided the pain of my past, it would continue to control me. Only once I faced it and owned it could I begin to transform darkness into light.

Every soul has a unique song — a unique mission composed from the strengths and challenges we were given. Every person experiences periods of lows and highs throughout their life. It is the harmony of the low and high moments that creates our life's song. Accepting the highs and lows of my life helps me understand that it is all part of the song that G-d intended my soul to sing. Each experience has shaped me into who I am today and has provided me with the insight to fulfill my mission of uplifting women, girls, and their families through teaching, coaching, writing, directing retreats, and creating inspirational resources. Transforming pain into purpose gives me a sense of *nechamah*, comfort and healing beyond the expression of mere words.

I am writing this book to inspire you to use your strengths to overcome and transform your struggles in life. I hope to empower you to reach out to another person in need with your support and love. Encourage someone to pray to *Hashem*, to sing a song of hope, to seek the song in their sorrow. Eventually, the song in sorrow will transform into a song of victory and redemption. May this song spread from person to person and very soon we will sing the song of redemption for all of mankind. We will merit a world of peace and love forever where everyone will sing and praise G-d.

I invite you to continue the conversation and join our global community at www.jewishgirlsunite.com.

With blessings,

Nechama Dina Wasserman-Laber

P.S. You can listen to many of the songs referenced in this book online at www.jewishgirlsunite.com/songinsorrow

CHAPTER 1

Childhood Memories of Love and Loss

THE LIGHT IN MY FIRST DECADE OF LIFE

"My father knew how to make Judaism a joy."

Growing up, I treasured the time I spent with my father. Each night, I'd eagerly wait to hear him walking up the stairs, humming a melody after his long day of teaching, and to see his smiling face when I greeted him at the door and he scooped me into his arms. When he wasn't spending time with family, he was preparing for classes, grading papers, studying, or *davening*. I loved going shopping with him for *Shabbos*; I gained so much from our time together, I didn't mind waiting in the long lines. My father cherished me, often telling me how proud he was of me and carved out time from his packed teaching schedule to tell me stories and to learn with me.

My family's home was quite modest, yet I considered myself wealthy because of the light and love that surrounded me. Our *Shabbos* table was filled with laughter and lively singing, and my parents welcomed people from all walks of life to join us. My dear mother, Daniella Wasserman (now Katzenberg) was of *Sephardic* origin, and grew up in Algeria in North Africa and Paris, France. My father was from Boston, Massachusetts. Together, they gave me the perfect blend of both worlds: my mother's delicious *Sephardic* dishes and enthusiasm combined with my father's passion for igniting souls through *Chassidic* teachings and songs created a home filled with a vitality that inspired men and women of all backgrounds. And, as much as I enjoyed the variety of guests at our table, I also have fond memories of spending quality time with my parents and siblings at our designated family-only *Shabbos* meals.

Once, during the holiday of *Purim*, my father brought home a Jewish beggar from the street. His clothes were oversized, his hair long, and he devoured the warm *Purim* meal set before him. He didn't stay long, telling us he had to return to his street corner to collect coins from those who were observing the *Purim mitzvah* of giving gifts to the poor. It was in moments like those that I learned from my parents how to love unconditionally.

Pesach Seders around a full table of guests, led by my father, were filled with deep and lengthy discussions on the Exodus from Egypt and lasted until the early morning. My father used to prepare and study the

My father leading a lively Purim party

My father's 2nd grade class at Lubavitcher Yeshiva in the 80's

Haggadah with many commentaries, and wrote notes on the margins of his *Haggadah* with great diligence. Why did I think that it was fun to stay up all night talking about the Exodus? My father knew how to make Judaism a joy. I remember clearing off the table after the *Seder*, marveling at the sun rising from my Brooklyn window.

Shortly before *Pesach* in 1984, at the young age of 35, my father was unfortunately diagnosed with a life-threatening illness. He did not let others know he wasn't well and continued to follow a rigorous teaching schedule with the strength of steel. That summer, he was hired by Rabbi J.J. Hecht, *z"l*, as Rabbi at Camp Emunah in the Catskills. I was already registered for camp and was elated when father told me that he was coming to serve as the camp rabbi. As a beloved and enthusiastic camp rabbi, my father broke out color war by composing an original song for the camp. Mattie Hecht, a former camper and friend told me, "I was in Camp Emunah the year your father was our rabbi. I remember his spirited songs, his laughter and smiles that lit up camp like the rays of the sun. I recall when he taught us the song he composed, 'Kingston Avenue.' It was the favorite song in camp. Who would have known that he was, in fact, struggling with a severe illness?"

The light of my father's soul touched every girl at camp. After eight weeks of camp, he had the privilege to speak publicly at the children's rally in 770, in front of the *Lubavitcher Rebbe*. He spoke about the impact of summer overnight camp to inspire future generations of Jewish leaders. He shared with me that he had treasured every moment and

My father speaking at the rally in 770 after camp

From left to right: Mendy, Tatty, Shalom, Mommy, Nechama Dina

he would love to spend future summers in camp. He was so in touch with his inner joy; his spiritual light enveloped everyone he met. My first overnight camp experience was a summer I will cherish forever.

A Letter to *Tatty* in the San Diego Hospital

June 19, 1985 - *Rosh Chodesh Tammuz*

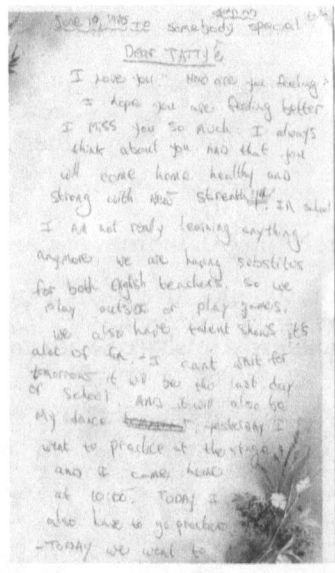

To somebody special

Dear Tatty,

I love you! How are you feeling?

I hope you are feeling better. I miss you so much. I always think about you. I'm waiting for you to come home healthy and strong with new strength. Amen!

I can't wait for tomorrow because it will be the last day of 5th grade and my dance performance. Yesterday, I went to practice at the stage and came home at 10 pm. Today we went to the Staten Island Zoo and it was a lot of fun. We went on a ferry and fed all kinds of animals.

I can't wait to tell you all about it on the phone. I love you! Refuah Shleimah. Get well quick.

I have no words to tell you how much I love you!! The next time I see you, I hope it will be soon, I want to see you healthy and strong with new strength like you never had before! Amen!

Love,

Your daughter, Nechama Dina

I love you & miss you a lot!!!!

PLUNGED INTO DARKNESS

"My world felt dark. I saw my dreams disappear before me."

It was only one year since the summer of a lifetime, and my world looked very different. I found myself in camp once again, surrounded by the same grass and trees, bunkhouses, and many of the same people, but this time the sun wasn't as bright for me. Alone and deep in thought, I rocked myself on a swing during rest hour. The next activity was announced on the loudspeaker: it was time to leap into the swimming pool on this beautiful, hot day in July. Happy, carefree girls ran back to the rustic bunkhouses holding treats from the canteen and laughing with glee. I wished I was one of them. I had other things on my mind. I had received the news that my father wasn't doing well. His condition had worsened as he lay in a hospital bed in San Diego, far from New York. I received the message to pray, and so I did. I yearned with my entire heart and soul for his complete recovery. I had been counting the days for his return. How I missed him! With hope in my heart, I held back my tears and joined the girls at the next activity.

In the early hours of the morning, I was suddenly awakened. I looked around, and it was still dark outside. Was it topsy-turvy day in camp? I didn't think so. My bunkmates were snoring away on the dozen bunk beds that lined the walls. In a whisper, I was told that Rabbi J. J. Hecht, the camp director, was waiting to give me a ride to Brooklyn. My family needed me; that was all the information I was given. In a daze, I gathered several of my belongings and entered the rabbi's vehicle. I felt like a leaf blowing in the wind. I had no idea how much time I would be spending at home. I refused to imagine the worst, yet I knew something was very, very wrong. Rabbi Hecht didn't say a word to me the entire two-hour ride from the Catskills to Brooklyn, and there was an eerie silence in the car.

As we traveled, I watched the cars pass me by, along with my carefree years of childhood. I reflected on my father's words to me two months earlier, before he boarded his flight to San Diego for treatment. He hugged me tight and told me that he was taking a trip to strengthen his health and would be back soon. I trusted him.

I was dropped off at my home on Eastern Parkway and ran up the four flights of stairs to our apartment. My mother's sad eyes met mine, and in her silence, I heard that my worst nightmare had come true, changing my life forever. My mind raced with questions. I vividly recall the first thoughts that entered my mind: "*Tatty*, why did you leave me? Who is going to teach me how to teach? Who will guide me? *Tatty*, we dreamed of having a large family. I wanted sisters. Didn't we imagine opening up a center where Jews would be nourished with Mommy's delicious food and your inspirational teachings, and each member of our family would play a role?"

My world felt dark. I saw my dreams disappear before me.

My dear father, Rabbi Azriel Yitzchok Wasserman, o"bm, returned his soul to his Maker on July 22, 1985, *Menachem Av* 4, at 8:30 a.m. in San Diego. With great courage and faith, my father had battled melanoma for one and a half years. He had departed to San Diego on June 16, *Parashas Shelach* (which means "send" in Hebrew), for medical treatment. Unfortunately, he was too ill to be brought back home to us in New York. He'd boarded his flight with complete trust in G-d that his condition would improve and that he would be back home in good health for his family and students. He told the *Lubavitcher Yeshivah* school principal at the end of the year when he handed in the student reports, "I will be back in September." However, this was not G-d's plan.

I was taken to the funeral by two friends of our family. They held my hands as we walked down the stairs to join the overflowing crowd on Eastern Parkway, escorting my father to his final resting place. I watched in disbelief as the coffin was covered by dirt and my two young brothers, ages five and seven, recited the *Kaddish* prayer. The remainder of the day was a total blur. I only remember walking down the "path of mourners" between two rows of people who were expressing words of comfort. I will never forget the tears on my paternal grandmother's distraught face, as she said to me, "It never dawned on me that he was so ill."

During the week of *shivah*, friends and relatives filled our home, bringing gifts and food. The reality of our new situation did not hit me. I was taken right back to camp immediately after *shivah*. When I returned to camp, I faced a wall of silence. I can't remember if anyone mentioned a word of comfort to me. Campers and counselors didn't know what to say. A friend mentioned to me that she remembers me sitting alone on a swing deep in thought. Sometimes I wonder if the silence hurt more than the loss itself. I must accept *Hashem*'s plan because *Hashem* knows best, but it is harder to accept people's lack of acknowledgment of the pain.

At the time of my beloved *Tatty's* passing, I was ten years old (three weeks before turning 11). My brothers, Menachem Mendel and Sholom Dovber, were eight and six. Three months later, on the first day of *Chol Hamoed Sukkos*, Tishrei 17, 1985, a precious baby boy was born to our family and named Azriel Yitzchok. Little Azriel was called "Baby" for a very long time because it was difficult for us to use my father's name. When he went to preschool, his teacher called him by name, but he didn't respond. His first preschool lesson was learning that his name was not Baby, Cutie, or *Tzaddik'l*, but Azriel.

I did not openly speak about my father for several years after his passing since it was a source of pain. I also felt that it made others uncomfortable — and I didn't want to be labeled as a person with "issues." I also did not want to be pitied. Most of the time, I locked my heart and ignored the pain. It hurt to feel, and it was easier to hide my sadness. There were specific occasions, like the *yahrtzeit*, that evoked

My brothers little Azriel Yitzchok, Mendy, Shalom

painful memories, and it felt as if I was reliving the searing pain of his passing all over again. During the Jewish holidays, we would recite the memorial prayer *Yizkor*; since I had never processed my feelings, it felt as if I was reopening a wound that never had a chance to heal.

I turned to my loyal journal, always waiting for me without judgment, a haven to express my emotions through self-reflection and poetry.

A PEEK INTO MY TEEN JOURNAL

I can't express in words how much I miss him.

April 23, 1989

Another Pesach without my Tatty. I feel his loss even more now and feel so alone without him. He is no longer leading our Seders or making Kiddush. It hurts to recite the Four Questions without his physical presence, though I know he hears me from his heavenly abode. Yesterday, I cried for him in bed. I wish he hadn't left us so soon. I see that life is so difficult for my mother and I don't know what to do. My energetic brothers are difficult to raise without a father.

April 27, 1989 *(Motzoei Pesach)*

Last night I had a dream about Tatty, and he was giving me advice, which I don't remember. I cried for him this morning. I can't express to you in words how much I truly miss him. Moshiach, please come already. We've had enough!

Today was Yizkor. Every Yizkor service is a huge ordeal. The shul was packed with guests, and the gabbai announced after the Torah reading, "Yizkor! All people with parents should leave." I'd dreaded this moment. I wondered which lady would be the one to instruct us to move out. Sure enough, an elderly woman with reading glasses perched on her nose and a big hat sitting on her head pointed to the exit, very annoyed. She ordered Mommy to take my little brother Azriel outside the shul. Mommy rolled her eyes at me and responded to the woman, "Don't you think I know what I am doing?" Later, we thought about revising our response for the next Yizkor. We will calmly answer, "We wish we didn't have to stay." It's hard enough not to have a father, and these shul women only make it more painful.

May 2, 1989

At times, my longing for Tatty, o"bm, makes it difficult to focus and concentrate on schoolwork. My friend Raizy came over tonight, and we were supposed to study together for a huge history test on many chapters, but instead, we ended up talking about our deceased fathers. Raizy lost her father when she was five years old. I didn't even study one complete page, and we have many more sections to review.

July 1990

Today was Tatty's yahrtzeit, and we had a farbrengen in camp with my bunk and the staff in his memory. I brought the cake, chips, and candy that my mother sent me for the farbrengen. We sang songs and learned with Rochel Schmukler, the head counselor, who led a beautiful gathering. I love and respect her. At the farbrengen, I showed no emotions outwardly. Honestly, when I walked in with the refreshments, I didn't know how to act because everyone was staring at me and I was very self-conscious. I sat near Rochel and contained my feelings.

I was speaking to one of the counselors during Shabbos lunch [the day after the farbrengen], and I burst out crying. We left the dining room together, even though the meal had not ended, and I shared memories of my father with her. Later, the camp director expressed her great disappointment when she found out that the counselor left in the middle of the Shabbos meal to talk to me.

After Shabbos, I courageously asked Rochel if I could speak to her privately. I shared my pain with her, and for the first time, I poured out my heart to an adult mentor. I told her that I never had a chance to say goodbye to my father and how much he'd meant to me. Rochel is the first adult that I've shared with so deeply; I feel that I can trust her.

Chanukah 1990

Tonight is the fifth night of Chanukah and my family gathered to light the menorah. My three brothers lit the candles, but there is no light coming from Tatty's menorah. Although we are celebrating the Festival of Lights, it still feels so dark to me. I long for the light of Tatty's menorah. The presents I received tonight don't compare to my father's presence. I wish I could bring back those days when we would listen to Tatty tell us stories and sing songs while strumming his guitar by the flickering flames of the menorah.

Shabbos January 1990

Tatty isn't here to help the boys when they need guidance with their schoolwork, so I try my best to help out. Tatty isn't here to take them to shul. Tatty isn't here to discipline them and show them right from wrong.

Every Shabbos without Tatty at the head of the table reciting Kiddush and Havdalah reminds me of our tremendous loss. When Shabbos is over, we go over to the neighbors, the Malachovsky family, to hear Havdalah. Although, the Shabbos candles are lit every Friday night and the Havdalah candle glows in the dark, it still feels so dark without my father's love and light.

Will my life ever feel right again? Will the light shine again in my heart?

The loss of a young life, especially when the deceased leaves young children behind, is tragic beyond comprehension. The only solace is in accepting that this is part of G-d's grand master plan, which we cannot grasp due to our limited human perspective. We don't see the full picture. It was only decades after my father's tragic passing that I began to heal my heart and discover the light in the darkness. Light emerges when we transform the pain into the pleasure of fulfilling our purpose. It is our difficulties that lead us to our future destiny.

MY FATHER PREPARED ME

"G-d gives and G-d takes; blessed be the name of G-d."

Sadly, experiencing loss was familiar to me even before I lost my father. In the early days of summer 1981, when I was eight years old, my father arrived home from the hospital on an early *Shabbos* morning and sat me on his lap to tell me a story. While I sensed his pain, with his hand holding mine, I felt enveloped by his nurturing love. I was always ready for one of my father's amazing stories — but this time, it felt different. This was no ordinary story time, and it is now etched in my mind forever. This was the story he told me:

> Once there was a woman named Bruria, and she had two sons. One Shabbos, while her husband, Rabbi Meir, was in the synagogue, sudden sickness struck the children, and they passed away before anything could be done for them. Bruria covered them up in the bedroom and did not say a word to anyone. After nightfall, Rabbi Meir returned from the house of learning and asked his wife, "Where are the children?" Bruria remarked that they had gone out. She calmly prepared the Havdalah — the cup of wine, the light, and the spices. She also distracted him while she prepared and served the melaveh malkah, the evening meal with which a Jew accompanies the departing Shabbos Queen. Then, after Rabbi Meir had finished eating, Bruria asked him for an answer to the following problem:
>
> "Tell me, my husband, what shall I do? Some time ago, something was left with me for safe-keeping. Now the owner has come to claim it. Must I return it?"
>
> "That is a bizarre question indeed. How can you doubt the right of the owner to claim what belongs to him?" Rabbi Meir exclaimed in astonishment.
>
> "Well, I did not want to return it without letting you know of it," replied Bruria. She then led her husband into the bedroom where their two sons lay in their eternal sleep. She removed the bedcovers from their still bodies.
>
> Rabbi Meir, seeing his beloved sons and realizing that they had passed away, burst out into bitter weeping.
>
> "My dear husband," Bruria gently reminded him, "didn't you say a moment ago that the owner has the right to claim his property? G-d gives and G-d takes; blessed be the name of G-d."

"My dear Nechamale," said my father, "G-d gave us a precious gift for seven months, and now he has taken our baby, Schmuel Yaakov, to his heavenly home. He is not ours. We, too, must return this gift to G-d."

Unfortunately, my seven-month-old baby brother, born prematurely, passed away on *Kislev* 8, 1981. I will never forget the gentle, thoughtful way in which my father revealed the heartbreaking news to me. And perhaps, he was preparing me for what was to come later.

Our Sages say, "The deeds of our forefathers are a sign for the children." In fact, these deeds are not only a sign — they also provide the strength for us to emulate their ways. I realize now, that on that unforgettable *Shabbos* morning, my father instilled in me the strength that would lay a foundation of faith for the rest of my life. He paved the way and taught me to see the gift instead of the loss. He was a gift from G-d in my first ten formative years. His brother, Uncle Lenny, remarked after reading this book, "Your father gave you more in ten years than many fathers give their children in a lifetime." It's so true. Although I experienced tremendous loss, my father's teachings imbued faith and resilience in me from a young age.

A THIRTY-FIVE-YEAR-OLD LETTER

"To live as a Jew—this is what is real, what has infinite value."

My father, a master educator, is still teaching. His lessons in faith continue to show up in my life in different ways. Years later, while preparing to teach the prayer *Elokai Neshamah* ("...You safeguard my soul within me, and eventually You will take it from me, and restore it to me in the Time to Come..."), I discovered a 35-year-old letter that my dear father had written to his mother after the passing of my baby brother. It fell into my hands by Divine Providence and was a reminder that my father is still guiding and teaching me.

August 1982

Dear Mom & Dad,

The preciousness of our children is inestimable, and if we didn't appreciate them before, we are making our greatest efforts to realize and properly value the great gift that children are. Even now, we consider the precious moments (seven months) that we spent with Schmuly to be more valuable than the most valuable of earthly treasures. We know that we were privileged to have him with us for even so short a time. His precious soul touched our lives, and we will never be the same. He has sanctified our life.

This whole experience, as bitter as it has been, has served to crystallize and clarify the reality of the Jewish perception of life, the world to come, Gan Eden, Moshiach, the revival of the dead. They are no longer theoretical concepts or vague hopes and dreams. Suddenly, with the swiftness of Schmuly's passing, the other world is as real as Schmuly was. Schmuly, my son, is there. Schmuly, my precious, beloved son, will return.

I feel connected to all those Jews who have suffered loss and silently accepted the will of their Infinite Father, who have lived with the faith and the knowledge that the promises of G-d, the visions of the Prophets will be realized.

Schmuel Yaakov lived, he touched our lives; he is gone.

Schmuel Yaakov will live again.

Our lives continue, blessed by the presence of three wonderful children who fill our lives with joy and nachas.

To live as a Jew, a life with Torah and mitzvos — this is what is real, what has infinite value. The ultimate tragedy is not that a child should die, G-d forbid, but that man should live unaware of his life purpose, in a world of darkness, pursuing falsehood, and harming his Divine soul, G-d forbid.

But we are also taught that as long as we have life, we can entirely transform the quality of our life and even change the past. The future is bright!

Take care of yourselves — write. Come here for a visit.

Love, Azriel

BODY AND SOUL

"Just as his children are alive, so is he alive.[1]"

From the time I was a teen, I spent many hours researching the meaning of pain and loss through the lens of *Chassidus* and the teachings of the *Lubavitcher Rebbe*. These concepts helped me battle negative feelings and stay soul connected to our loved ones. The *Rebbe* was a constant source of strength and inspiration for me and my family. I spent many hours on *Shabbos* and sometimes during the week listening to his talks, also known as *farbrengens*. We studied his teachings for hours in Beth Rivkah school, as well as out of school. His holy teachings still keep me going through the lows and highs of life.

I always found the *Rebbe*'s explanation on the name *Parashas Chayei Sarah* very interesting. If the *sidrah* begins by talking about Sarah's passing and how Avraham mourns her death and purchases her burial place, why is it titled "The Life of Sarah?"

The answer given is because the *parashah* expresses Sarah's legacy — the fulfillment of all her prayers and dreams during her lifetime — and so it is called "The Life of Sarah."

The *Rebbe* teaches: When a person shared love, wisdom, and kindness with others in his years on earth, his life did not end. His spirit is still alive. Our loved ones never leave us; our purpose is to keep them alive by living in their ways. When the Torah mentions the passing of our Patriarch Jacob, it says, "And Jacob finished commanding his sons, and he gathered up his feet into the bed and expired, and was gathered unto his people.[2]" The Torah does not state "he died" and the Sages declared, "Our father Jacob did not die... just as his children are alive, so is he alive — *mah zar'o bachaim, af hu bachaim.*" When we live the way

---
[1] Talmud, *Taanis* 5b
[2] *Bereishis* 49:33

they lived, *zar'o bachaim*, we can see that *hu bachaim* — they are alive in the world![3]

The *Rebbe* wrote to a widow whose husband was a fallen soldier during a war:

> *In the World of Truth, the soul of the departed has great pleasure in seeing the members of his family recover from the tragedy, make every effort to set their lives in order, and act as an inspiration and encouragement to others.*
>
> *A bullet, a shell fragment, or a sickness can damage the body, but it cannot hurt or affect the soul. It can cause death, but death is only a separation between body and soul.*
>
> *The soul continues eternally; it continues to have a connection with the family, especially with those who were particularly dear and beloved. It shares in their distress and rejoices at every joyous event. It is only that the members of the family living in this earthly world cannot see the soul's reaction with their flesh-and-blood eyes, nor can they touch it or feel it with their hands — for the physical connection has been broken. The soul of the departed derives special satisfaction from seeing his children being reared in the proper Torah-spirit, free of any feelings of despair or depression, G-d forbid, but rather (as the traditional expression goes) to raise them to Torah, to chuppah, and to good deeds.*[4]

This concept — knowing that our loved ones are still spiritually alive — gives us a foundation for healing. The challenge is to internalize these lessons. In addition, belief in the resurrection of the dead provides us with the hope that one day we will be reunited physically with all of our loved ones. G-d's promises come true. Death is not the end.

---

[3] From an address by the *Rebbe*, Shevat 10, 5726
[4] *Likutei Sichos*, Vol. X, p. 212

MY FATHER'S IMAGE

"My father's words were instilled in me."

During the week of *shivah*, I was told by a family friend that the *mitzvah* of honoring my father applies at all times and in all places, for he is always watching me, no longer bound by physical limitations. I often thought about this concept.

My father's words to me shortly before he passed away stuck with me and shaped my actions later on. On Father's day, I presented him with "#1 Father" mug and he accepted my gift with tears in his eyes, and in his sweet and gentle way, he implored me, "Please honor your teachers and elders and always be respectful."

When I was in sixth grade, on an ordinary afternoon, my classmates were looking for some excitement, and so they plotted to hide from the teacher after recess. The recess bell rang, and my classmates hid around the school building. I remember my inner conflict: "Should I join or not?" My father's words echoed in my mind: "Nechama Dina, please respect your teachers always," and I gathered the courage to return to class. I sat down at my desk and my confused teacher asked me with questioning eyes, "Where is the rest of the class?" I looked up and felt terrible for my teacher, who was new at the job. It was just me and her — and of course, my father was there too, watching and smiling from above. How could I not honor his wishes? After all, wasn't he with me at all times? It was in those moments that I felt even closer to my *Tatty*, in a way that is beyond this world.

This concept reminds me of the story of Yosef in Egypt. Yosef is termed righteous, a *tzaddik*, because of the episode when he was able to withstand the advances of Potiphar's wife. The *Gemara* famously depicts this event: "At the moment when Yosef was prepared to sin, the image of his father appeared to him.[5]" The *Gemara* teaches that Yosef was able to withstand the enormous pressure because he saw the image of his father. This vision enabled him to look beyond the immediate situation and gather the necessary strength to resist the temptation.

Gazing at my father's image as a girl with deep longing for his warm embrace also gave me strength to make the right choices, even when it was difficult. I wrote this short poem when I was 14 years old:

My Father's Photo

Gazing at a photo of my dear father's face,
I truly long for his warm embrace.

Although years have passed since then,
I just had the urge to pick up a pen.

To write about my father so dear,
Taken to heaven, going back five years.

Every day at Tatty's smiling picture I do stare,
His loving blue eyes are so crystal clear.

He reminds me to love and fear Hashem,
And that every Jew is a precious gem.

He implores me to respect others and learn well,
And to do my part as a member of Am Yisrael.

"Ashreinu," how fortunate I am to possess
A father who lived with love, faith, and happiness!

---

5 *Sotah* 36:2

STRENGTHS AND STRUGGLES

"A person's strengths are the solution to the struggles in life."

Expressing one's strengths allows the soul's unique light to shine through the darkness, serving as a bridge between the cold intellect and passionate heart. It is helpful to create a peaceful oasis in order to take on life's battles. I think of this as my own version of "Sarah's tent." Sarah's tent was her space to create and gather strength, and as a result, miracles abounded. Sarah's candles burned all week. Similarly, her light never dimmed even though she faced many challenges. Her actions always benefited others and she baked the freshest and most satisfying *challah* for her guests. As a result, she created a beautiful dwelling for *Hashem*. This was evident from the cloud hovering above her tent. "It is most vital is to create a peaceful oasis — a space, a moment, a corner, in which you have the ability to stock up, gather strength and reinforce yourself before you face the realities around you," says Rabbi Simon Jacobson.

My mode of creative expression as a teenager was writing poetry and journaling. Writing helps me internalize my inner truth and the reality of G-d's constant guidance in my life. I still treasure my notebooks from high school, where I wrote poems and essays to express my thoughts and feelings in times of sorrow and joy. Through creative outlets, we can explore the meaning in the struggle until it becomes a new bright light for the world.

Our gifts from G-d are the exact tools that we need to overcome life's challenges. It may seem strange that a person's strengths are the solution to the struggles in life, but I have learned that my light — my unique strengths — and my darkness — my struggles — are all part of my one mission. Every song is composed of highs and lows. It is the harmony of both that creates my life's song - my soul's mission.

Each difficulty is another opportunity to give voice to the song of our soul and tap into the unlimited powers we possess within to heal ourselves and the world. As it says, "G-d doesn't give us anything we can't handle; along with the challenge, we are given the inner strength.[6]" We don't need to look outside ourselves for the solution; the strength is within the recesses of our soul if we only take the time to search and find it.

Rabbi Simon Jacobson, head of The Meaningful Life Center, says, "You must always know that each challenge, no matter how difficult, comes with tools to face that challenge and come out stronger. Since struggle is the purpose of life, and not just some incidental distraction, you are provided with all the resources you need to deal with your struggles. Whatever difficulty and hardship come your way, whatever loss or setback you are experiencing, you must always know that you have the tools necessary to face the struggle and prevail. Not just prevail but thrive and grow and transform your corner of the world."

COMFORTING OTHERS

"The living shall take to heart.[7]"

From a young age, I found comfort in comforting others, even though my heart was still hurting. I was being strong for others. My high school friends and I once visited a classmate sitting shivah for the loss of her little brother. There was an uncomfortable silence, as no one knew what to say. I remember gathering the courage to share words of comfort with our bereaved friend. My reflections on the soul's journey and the afterlife had given me a voice to comfort others.

---
6 *Talmud, Avodah Zara* 3a
7 *Kohelet* 7:2

When I was in high school, there were twin sisters in our shul who had moved from Australia to New York. Although they were several years older than me, we felt a special connection. I was heartbroken upon hearing about the sudden passing of their beloved father on a business trip to Australia, and I was moved to write them this poem. I saved it in my poetry journal and share it with you now, so many years later.

A few words I wish to impart
Coming from the depths of my heart
I feel the pain you're going through
Because I lost my dear father too.

It seems to you, "How will we survive
When our beloved father is not alive?"
Feeling at the edge of despair
As your eyes well up with tears.

With great sorrow, you weep
For this pain is ever so deep
"G-d," we can't help but ask, "Why?"
As we breathe a painful sigh.

It's impossible to understand
G-d's reasons for trials on this land
Please remember, G-d forsakes you never
He has His plans; He's at your side forever.

Everything G-d does is (ultimately) for the best
He gave us the tools to handle every test
And in G-d you must
Have complete faith and trust.

Please keep strong
Forge ahead and move along
When you feel down and blue
Know your father is with you!

Father is guiding you in every way
From above, every single day
Sending you his love
From the heavens up above.

"V'hachai yiten el libo[8]"
These famous words we do know
Live his legacy every day
To follow in his noble ways.

Our fathers sit by G-d's throne of glory
For Moshiach they do beg and plead
Please, G-d, unite our nation
Bless us with inner joy and Your salvation.

    I tell my story today to inspire and uplift those yearning to find comfort and to turn pain into the joy of purpose. I praise *Hashem* and acknowledge each person who illuminated my path. The Talmud says, "Whoever saves one life is considered as if he saved an entire world.[9]" I am just one, yet my life today impacts my family — my husband, 11 children, and grandchildren, *ka"h* — and a global community of women and girls who attend our classes and retreats. When you help just one person heal, you truly heal the world.

---

8 "And the living shall take to heart." (*Kohelet* 7:2)
9 *Sanhedrin* 37a

MY SOUL STRUGGLED TO SHINE

"She listened and understood my plight."

As you may have realized, my father was so much more to me than a father. He was a mentor, teacher, and guiding light. I looked up to him and often shared my deepest feelings with him. He believed in me and encouraged me to never stop dreaming. The void that I felt when he passed away is hard to describe in words. Grief comes with isolation. I felt isolated and alone in my pain and did not feel that anyone really understood me. I was the oldest child and the only girl in my family, and I didn't want to burden my mother or anyone else with my raw pain. For years, I concealed the emotions in my aching heart and avoided talking about the loss, except to a close peer who had lost her own father at age five.

I was a happy and capable teen and did well academically. Yet on the inside, I experienced waves of sadness. Suppressing my feelings of sorrow caused my emotions to unexpectedly erupt at certain times. I needed support and a safe space to share my feelings with someone I could trust. However, I was under the impression that opening up the issue would make it worse, and that I could make it disappear by not talking about it. I wonder how different I would have felt if I would not have waited until ninth grade to reach out and confide in my head counselor, as described in my teen journal.

When I was in grade ten, my assistant high-school principal, Mrs. Rivkie Piekarski, noticed that I wasn't myself. After I arrived to school late on several mornings, she called me into her office. Fighting back tears, and my heart beating rapidly, I took a seat in her private office. Instead of rebuking me for my lateness, she asked me if everything was okay. I burst out crying. I told her how difficult it was to be okay because of my circumstances. I told her that since the summer I didn't feel connected to anyone in the class because I had not been able to join my friends in camp. (My life had been miraculously saved when I was hit by a van and broke my right leg; I spent three months in a cast from my toes to my hip.) I told her how lonely I was at home and that I missed my father with every fiber of my being. It was sad for me to watch my mother struggle to raise three young boys without a male role model. Although I helped my mother in every way I could, I felt that I never did enough.

I had always been a serious student, but following that difficult summer, I lacked the will and energy to get up in the morning. Mrs. Piekarski listened and understood my plight. She encouraged me to see beyond the present challenge and gave me hope by teaching me to look ahead and envision a bright future with a wonderful husband and family of my own. She lit a candle in my heart that day, and subsequently checked up on me every so often, even calling me out of class to schmooze.

Thank G-d, my world became brighter. I made new friends, including an out-of-towner, named Chanie Pinson, from France. In grade 12, she boarded in my home and we became as close as sisters. I am forever grateful to Mrs. Piekarski for showing me kindness and understanding, and being a candle in the darkness.

My journey has led me to believe that the emotional and psychological damage of not dealing with pain may turn out to be worse than the actual trauma. I totally understand why teens would think that if they seek help, they are losers who deserve to be cast off on an island for misfits. I used to think this way too. However, today I understand that it is a sign of strength to ask for help, and not weakness. It takes courage to be vulnerable and reach out or even accept support and guidance from others who offer to help us.

Often, teachers and counselors ask me, "What should I say to a student who has suffered a loss?" They think to themselves, "I don't know what to say. I don't want to go there and open up a can of worms. Who am I to reach out? Thank G-d, I don't know what it's like, and don't have the experience." My response to them is, "If you have love in your heart and a trusting relationship, you have an opportunity to deepen your bond when it's needed most. The most successful way to help others is by showing them that you are in it with them. Reach out with love and ask G-d to guide you to express the right words. One can never truly estimate the value of a loving and caring adult in the life of a child or teenager."

Since Shabbos and holidays can be a reminder of the loss, I also encourage those who can to extend an invitation for a meal. The first Pesach after my father's passing was especially difficult. My mother's best friend from seminary, Chana Raizel Kagan, invited our family to join her large family in Montreal. The following years, Rabbi and Mrs. Chaim Meir and Sarah Lieberman invited our family for Pesach *Seders*, and one year we even moved into their home for the holiday. Although I loved hosting others in our home, this was much easier on my mother. She didn't have to worry about making Kiddush or leading the *Seder* and the excitement of being surrounded by a large family and new friends helped take my mind off our loss. The Liebermans hardly knew our family and already had over a dozen children of their own, yet they reached out to us with love at a time that we needed to be embraced by another family because we did not have any relatives in Brooklyn. We will never forget their kindness. These experiences also gave me a glimpse into how a large family operates. I pay it forward and we share our home, Shabbos, and holiday meals with others, too. Today, our family welcomes our guests as family, just like we experienced at the Kagan and Lieberman homes.

LET THERE BE LIGHT

"When you are emissaries of the King of Kings, the Holy One Blessed Be He, there is no room for sadness."

Why do I share my story? Why don't I just forget and wash away the painful past?

Everything in our lives — that which appears good and that which appears bad — is part of who we are. My loss is part of me and my purpose in the world. It is part of the unique song that my soul sings. If I suppress my story, a part of me, a part of my soul is not fully expressed. When I share the meaning in my loss, my soul feels free.

From the time I was a teenager, I contemplated the existential question: What is the purpose of pain, struggle and dark moments in life?

The answer is revealed to us in the first words of the Torah:

> *In the beginning, G-d created the heavens and the earth. And the land was empty, and darkness was on the face of the deep, and the spirit of G-d was hovering over the face of the water... G-d said, "Let there be light," and there was light!* [10]

G-d did not create the luminaries themselves until the fourth day of Creation; clearly, they weren't needed before the rest of the world was brought into existence. So why did He still begin Creation with the light?

The first step to any project is articulating a mission statement, defining the purpose of the endeavor. So, too, with our Creator; G-d defined the mission statement for all of Creation: Why a world? What is the purpose of all these magnificent creations? What is the purpose of all of life?

---
[10] *Bereishis* 1:1

"Let there be light!"

G-d began Creation with the instruction to transform darkness into light, to discover the hidden light within every physical object, every situation, and every person. It is the contrast between light and darkness that gives us a greater appreciation for the light.

Rabbi Simon Jacobson teaches, "It's an illusion to think that life is easy and that faith is bliss. On the contrary — life is a battle. And it is precisely this battle that we were designed to face. Therefore, do not be disturbed or demoralized by your challenges, by your inconsistencies, and by your weaknesses. Do not be discouraged — because this struggle is the fundamental purpose of all of existence."

In their first year of marriage, my parents had a private audience with the *Lubavitcher Rebbe*. Amongst other questions, in a joint letter to the *Rebbe*, my mother included the fact that she was sad because she missed her family in France. She was having a hard time adjusting to a new country and a new language.

The *Rebbe* answered all the questions on the paper with his head bent down. When he came to the last question concerning my mother's feelings of sadness, the *Rebbe* lifted his head, and looked up at my mother with a huge smile radiating from his holy face. He gazed straight into her eyes and answered, "When you are *Shluchim shel Melech Malchei Hamelachim HaKadosh Baruch Hu* (emissaries of the King of Kings, the Holy One Blessed Be He), there is no room for sadness."

My mother says that she still lives with that smile, and she felt the *Rebbe* reaching deep inside of her to banish all the sadness. This encounter gave her the strength to overcome the many challenges in her life.

The guidance my parents received from the *Rebbe* applies to everyone. I ponder the meaning in my own life and recognize that I was given a unique mission to search for the light within the darkness of losing a parent at a young age. G-d challenges us, yet He also gives us the strength and believes in us to fulfill His mission.

We say of G-d in the morning prayers, "Who forms light and creates darkness, who makes peace and creates all things." He created everything, both the darkness and the light. While we would all rather avoid the "dark" moments in our lives, ultimately, it is through these experiences that our soul sings a new song. When we acknowledge that G-d created the darkness as well as light, and search for the Divine, we bring peace to the world.

G-d blessed the children of Avraham to be "like the stars in the heavens," because we can't see stars during the day when the heavens are full of light. It is only in the darkness that stars shine the brightest. We can all be a star when we choose to light up the night. This song, which I sang years ago with my campers, is a good reminder of the choices we have in the face of challenge.

Shall we walk in light or darkness?
Night must fall; still, the choice is ours
To look and just see shadows
Or raise our eyes and search the sky for stars

Let there be music, oh yes, let there be joy and light
Laughter and song to brighten the darkest night
Trust in Hashem that everything's going right
"Ivdu es Hashem b'simchah! [11]*"*

---

[11] "Serve G-d with joy" (Tehillim 100:2)

CHAPTER 2
SINGING IN SORROW

MY BLENDED FAMILY

"We too can rise above our challenges with song."

Throughout my teenage years, I often wondered what would happen if my mother remarried and worried about how my life would change if she did. I feared the unknown. I understood that my mother was lonely and knew that remarriage was inevitable. I told myself to trust in G-d and prayed for a bright future. As I matured, I became concerned about leaving my mother when I graduated high school and hoped that she would find a kind man to marry before I left for seminary, so I kept my eyes open for potential candidates.

When I was in grade 11, our school hosted other high schools from around the country for a convention. During that memorable weekend, each school presented their talents. The Montreal Beth Rivkah School performed a song titled, "Three *Malachim* Came..." which was about the noble ways of our Matriarchs, Sarah and Rivkah. The song had been composed by Racheli and Ziva Katzenberg, and their mother, Mrs. Bracha Chaya Katzenberg, o"bm, several weeks before she passed away. Unfortunately, they did not attend that year's convention, due to her untimely passing, but before the Montreal choir performed, they announced that their song was dedicated in memory of Mrs. Katzenberg.

After hearing about these talented sisters, I assumed that their widowed father was probably a great person too. So, I suggested to my mother that she inquire about Mr. Yitzchok Katzenberg. This idea took off, and they were married less than a year later. My mother packed a suitcase and moved with my brothers to Montreal, after living in Brooklyn for over 18 years. I was in grade 12 and still had to graduate from high school so I couldn't relocate with my family. Together with Chanie Pinson, the girl from France who had been boarding in our house, I moved into the Lieblich family's basement until we graduated high school.

A song blends many different notes to create the perfect harmony. Similarly, it was a song that changed my home environment and blended two families together when my mother married Yitzchok Katzenberg, the father of three beautiful daughters, Racheli, Ziva, and Dina Tova. Their father became my Daddy and my mother became their *Ima*. We were welcomed into a world of song and harmony; I remember our first *Shabbos* together and their special *Shir Hamaalos* melody and *Shabbos zemiros*. These songs had survived the Holocaust with Daddy's father, Daniel Avraham Katzenberg, o"bm, and it was the highlight of every meal, with the three sisters singing in beautiful harmony accompanied by Daddy, an expert *chazzan*. Daddy told us that singing these songs brought back memories of life in his parents' home and thoughts of what it must have been like in his grandparents' house, back in Germany before the Holocaust, and all those who sang these same Jewish songs going back many generations.

My new family taught me the incredible power of song to uplift the heart and soul and to preserve our faith and spirit. I learned that with joy, we can overcome difficulties and turn our highs and lows into a song. Just like Daddy's father who never stopped singing the songs he learned from his father before World War II, and his granddaughters, who continued singing songs to inspire others, we too can rise above our challenges with song and a joyful approach to life.

A LEGACY OF TEACHING

"Every cloud has a silver lining."

My dream was to spend a year after high school studying in the Holy Land. I registered in a seminary in Israel and I was extremely disappointed when the school decided not to accept students who lived in a location where a seminary existed. My next option was to enroll at the Beis Chaya Mushka Teacher's Seminary in Montreal. I moved into my mother's new home and when I walked in, there was a welcome sign that read, "Welcome to the Katzenberg-Wasserman Home." With three floors, the boys slept in the basement and the girls had rooms on the third floor. In retrospect, if I had gone to Israel, I would not have had the opportunity to bond and become a part of my new family. I loved Daddy's daughters, Racheli, Ziva, and Dina and was thrilled to finally have sisters.

I was in the same seminary class as Racheli and we quickly became fast friends. We shared a common goal and desire to work with children. Our parents had both been teachers; Racheli's mother had been a beloved Jewish studies teacher and my father's passion for education inspired my desire to become a teacher of Judaism. Our bond developed so much so that our seminary teacher, Mrs. Tzivi Zaklos, *a"h*, once remarked to us about our friendship, "Every cloud has a silver lining." Our huge losses had a silver lining, for we had each other.

Our *Metodika* instructor, Mrs. Sima Mockin, once asked the class, "Who wants to teach after seminary?" Racheli and I both immediately raised our hand, and only a few other students joined us. Out of our class of 18, some were in seminary to study about Judaism, not necessarily with the intention to go out and teach. Our teacher informed us we would be preparing lessons and teaching in the elementary school to complete the course. Although it took courage to give model lessons, Racheli and I welcomed the challenge which would lead us on our teaching path, thus carrying on our parent's legacy. We gave each other ideas and repeatedly practiced our lessons in front of each other.

It amazes me today that my first *Chumash* model lesson, supervised by Mrs. Sima Mockin, was on the verse, "And Miriam the Prophetess, the sister of Aharon, took the timbrel in her hand." The teacher could have assigned me any verse in the *Chumash* to teach. It was certainly a message from Above that this theme would define my life's mission to help Jewish girls discover their souls' songs and the strengths of Miriam within. Perhaps, it was also a message from above guiding me to learn from Miriam to heal and find the song in my childhood sorrow.

Miriam inspires me because she had the ability to listen to the music within the chaos of the dark Egyptian exile. Her clarity of vision to stay on the path to fulfill her G-d-given mission gives us the strength to keep singing the unique song of our soul.

The Talmud says, "In the merit of the righteous women, we were redeemed from Egypt, and we will once again be redeemed in the merit of the women of today.[12]" My purpose was given to me with my very first lesson plan, to cultivate and nurture the strengths of Miriam within myself and our daughters — our future mothers and leaders, who bring unity, healing, and redemption to our world.

---

12 *Sotah* 11b

TEACHING WITH LOVE & JOY

"Words from the heart will enter the heart."

My father was very expressive in his love and affection. His tragic passing shattered my heart so intensely precisely because he had loved me so intensely. It was a love that no one could replace and I felt deprived of his love. Today, I have learned to shift my perspective. The love that was poured into me in my formative years is eternal and remains with me to share, especially with my children and students. I am energized when I pass on the unconditional love that fortified me in my early years, and my heart feels full instead of sad and depleted. We have a choice to think as a victim or a lamplighter. A victim says, "I was deprived of love," and a lamplighter says, "I will share the love I received because I know the feeling of lacking love."

My father once asked the Lubavitcher Rebbe in a special private audience, "How do I achieve success with my students?" The Rebbe gave him three tips for success as a teacher and he dedicated his life to these three principles:

1. Words from the heart will enter the heart.

2. Teach with joy.

3. Be a living example of what you teach.

These principles guided my father's life mission and inspire my teaching today.

My father internalized the *Rebbe's* teaching, "If we do not succeed in igniting their soul and touching their heart, it only means that we have not spoken the words from our heart." As a beloved teacher to children and adults, he could melt a heart of stone. A student named Mindy wrote to my family: "As a teenager, Rabbi Wasserman mentored me with such deep love that it caught me off guard. He thought I was some kind of wonderful person, while I thought I was maybe even a waste of time. I don't know where I would be today if not for his love and guidance."

I wrote the following poem to express my father's unconditional love that I strive to share with others.

My father shared unconditional love
It was a love for being YOU, not for what you do
He saw your beautiful soul deep inside
He spread G-d's infinite love far and wide

My father's passing concealed a love that was so pure
I craved his love and allowed pain in my heart to endure
Is it possible to fill the void when loss we do face?
The truth is that only G-d, our Creator, can hold the space

When I let go of the pain of the past, buried deep inside
And no longer let negative thoughts fester and hide
The veil lifted and my father's eternal love did reappear
A love that mirrors G-d's love for His children, so dear

Thank you, Tatty, for sharing the gift of unconditional love
A G-dly love that still flows from the heavens above
You taught us to believe in ourselves the way G-d believes in us
To trust in G-d and know that approval from others is just a plus

Tatty, You gave me strength to transmit G-d's love to the next generation
A pure love that is not bound by approval or expectation
I will love G-d's children who need love and healing too
My genuine love and acceptance will pull them through

Love will fuel and empower their soul to be free
With unwavering confidence to be all they can be
You showed me how to reach out with love, a smile, give a call
Dear Tatty, your light and love still shines upon us all

With a LOVE...
that is boundless
that spreads happiness
that is so pure
A love that will forever endure.

For many years, I missed my father's love. He had cherished me and often told me how much I meant to him, sharing his love and dreams with me. Today, his dreams are my dreams. I know that his love for me is forever!

I share the journey that helped me reconnect to my father's eternal love, legacy, and light. Today, we celebrate his love, which fills my heart and all those whose lives he continues to impact.

Remember, friends, to tell your family members that you love them so they will never forget. Love is forever!

In Kharkov, Ukraine. Tanya is at my side in the white hat.

ON A MISSION TO KHARKOV, UKRAINE

"We gained a new appreciation for the small things in life."

Racheli and I worked together and supported each other on our path to become camp head counselors and teachers from 1992-1995. We helped each other prepare for our weekly Hebrew School classes at Free Hebrew for Juniors in Montreal and spent summers volunteering at various Gan Israel summer camps, including Denver, Colorado; Rochester, New York; and Kharkov, Ukraine.

In the spring of 1994, we were sent by our seminary on a mission to help the *Chabad Shluchim*, Rabbi Moshe and Miriam Moscowitz, in Kharkov, Ukraine. Together with my sister, Racheli Katzenberg (now Jacks), and Sara Kulski from France, we departed filled with ambition and excitement to revive the flame of Judaism in a country that had lived under Communism for so many years.

During our four-month stay from May through August, we taught in the Jewish school, gave classes to women, directed youth clubs and hosted *Shabbatons*. In the summer, we ran a day camp followed by a three-week overnight camp for 125 girls. Although the food was very different and there was a language barrier, knowing the importance of our mission carried us through. We gained a new appreciation for the small things in life, like soft toilet paper and hot water. In this abyss of materialism, we connected more deeply to our spirituality and our G-dly mission. This life-changing experience helped shaped me and still inspires my work today.

Although we did not have all the luxuries we had back at home, we loved every moment. More importantly, we loved the extraordinary people we met. We were inspired by their intense passion and sincere desire to discover their Jewish roots. The young girls in Kharkov were eager to learn, yet some of the adults who grew up under Communism had a more difficult time believing in G-d. I remembered the words of the *Rebbe* to my father, that "Words from the heart enter the heart." We learn this from the story with Akiva, the once-ignorant shepherd. One day while attending to his flock, he saw water dripping onto a rock, piercing a hole. He realized that at 40 years old, it still wasn't too late — his mind and heart could similarly soften up and be penetrated by the wisdom of Torah. With the love and encouragement of his wife Rochel, he went to study Torah, returning with 2,400 students and becoming one of the greatest teachers of his time. At times, the heart of a student or camper may seem hard to penetrate, like a rock, yet with words from our heart, we can be sure that our efforts will not be in vain.

There was a woman named Tanya who served as my translator, and her daughter was a camper. Although her daughter and husband embraced a Jewish way of life, she had a harder time accepting the concept of G-d, since she grew up learning scientific atheism in school, which attempts to prove that G-d does not exist. We had many conversations, and she often debated our Jewish beliefs. I treasure this precious poem that she wrote, which reminds me to never give up on anyone, even if it appears as if they are not receptive to the message.

Singing in Sorrow 49

There is a girl, her name is Nechama
She is trying to wake up my Jewish neshamah
It's a difficult task, no denying
But don't give it up, keep on trying
I'm a bad pupil, I don't know all prayers
But I'll remember your shining eyes and smiling faces
Because sometimes a friendly look
Is more convincing than a book
We wish you forever and ever be happy and pretty
We welcome you again in Kharkov city
Let G-d bless you with a husband and a lot of kids
And let Hashem permit
In Eretz Yisrael, we meet.

On June 12, 1994 (3 *Tammuz*) we received the heartbreaking news that our *Rebbe* had returned his soul to His Maker. Once again, my world seemed so dark. We felt so far away from Brooklyn, where the funeral was taking place. I remember walking outside and thinking, "How is the sun still shining?" We joined the *Shluchim* on a trip to Haditch, where

the first *Chabad Rebbe* is buried. We sang the *Rebbe's niggunim* and cried for those days when we'd waited in long lines to receive one-dollar bills with blessings and watched the *Rebbe* dance with the Torah and speak for hours on end at *Shabbos farbrengens*. It was pure, G-dly revelation.

The next day, we were back at the camp with the girls. We had all lost our spiritual father; all we wanted to do was cry, but we were on a mission. I thought about how the *Rebbe* felt the joy and pain of the thousands who sought his blessing and counsel. With his holiness, he ignited the soul of each individual he encountered. He taught us to transform every moment and every encounter into one of love, kindness and meaning, and to seek every opportunity to help another. And so with tears in our eyes, we continued to teach and sing with the precious Jewish children, thereby connecting to the *Rebbe's* eternal light. We felt so close to our *Rebbe*, our spiritual father and leader who gifted us with the awesome ability to change the world for the better.

ALL BEGINNINGS ARE HARD!

"His teaching insight gave me strength years later."

Racheli and I returned from Kharkov in August 1994 with a rejuvenating stop in Israel, and jumped into preparing for our first position, teaching sixth grade in Beth Rivkah Montreal. There were two classes and Racheli and I split the subjects. Teaching *Chumash*, Hebrew, and Jewish values involved hours upon hours of preparation. My *Metodika* teacher, Mrs. Mockin, became my school principal, and every Monday morning we submitted our weekly lesson plans for review. It took enormous effort to craft each lesson, learn the many commentaries on the *Chumash*, and make it interactive and engaging for the students. In addition, we had a challenging group. My first students taught me important lessons that helped me grow as an educator.

At times, I wished that I could receive guidance from my father in dealing with discipline issues or tips to motivate girls to learn or pray. I remembered that when he began teaching grades two and four at the *Lubavitcher Yeshivah*, he told me that his first year would involve numerous hours of preparation. I understood that the first year requires more time to adjust and prepare. Certainly, this teaching insight gave me strength to persevere as I embarked on my path as an educator, years later.

I composed this poem in my journal during the early days of my teaching.

The Joys of Teaching

As difficult as it does seem
To be a teacher, I always did dream

To teach, enrich and inspire
And awaken in them a burning desire

To grow and to learn
And for Moshiach to yearn

Now that this job has become real
There are so many emotions that I feel
Am I truly achieving success?
Reaching every student, and nothing less?

At times, I am filled with frustration
From all the work and preparation

There is so much to teach
Some are so difficult to reach

In my mind, the Rebbe's words to Tatty do echo
Something that every teacher must know

Teaching is surely no breeze
Yet, don't be phased by the difficulties

Polishing diamonds is no easy task, you see
It's the holiest profession that can be

Each and every day to You, Hashem, I pray
May my lessons be successful in every way

MARRIAGE MILESTONE

"I trust You, Hashem.[13]"

In the middle of my first year of teaching, I was introduced to my future husband, Rabbi Avraham David Laber, through our mutual friends, Mendy and Batya Rosenblum and Batya's mother, Mrs. Raizel Wolwovsky. I was 20 years old and Avraham was 24. On our first date, we spent a long time sharing stories from summer camp: I had spent four months in Kharkov, Ukraine and he had spent four summers in Moscow, Russia. Sharing our experiences lead us to realize that we had the same values and life goals. We dated for a couple months in New York and Montreal, and we celebrated our engagement on October 30, 1994.

My engagement was a time of highs and lows, and felt like an emotional roller coaster. Although I was excited to establish my own Jewish home, a vision I'd had for many years, I was about to leave my teaching job in Montreal and was searching for a new position in New York City. I worried about what the future would bring and how would we financially support our life together.

A few days before the big day, my father appeared to me in a dream and wrapped his loving arms around me. He said, "Nechama Dina, you must trust in G-d that He will provide for all your needs. Just like G-d sent manna to the Jews in the desert, G-d will provide for you too!"

In the morning, I couldn't believe that it had been only a dream because it had felt so real. The manna is a symbol of our sustenance and faith, as the way it was given was meant to arouse — and thereby test — the people's trust in G-d, for it demonstrates that man's food, like all his needs, comes from G-d alone.

---
13 Psalm 55

My father taught me (and so many others) to have trust in G-d. As a child, when I would complain about being teased or hurt, he would say, "It's better to be hurt than to hurt another." He suggested that the next time it happened, I should say, "I trust You, G-d!" He promised me 25 cents each time I responded this way.

My father's words, "Trust in G-d," were thus planted in my subconscious mind and heart. When I find myself wishing that he were still here to reinforce my faith when feeling down, I remember that he *does* manage to send me his messages from Above. As I embarked on building my own home, I needed to do my part, then let go and trust in G-d.

We celebrated our wedding on a freezing February day. I was thrilled to join a large family, gaining four Laber sisters and five Laber brothers. After a week of celebration, I bade an emotional goodbye to my dear family and friends in Montreal. I would especially miss my teaching partner and sister, Racheli.

Bottom: Daddy Katzenberg, Avraham, Azriel, Nechama Dina, Mommy, Bubby Wasserman
Top: Mendy, Shalom, Daddy's Mother, Même, Racheli, Dina, Ziva

We rented an apartment in the Crown Heights neighborhood of Brooklyn, New York. *Baruch Hashem*, I found a job teaching special education in my alma mater, Beis Rivkah. My husband continued his Rabbinical studies and I also attended Touro College twice a week in order to learn more about education.

Living in Brooklyn was just a stop on our journey to search for a location where we would go out into the world as *Shluchim*, emissaries of G-d, illuminating the souls of Jews with the light of Torah and *mitzvos*. Rabbi Sholom DovBer, the fifth *Lubavitcher Rebbe*, compared a Jew to a lamplighter. "The lamplighter," he explained, "walks the streets carrying a flame at the end of a pole. He knows that the flame is not his. And he goes from lamp to lamp to set them alight."

Eighteen months after our marriage, we moved to Troy, in upstate New York, where my husband had been offered a position as a rabbi in an Orthodox synagogue. A few months after we moved, our first child, Chaya Mushka, named after the wife of the *Lubavitcher Rebbe*, was born. We felt blessed to be parents and elated to teach and spread Judaism. We hosted numerous guests, revived the Hebrew school, founded a Bat Mitzvah Club[14] and Bat Mitzvah Camp, women's programs, and much more. I thrived in this role and loved hosting and teaching Jews of all backgrounds. I finally felt that I was reclaiming another part of my father's legacy, sharing the beauty and joy of Judaism with others, just like we did in my childhood home.

---

14 Capital Region Bat Mitzvah Club is a branch of Bat Mitzvah Club International, founded by Esti Frimerman.

Members of the Capital Region Bat Mitzvah Club, 2001.

BAT MITZVAH CLUB BEGINNINGS

"One good deed had a ripple effect and touched many souls."

In 2001, Emunah Sohn moved to New Jersey from Albany. When her eldest daughter, Eliana, neared her twelfth birthday, Emunah asked her how she would like to celebrate this special event. Emunah was taken aback by Eliana's response. "Oh, Mom, no big party," Eliana replied. "I'd rather just take a couple of friends to Disney World."

Emunah was surprised that a trip to Disney World was her daughter's idea of an appropriate way to celebrate becoming an adult in Judaism. Although Eliana attended a Jewish day school, Emunah realized that she needed to supplement her daughter's education in this area. And so, Emunah reached out to me, as I had been Eliana's teacher at the Maimonides Hebrew Day School[15] when the Sohns lived in Albany. Emunah knew that I had organized a Bat Mitzvah Club for local girls in the fifth and sixth grades, to help them learn about the special journey they were about to embark upon as young Jewish women. She was sure that if her daughter would be a part of the Bat

---
15 Directed by *shluchim* Rabbi Israel and Morah Rochel Rubin

Mitzvah Club experience, she would grow and mature as a young Jewish woman.

Emunah asked me if I was still running a program for bat mitzvah-age girls. I explained that for various reasons, I had not intended to run the club that year. She offered to sponsor the first club meeting at her mother's home in Albany if I agreed to undertake organizing the club. The first monthly Capital Region Bat Mitzvah Club event was publicized at the Maimonides Hebrew Day School and at the Hebrew Academy of the Capital District. We expected about eight girls to attend the initial meeting, and were delighted when 20 girls showed up. Mrs. Sohn and Eliana continued to travel from New Jersey for our monthly BMC meetings and celebrated a spiritually meaningful bat mitzvah.

Thanks to one mother's determination, many new girls joined from both schools and this program united girls from across the Capital Region. We see how one mother turned her low into a high with one good deed that had a ripple effect and touched many souls. This program lead me on my path to focus on inspiring Jewish girls to become leaders.

FROM BAT MITZVAH CLUB TO BAT MITZVAH CAMP

"How can we inspire Rebecca to build a Jewish home one day?"

Every Sunday morning, my husband and I would wake up early and drive to the synagogue to teach in Hebrew School. For several years, we only had approximately seven children enrolled and sometimes it was even less. But my husband believed that as long as even one child needed a Jewish education, we would keep it going.

One of the founding students in our Hebrew School was a bright and cheerful girl named Rebecca Hertzberg. Each Sunday, the

Bat Mitzvah Camp counselors with Rebecca Hertzberg, center.

Hertzberg family would travel 20 minutes to attend Hebrew School. The family began to grow in their interest and Jewish observance. They spent *Shabbos* and holidays at our home. Rebecca was also a member of our newly opened Bat Mitzvah Club. She celebrated two bat mitzvah parties: an Orthodox one in our synagogue at age 12, and she read the Torah at her Conservative synagogue at age 13.

I thought to myself, "How can we inspire Rebecca to build a Jewish home one day? Hebrew School once a week and Bat Mitzvah Club once a month are not enough. Rebecca needs a summer camp where she could bond with mentors and be immersed in a Jewish environment." And so, with the encouragement of Rebecca's mother, Lori, all the BMC members were invited to register for an unforgettable summer at the Bat Mitzvah Camp, founded in 2001, for Jewish girls of all backgrounds.

After eight years of Hebrew School and summer camp, the Hertzberg family took a major step again and decided it was time to send their children to a Jewish day school. Although the school was a 30-minute ride from their home, they managed to bring their children to Maimonides Hebrew Day School in Albany. A couple of years later, they moved to Pittsburgh and became part of the vibrant Jewish community there.

LOSS OF OUR POSITION

"This challenge opened up unhealed childhood wounds."

In 2005, after ten years of devoting heart and soul to the community and synagogue in Troy, the board announced at a *Chanukah* meeting that due to the decline in membership as a result of an aging population, they would be eliminating the position of rabbi. In addition, it was made clear that the building would not be available, even on a voluntary basis, to host programs, such as our vibrant Hebrew school, women's events and thriving Bat Mitzvah Club and Camp.

I found this decision extremely painful and difficult. It felt like my dream to kindle Jewish souls was disappearing before my eyes. We were unsure of our future. We had a very busy household with six children under the age of seven. My husband and I had to figure out how we would support our growing family and sustain our outreach activities without any infrastructure. I was on a meager teacher's salary. My husband was working on building Jewishdata.com, a subscription-based database with Jewish genealogy records.

My inner turmoil was not just because of financial pressures and the loss of a position; this challenge opened up unhealed childhood wounds. As a young girl, I had worried about how our changed circumstances after my father's passing would impact our family. How would we manage? Now, the unresolved emotions that had been suppressed for years resurfaced. As a child, I had tried to be strong and had thought the best way to handle my personal loss was to keep busy with schoolwork and friends. Once I got married, I was blessed with children and didn't have time to think about my own feelings. The problem with grief, though, is that if we fail to deal with the emotional pain, it can build up, waiting deep inside to resurface later.

The truth is that when something triggers and hurts us, G-d is sending us a message to mend our wounds and access new strengths. G-d's command to Avraham is for every Jew: "*Lech Lecha* - Go to yourself.[16]" 'Reach into the deepest, innermost part of your soul; go out of your comfort zone, and push past your natural inclinations, so you can discover the real YOU!'

This darkness spurred me to increase the light. I resolved to continue to host Torah classes, Bat Mitzvah Club, the Hebrew School and guests for *Shabbos* and holidays in our modest home. My parents had instilled in me the importance of an open home with many guests of all backgrounds. My father's dedication to Jewish education also fueled my passion to not give up and go out of my comfort zone to spread the light of Judaism.

A SONG WOKE UP HIS SOUL

"Inside of me, I felt something that was purely Jewish."

I'm filled with warm memories, picturing my father sharing words of inspiration and singing *Chassidic* melodies, which he loved, while banging his fist on the *Shabbos* table. It pained me that after his passing, many friends and students who were often guests at our *Shabbos* table faded from our lives. Instead of our own joyful *Shabbos* table with my father at the head, we were often guests at the home of others. When we stayed home, our *Shabbos* table just wasn't the same without *Tatty's* exuberant singing, dancing and enthusiasm for Torah and *mitzvos*.

Why was my father always singing? The *Tanya* says that when we genuinely experience an attachment to G-d, we naturally burst into song.

---

16 *Bereishis* 12:1

My father grew up in Boston, Massachusetts, and while he was in his senior year at Brandeis University in 1969, he borrowed a Jewish record from a friend. By Divine Providence, it was a *Chabad* record and the *niggun* "*L'chatchilah Ariber*" was on it. He later reminisced on a tape recording that he would listen to the melody while he did yoga, "Inside of me, I felt something that was purely Jewish. I felt something that was so beautiful, noble, and great."

My father was a typical American boy in college and it was this *niggun* that aroused his soul. He followed this *niggun* to Brooklyn, where he spent his first *Shabbos* at the home of Rabbi Moshe and Esther Goldman. He arrived as a hippie and vegetarian and after attending the *Rebbe's Shabbos farbrengen* at 770 Eastern Parkway, he walked out as a *Chassid* and enrolled in Hadar Hatorah, the world's first *yeshivah* for Jewish men returning to their roots. He had found the three things that he was seeking in life: a leader, a community, and eventually, a wife with whom to build a Jewish family.

My father taught himself fluent Yiddish so he could understand the *Rebbe's farbrengen*. He would stand on the bleachers in the back of 770, and translate the *Rebbe's* words as he spoke between singing *niggunim*. He was able to hear the *Rebbe* on *Shabbos* when there was no microphone and translate word for word for the people standing nearby. Many people were amazed at his skill as a Yiddish translator.

My father was often singing *niggunim*. He would hum a melody as he danced down the street, and sometimes his singing even embarrassed me. Each week, he would teach his students a "*niggun* of the week," and they would perform at senior group residences. My father was passionate about educating Jewish youth to sing the song of our heritage because he himself had not discovered it until he was an adult. He could not sit by and let future generations forget about their souls.

LEAP OVER THE OBSTACLE

"The words 'l'chatchilah ariber' were ingrained into my soul."

It is no coincidence that my father's soul was set free through a meaningful *Chassidic* melody that defined his purpose and the strength he transmitted to his children and students. "*L'chatchilah Ariber*" is based on a motto that originated with the *Rebbe Maharash*, who explained, "The world says that if you cannot crawl under an obstacle, try to leap over it. However, I say leap over it in the first place!" The message is that we can jump over a problem and use it as a stepping stone to reach higher. When we strengthen our resolve to keep moving forward with determination, we can overcome all obstacles.

My father lived by this motto. He worked on himself to not let the troubles in life depress him. He continued to teach and inspire others despite his illness. I recall holding his hand as we climbed the stairs to our fourth-floor apartment, while he would be swaying to a *Chassidic* melody. I realize now that he was able to sing, though he was in great pain, while taking each step up those many flights. He exemplified using each difficulty as a stepping stone. Instead of complaining, he sang with his heart and soul and uplifted many others with a joy that was contagious.

The words "*l'chatchilah ariber*" were ingrained into my soul as my *Tatty* hummed the *niggun* while rocking me to sleep. As I faced obstacles that seemed insurmountable on the path to fulfill my life's mission, I remembered "*l'chatchilah ariber*" — to leap over them. Whenever I listen to this *niggun*, I picture myself overcoming the obstacles in life with the strength that my *Tatty* passed on to me. It is a tremendous source of strength and arouses my soul powers to use my challenges to lift me higher.

ASK FOR HELP

"Make for yourself a mentor and acquire a friend.[17]*"*

I felt extraordinarily unsettled and alone and needed guidance to figure out where to focus my energy once we were no longer associated with the synagogue. When I don't have the clarity or strength to uplift myself, I reach out to a mentor. We are taught in *Pirkei Avot*, "Make for yourself a mentor and acquire a friend." While it can be very hard to ask for help, asking for support is not a sign of weakness, it is strength.

I had always admired Leah Namdar (neé Lowenthal), who was a mentor to many girls when I was in high school. I remembered being welcomed to her apartment for the occasional *farbrengen* and being moved by her captivating stories and songs. As a girl, I had spent countless hours at 770, waiting for the *Rebbe* to speak. I remember listening

---
[17] *Pirkei Avot* 1:6

to Leah teach and inspire while we guarded our seats for the *Rebbe's farbrengen* and waited for the action to commence.

I never had the opportunity to share my innermost feelings with Leah back in high school. Nonetheless, her warmth and sincerity had left a strong impression on me. I recall telling my mother one day, "I want to teach and inspire girls, just as Leah inspires me." I remembered feeling excited when she got married and became Mrs. Leah Namdar. Soon after, news circulated among my friends that she moved on *Shlichus* to Sweden to strengthen and build up the Jewish community.

Fast forward a couple of decades to the annual international convention for *Shluchos*, which I am fortunate to attend every year. Before the weekend, I had the option to schedule a one-on-one meeting with any mentor from a list of mentors. I was not surprised to find Leah Namdar listed, and so I made an appointment to speak with her.

We met at the conference, and Leah listened as I described our situation. I told her that we only had a few months left at the synagogue and that we added a one-week overnight camp to our three-week day camp as a pilot program. Leah suggested that we focus our efforts on the overnight camp; she sensed that the camp had incredible potential. She encouraged me to have *simchah* and trust in *Hashem*. She loved our big vision to one day purchase a property for the camp. She said, "You are becoming a place for others to send people to learn and grow, which fills an amazing need." She emphasized the *Rebbe's* teaching that since women are the foundation of the home, when you inspire the girls, you are also impacting their brothers, future husbands and sons. She pointed out that a side benefit of living in a small Jewish community was that we had more time to focus on building a camp community. Leah stayed in touch and even sent a teenage camper from Sweden to our camp. I always felt strengthened after speaking to her.

A SHARED MISSION

"You are never too young to change the world."

It was early September 2006, and for the first time in ten years, all six of our children were attending school, and we were going away to family for the High Holidays, instead of hosting our local congregation. It was very quiet at home. In the quiet, I listened to the whispers of my soul. I thought about how much my father had cherished the last summer of his life as camp rabbi and remembered how the *Lubavitcher Rebbe* encouraged the founding of Jewish overnight camp. I reflected on the Bat Mitzvah Camp we had just organized and remembered my mixed emotions on the last day of a very successful summer.

As soon as camp ended, we had packed up all of our camp supplies and bade farewell to the synagogue where we had spent numerous hours teaching and directing programs. It was now time to grow the Bat Mitzvah Camp program that was still a seedling and cultivate the new relationships we were fortunate to create.

One of our remarkable teenage campers had been Leah Larson from Sharon, Massachusetts, founder and editor of *Yaldah*, a quarterly magazine for Jewish girls by Jewish girls, when she was 13 years old. She showed the girls that you are never too young to change the world. Leah had interviewed me for her magazine about our Bat Mitzvah Camp and decided to register for the summer. During camp we discussed our shared mission to inspire and connect Jewish girls and I had been deeply impressed by Leah's talents and maturity. At the end of the summer, we'd promised to stay in touch.

Around this time, I noticed this letter from the *Lubavitcher Rebbe*, which was a reminder about the importance of continuing to grow our camp.

Regarding the camp, since in the past year, you saw the necessity for this activity, specifically in New England, it is understood that it is worthy to invest the effort to continue the camp for girls in the upcoming year. Since at this time, there are several months until the summer season, certainly, the right attempt will result in recruiting campers from those who can pay what is required to ensure that there is no deficit and even extra funds to pay the debts from before.

You write that you want to continue the camp for the sake of Heaven, yet we see that for something to last, the budget needs to be sustainable. Therefore, it is imperative to do all that is necessary within nature to accomplish this. Since our Sages say, "All beginnings are difficult," the beginning has already passed, and so it will become easier.

With blessings for good news in all that was mentioned through harmony and gladness of heart.

My next step was clear: I immediately contacted Leah Larson. We had a warm conversation and decided to team up. As a first step, we created a new brand that would combine both of our missions, merging Bat Mitzvah Camp with *Yaldah* to become the Jewish Girls Retreat: "Where Heaven and Earth Meet." Leah designed the logo, website, and a beautiful brochure, and wrote about the winter camp in her magazine. She contacted the *Yaldah* subscribers and recruited many new girls; and her talented mother, Evelyn Krieger, also helped us spread the word. We brainstormed for many hours and planned the program together. My sister Racheli composed our retreat theme song called "Be a Star."

Baruch Hashem, thanks to our collaboration, we had 50 campers from all backgrounds for the inaugural JGR Winter Retreat in 2006, where every girl became a star! I still remember the brightly lit sky at night filled with glowing stars at our rented campus in Silver Bay, New York. This retreat taught me how even the darkness can be beautiful — a bright light was emerging from the darkness. BMC members and *Yaldah* readers from around the world, some from very remote Jewish communities, found friendship and connection at the Jewish Girls Retreat.

Several *Yaldah* readers and writers became summer retreat campers and staff members. We grew from 30 campers in summer 2006 to 60 campers in a larger location at the Sage College campus that was down the block from the synagogue where our programs were no longer welcome. One of our challenges was that we didn't have an onsite kitchen; we rented refrigerators and created a makeshift kitchen in the gym, which we used as our dining hall. The food was cooked in various kitchens outside of camp, such as at Shabbos House in Albany and at our home, and had to be brought in each day. My husband, who took care of all the shopping, had to know which location to unload the ingredients for cooking or for camp use. All this required a lot of organization, in addition to planning the daily schedules and activities.

In the winter of 2008, Leah won a $100,000 prize from Wells Fargo at the Wells Fargo History Museum in San Francisco for her work on *Yaldah* and she generously donated ten percent of the prize money to the Jewish Girls Retreat. Thanks to *Hashem*, our summer and winter retreats for girls of all backgrounds grew to 90 campers within a few years.

With help from Above and the power of unity, we continued to inspire Jewish girls through singing Jewish songs in camp, just like my father did in his lifetime. Not only did my father's singing inspire many in his lifetime, he continues to inspire through song, as you will read in the following story.

MUSIC IS THE ANSWER

"Song is the pen of the soul."

"If words are the pen of the heart," taught Rabbi Schneur Zalman of Liadi, "then a song is the pen of the soul." That is why niggunim have no words. Words limit and define, but the niggun expresses the soul beyond all bounds. Beyond words. Listening to a niggun quiets the chatter of the mind so we hear the whispers of our soul.

In August 2014, I was a guest at a Friday night *farbrengen* with Rabbi Shais Taub at a retreat for Jewish teen leaders. They argued and asked him many questions about G-d, Torah, and faith. However, they were not open to hearing his answers and could not absorb them.

Rabbi Taub related a famous story about the *Alter Rebbe* that occurred in the early days of the *Chabad* movement, when the first *Chabad Rebbe*, Rabbi Schneur Zalman of Liadi, faced strong opposition to spreading his *Chassidic* teachings. Once, he arrived in a city full of Torah scholars, and he invited everyone to gather in the main synagogue where everyone had a chance to ask their questions and voice their arguments against him. He assured them that he would answer every question and that he wouldn't leave until everyone was satisfied.

After everyone had asked their questions, the *Alter Rebbe* ascended the platform and gazed at each person in the crowd. Instead of speaking, he sang a *niggun* from the depths of his soul, a song that was not limited to words. Soon, the entire crowd was singing along with him.

After several long minutes of singing, everyone opened their eyes. "Do you still have questions?" the *Alter Rebbe* asked. "No," they responded; everything was clarified, so they didn't have any more questions. Their arguments seemed resolved and he was free to go.

Soon after, all their questions returned as they came down from their enraptured state. They ran after the *Alter Rebbe* and cried, "What have you done to us? We still have our questions!"

The *Alter Rebbe* answered, "There are gates in heaven that cannot be opened, except through song. I wanted to show you that there is a higher level than intellect, which we reach through song. By singing the *niggun*, you were able to feel the soul that has no boundary; when you feel the soul, your faith is revealed, and there are no questions or doubts."

Rabbi Taub suggested that it was time to sing a *niggun* to help them focus on the real questions and accept the answers, and they sang the *niggun* "Keili Atah - You are my G-d[18]" together. After the song, the teens argued that the niggun didn't open their hearts and they continued to question without being receptive to the rabbi's answers. They did not yet hear it or feel it.

---
18 *Tehillim* 118:28

I offered to share a personal story about my father and told them about his experience with the *niggun* in his senior year in college. The teens received the message, and with great enthusiasm, this small group of young American Jews from every background closed their eyes and sang the same *niggun* "L'chatchilah Ariber" from the depths of their souls. When they opened their eyes, they had reached a whole new appreciation for their faith and their souls were ignited. The "Ask the Rabbi" *farbrengen* continued until 6:00 a.m. Their hearts were opened so that they could hear the answers to their questions. And so their night turned into day, and their darkness (confusion) turned into light (clarity). And in the morning, the rabbi and several teens thanked me for sharing my father's story. I thanked my *Tatty* again for guiding me to inspire others through the *niggun* that helped him discover his soul.

Song preserves our faith and spirit, it opens our hearts and reminds us to return to our true selves. In those times when it's easy to lose faith and trust in G-d's master plan, we can sing a *niggun* or a song with a message of hope and faith in *Hashem*. Songs repeat themselves over and over until the message becomes integrated and a part of us. Faith is embedded in our soul as an inheritance from Avraham and Sarah; our purpose is to find it and express it.

SINGING WITH MÊME AND MIRIAM

"Hold on to Miriam's tambourine."

During a bleak and cold winter, on *Shevat* 7, my beloved maternal grandmother, *Même* Rachel, returned her precious soul to her maker. She was 93 years old. My sister-in-law Leah told me that when she notified her family, they immediately asked, "Is that the grandmother who danced at your wedding and was the life of the party?" She rejoiced and danced at all of our family celebrations well into her 80s!

Singing in Sorrow 71

Même dancing at a family simchah.

The week of my grandmother's passing was *Parashas Beshalach*. In the Torah reading it says, "Miriam the Prophetess, the sister of Aharon, took the timbrel in her hand; and all the women followed her with timbrels and dances...[19]" Miriam prepared the instruments while her people were suffering in Egypt. When Pharaoh decreed to drown all the baby boys in the Nile river, husbands and wives separated so their children wouldn't be killed. But five-year-old Miriam prophesied and told her father, "Mother will have a baby boy who will redeem us from this darkness."

Amram listened and remarried Yocheved. Miriam danced with the same tambourine at the remarriage of her parents, Amram and Yocheved, that she used to sing at the splitting of the sea years later. Moshe was born, but the darkness of the Egyptian slavery became more intense. Nevertheless, Miriam held onto her timbrel, and proclaimed, "We will be redeemed, and we will dance with our tambourines." All the women prepared their instruments just like Miriam. Miriam's name means "bitterness" and "rebellion," from the root "*meri*." Miriam rebelled against the bitterness of her time with faith and joy.

I was feeling overwhelmed by the darkness, and the Torah reading reminded me to have faith and hold on to Miriam's tambourine and dance. Similarly, *Même* Rachel's life was fraught with hardships, but she never stopped dancing. Her family had to restart their life in France after fleeing Constantine, Algeria in 1962 because of the Arab militant takeover. In France, she faced financial struggles and worked hard to

---
[19] *Shemos* 15:20-21

Même, center, at my brother Shalom's wedding.

raise her family. Later in life, she faced health challenges and loneliness. Nevertheless, despite all the difficulties she encountered, she was always ready to party, and her eyes sparkled with joy as she sang to her grandbabies and danced in the middle of our dining room, turning an ordinary day into the extraordinary.

Even in her later years, *Même* Rachel sang and clapped her hands from her wheelchair. She rejoiced in our *simchos* and cried with us in our sorrows. We thankfully spent time with her once we no longer worked for the synagogue and had the chance to visit her in Montreal on the holidays of *Sukkos* and *Shavuos*. She was the regal matriarch of our family and helped raise her grandchildren and great-grandchildren with love and laughter.

I was in Troy, New York, feeling despondent and teary-eyed, while my mother and extended family were sitting *shivah* in Jerusalem. Baby Baruch was crying more than usual and my two-year-old son, Schneur, kept asking me, "What happened, Mommy?" I thought to myself, "What would *Même* do to cheer us up right now?" Hanging on my wall were beautiful hand-painted tambourines decorated at camp. Baruch and Schneur held a tambourine as we danced with *Même* in our hearts, and we sang some of her favorite songs. My precious children smiled and laughed, and I knew *Même* was smiling and laughing along with us. This, I realized, was how I could keep my father's and *Même*'s legacies alive: by singing, dancing, and spreading joy, just like they did, through the highs and lows of life.

Miriam and my *Même* give me the strength to hear the music in the noise of life. A song includes highs and lows. Similarly, the ups and downs of life are all part of the one beautiful song of our souls. When life is experienced as a song, it is much easier to maintain faith in difficult times. We keep singing, even in the sorrow and disappointment, and eventually compose a new song expressing our greatest joy.

CELEBRATE POTENTIAL

"We descend in order to rise higher."

I traveled to Montreal on *Tu B'Shevat* (*Shevat* 15), when we celebrate the new year for trees, to be *menachem avel* my mother, who had just returned from Israel to finish sitting *shivah* at home with her family and friends. It was cold, and the trees and ground were covered with snow. I reflected on the conundrum of why we celebrate the birthday for trees in the middle of winter, when it is still cold and the trees are bare without any sign of growth.

When I looked around, I saw so much pain in the world. My dear mother was mourning the passing of her mother. A special friend, Miriam Rav-Noy, who was my student and first camp counselor, had lost her husband, Rabbi Ariel, and was left with seven young children. My friend, Emunah Sohn was mourning the passing of her father.

How can we celebrate when the good in life is concealed from us?

Tu B'Shevat reminds us that there is more to life than what meets the eye. We enjoy the taste of sweet fruits and renew our hope and faith in the coming of spring and the end of the cold winter. On this day, when the sap is beginning to flow deep within the trees, we celebrate potential — our faith in a brighter future.

This message is especially meaningful to me as a Jewish educator working with bat-mitzvah-age girls. When a Jewish girl becomes bat mitzvah at age 12, we celebrate the wonderful potential within her. On this day, she is given her complete soul, with all the power to blossom into a beautiful daughter of Israel.

My life's journey demonstrates this lesson, that in the concealment and quiet, there is growth and expansion. When the world seems bare and cold, underneath is the beginning of a new era. This is the process of growth, just like a caterpillar in a cocoon or an infant in the mother's womb. Similarly, the Jews had to descend into Egypt in order to rise to greater heights and become the Jewish Nation to receive the Torah on Mount Sinai. "*Yeridah l'tzorech aliyah*" — we descend in order to rise higher.[20] My father's words ring true, "In the lowest moments, we can access our highest potential."

My friend Chana Cotter taught art at Bat Mitzvah Camp during our transition year from the synagogue. When I reminisced with her about those days and shared the inner turmoil that I felt at the time, she remarked, "I would never have known that you were experiencing pain. You were totally immersed in teaching your students and caring for your children." I reflected on her words. My father and my mother both taught me to be strong and to carry on with my mission, with a *L'chatchilah Ariber* approach, despite my personal circumstances. My mother devoted herself fully to her family despite the sadness and emptiness that she felt inside when she was alone.

Rabbi Levi Goldstein, colleague of my father, shared the most valuable teaching tip he learned from my father: "When you walk into the classroom, you leave your personal baggage behind. You are there to fully focus on each student's needs." This vital skill to stay on the path of purpose even in the low of life and keep singing, was ingrained in me at an early age by both of my parents.

---

20 *Torah Or, Bereishis* 30a

CHAPTER 3

Legacy: A Truly Long Life

BITTERSWEET MEMORIES

"Who will tell the stories to the future generations?"

Mazal tov! It was *Erev Sukkos* 2010 and we were celebrating the engagement and birthday of my dear brother, Azriel, in Montreal. My future sister-in-law Chana and I were getting acquainted. "Azriel doesn't know anything about his namesake," she said. "When he tells people his name is Azriel Wasserman, they say to him, 'Your father was a great man.' And that's all he knows."

Her comment brought me back to *Sukkos* 1995, a mere three months after my father's passing, when Azriel was born. I had wished my father was alive to meet our new baby boy. I remembered how elated he had been to share the news that my mother was expecting. Azriel's birth filled a huge void. The joy and distraction of a new baby also served to remove some measure of our pain.

Chana's comment made a deep impression on me. I thought about it and asked myself, "Who will be the one to pass on the memories?

"Who will tell the stories to the future generations?" I had just turned 37, the exact age my father had been at the time of his passing, and felt responsible to keep his legacy of love and joy alive. I committed to preserve

Chana and Azriel at their wedding

and present his memory for the sake of Azriel, my brothers, grandchildren and future generations.

After decades of silence, I yearned to reconnect with my father's legacy. Unfortunately, because his passing occurred at such a young age, his memory evoked much sadness. I realized he would not want his memory to be a source of sorrow when his life had been one of tremendous joy. I excused myself from the hustle and bustle of the holiday preparations, and with my husband's help, I spent numerous hours scanning and compiling pictures and writing stories to go along with photos. It was time to uncover his legacy of love and joy.

About a year and a half later in January 2012, I presented a 60-page memory book filled with pictures and stories to my three brothers, Mendy, Shalom, and Azriel, and their families. I also sent them the audio recordings of my father; these were tapes he had recorded for his parents before long-distance phone calls were free. We had them digitized, and for the first time, at the age of 26, Azriel heard our father's sweet and powerful voice and got a glimpse of the father he had never met. He remarked that he never realized how much he was missing. Thank G-d, the timing was right and the newly-explored void in his life was filled with the blessing of his first child, a baby girl named Eliana Leah after my father's mother, Bubby Leah Wasserman.

A GLOBAL MEMORIAL GATHERING

"They don't want to be forgotten."

Our next project to honor my father's legacy was a memorial organized the following summer for his 27th *yahrtzeit* on August 20, 2012. It wasn't easy to gather family and friends after so many years and share memories about my father. I prayed that the memorial would go smoothly. While I shopped for the refreshments, I met Mrs. Hinda Gurary, whom I knew from Montreal and was visiting her New York family. She asked me why I was in Crown Heights and when I told her the reason, she shared with me a message straight from heaven. She related to me that her mother passed away when her youngest brother, Rav Sholom Ber Chaikin was a newborn. Once, after a long and exhausting trip to her mother's burial spot in Belgium, she asked her older brother, the Chief Rabbi, "Is this worth all the effort?" Her brother, whose name is Azriel, replied, "Yes, it is worth all the effort because they don't want to be forgotten!" In her words, I heard my father thanking me for sharing his life with others so he will never be forgotten!

How does it happen that loved ones are forgotten? The answer is that often, our experiences of pain and loss become a barrier between the past and present. Since it's too painful to face, we limit our connection to the precious memories of our loved ones. Unfortunately, treasured memories are lost or become tainted by the pain. Yet, when we push through the pain and share the precious memories, the beauty of the person's life returns to our lives. We feel a new sense of freedom from the pain in our hearts.

A TRULY LONG LIFE

"I shall dwell in the House of the L-rd for many long years.²¹"

At the memorial, we were spellbound as friends, family, and students shared the lasting impact my father had on their lives. The lineup of illustrious speakers included Rabbi Beryl Epstein, *Rosh Yeshivah* Hadar Hatorah Rabbi Yakov Goldberg, Rabbi Levi Goldstein, Avraham Kamman, Rabbi Shmaya Katzen, Meir Langer, Rabbi Shmuel Metzger, Rabbi Abba Paltiel, Mark Powers, Meir Rosenberger, Rabbi Schwartz, and Mendel Shagalov. As we celebrated my father's life and his shining legacy, the Torah Cafe team live-streamed the event, which was held in Brooklyn, and it was uploaded to YouTube.

It had already been 27 years since my father's passing, yet from the way people spoke, it felt like it was only 30 days. I was comforted, knowing that after so many years, my father was still alive in people's hearts and he was not forgotten. I heard from all the speakers a similar message: "Rabbi Wasserman accomplished more in 37 years than many others in a lifetime." **This** is the meaning of a "truly long life," a life that keeps giving and empowering others even after the person's physical passing.

Once I began to share my father's legacy, his light was reflected back at me. Many people whose lives he touched continued to share their memories with me after the memorial. I was

---

21 *Tehillim* 23:6

grateful for the opportunity to honor my father's memory in this unforgettable way.

Benzion Welton, my father's learning partner, wrote this letter to our family in response to the memorial's announcement:

> *I think about Rabbi Wasserman on Shabbos every time I say "Mizmor l'Dovid." When I heard him say this, I did not know that he was in pain. How could I? I saw his shining countenance repeating the last line, over and over again, with meaning in every word. The Sweet Singer of Israel, Dovid HaMelech, and your father say, "Only goodness and kindness shall follow me all the days of my life, and I shall dwell in the House of the L-rd for many long years." Your father lived a truly long life, for he still has an impact on people today and will continue to have an impact for "many long years."*

I now understand the meaning of "a truly long life" and shared my father's legacy with the intention to inspire others and, in turn, others inspired me. It was a joy to reconnect with my father's legacy and the friends and students whose lives he impacted. This was another major step in my healing journey of turning the pain of loss into the joy of legacy.

LESSONS NEVER FORGOTTEN

"This is life; you gotta take it as it comes!"

During this time, we were staying at the home of Yakov and Tzivia Chaya Rosenthal in Brooklyn. She related that one *Shavuos*, on the way to hear the Ten Commandments in *shul*, it was pouring buckets. (The *Lubavitcher Rebbe* encouraged everyone to attend *shul* for the reading of the Ten Commandments, including very young children.) She saw my father standing at the intersection with my family, waiting for the light to turn green, while cars rushed by, splashing gigantic puddles in our faces. After this happened a couple of times, my father smiled and said,

"This is life; you gotta take it as it comes!" He taught us that even in the storms of life, we can smile because the sun will always come out again.

Dobra Spinner, one of my father's students at Machon Chana, gave me a treasure at the memorial gathering, She handed me a folder and said, "I have been holding on to these notes from your father's last classes before his passing and now I'm giving them to you." This was a gift from my father for my efforts to share his legacy with the world.

The topic of his last classes on earth was "The Power of Thought: Think Positive, Rise Above the Challenges"!

The very last paragraph in those notes read, *"If a chassid[22] developed a potentially fatal illness, it wouldn't change him. It would motivate him to work harder to overcome any negative thoughts with a positive mindset. He would recognize his even greater need to counteract the darkness with more light."*

His students had not had any idea that he was suffering from a life-threatening illness. Although he wasn't well, he expressed joy until his last day on earth. I used to wonder why he never wrote us a letter with his final message to us. These notes are my answer. They portray his faith, so real, until his last moments, and since he never gave up hope, a goodbye letter was never written. These notes are his last words, inspiring us to live with faith and joy.

Why weren't these 30-year-old notes revealed to me earlier in my life? Because I wasn't ready... but I was ready now! The time was right for me to receive these teachings for my own healing and to share my father's legacy with the world. At times I felt overwhelmed and stressed by all my responsibilities. I read the notes and wanted to turn the inspiration into action and to internalize my father's positivity and secret

---

[22] A *chassid* is a pious person — one who goes "beyond the line of the law" in his duties toward G-d and man. A *chassid* is someone who relates to the soul of a thing rather than its body, to its inner essence rather than its external manifestations.

for consistently living with joy. I typed out the notes and shared them with the JGR staff at the winter retreat and they resulted in deep and meaningful discussions.

Before we left New York, we went to visit the *Ohel* of the *Rebbe*, where my father is buried close by. I reread my father's monument which said, "*A G-d fearing man involved with the work of Heaven with faith, teacher at Tomchei Temimim and Machon Chana. Dedicated his heart and soul until his last day to bring Jewish people closer to their Father in Heaven.*" I had a heart-to-heart conversation with him as tears streamed down my face. "*Tatty*, I feel so much closer to you and miss you so much more. I reconnected to you through so many people who were impacted by your life. I met people who watched the live broadcast (of the memorial) and told me how much it inspired them. Your legacy is strong!"

Shortly after, I received a call from a mother inquiring about the summer retreat. At the end of the conversation, she realized I was the daughter of Rabbi Wasserman, her beloved teacher in Machon Chana. She shared with me three lessons that my father taught her. He explained in his classes that it is easy to judge another person and see how they are different than you. It is natural to notice external qualities that may not be so appealing. Yet, we can — and must — look deeper and see the beauty in each person.

I told her that this is our mission at the Jewish Girls Retreat, where we treat every girl like a precious diamond and help her shine brightly. It is comforting to hear again and again that my father's teachings are still a guiding light for his students.

I mentioned to her that a student from Tzohar Seminary was writing a script for the camp movie production, which was about how my father mentored a teenager.[23] She replied, "I don't know much about the Tzohar school, but I do remember your father teaching us a lesson

---

[23] The movie was called *A New Leaf* and is available for purchase in the JGU Shop.

using the word "*tzohar*." *Tzohar* refers to the stone on top of Noah's Ark that provided light. The letters of *tzohar* also spell *tzarah*. Your father would say, '**Every *tzarah* (pain) can be transformed into the *tzohar* (light) in your life.**'"

The third lesson that Miriam remembered was from a class that had been momentarily disrupted by teens playing loud music outside on their boomboxes. Most teachers would have been annoyed by the disturbance, but my father just smiled and told his students, "*Chassidus* must be the boombox that we share with the entire world."

As we see from the stories above, my father's teachings are alive and so he is alive in so many hearts. It is comforting to witness that the seeds he planted in his students and children continue to bear fruit until this very day.

MY FATHER'S VOICE SAVES ONE SOUL

"A Jew is a Jew and a non-Jew is a non-Jew... they each have a purpose in the world."

Shortly after the *yahrtzeit* gathering, my father's voice had a tremendous impact on a Jewish girl in our community. The daughter of Jewish immigrants from Russia, Shulamit (not her real name) attended Maimonides Hebrew Day School. After high school, she attended a local community college and was involved with the Friendship Circle,[24] a community for children with special needs. One Sunday she offered to drive my daughter home from volunteering for Friendship Circle. We were excited to see her, as we hadn't seen her in almost a year, and invited her to stay for dinner.

---

[24] Friendship Circle is an international organization founded by Bassie Shemtov. The Capital Region Friendship Circle was directed by Liba Andrusier at the time.

We schmoozed while we waited for the food to heat up in the oven. I asked her about college and she told me that she was very busy. An idea popped into my mind to play the recording I had recently digitized of my father speaking about intermarriage and the purpose of a Jew, over 40 years earlier. He recorded these words on an old tape recorder for his mother because someone he loved was going to intermarry. I thought that since this girl was in a college with very few Jews, she could use the inspiration and reminder to stay strong.

I played the track of my father speaking these words from his heart:

My relationship to Torah is one that is true and everlasting. Torah is the basis of our existence. A Jew is a Jew and a non-Jew is a non-Jew and they each have a purpose in the world. A Jew's purpose is not fulfilled by marrying a non-Jew and a non-Jew's purpose is not fulfilled by marrying a Jew. If they do marry, it is not a marriage according to Torah. The Torah doesn't accept her as part of our family unless one day she will convert. I know this is a great source of pain. I have a Torah that I live by and it's more important to me than my own life. Torah goes beyond human life. It's from G-d, it's the most important thing in life. There is a G-d and Torah and all sins will be forgiven. We will go out of exile with all Jews, even those Jews who don't know they are Jews.

Shulamit listened very intently and left, thanking me for sharing my father's voice with her. I told her that I hoped to see her again soon. One week later, I was surprised to see Shulamit at a *Chabad* women's event. Shulamit came to sit near me and told me she had something to tell me. She revealed to me that on Monday, the day after she was at our home, her non-Jewish boyfriend presented her with a diamond ring and proposed to her. She had been in a relationship with him for over three years, and he had finally saved up enough money for the ring.

My father's words echoed in her head and she said, "I cannot marry you," shocking him with her refusal. "But we've invested so much time into each other," he said. "We are meant to be together!" He went crazy. He couldn't accept her answer. So she told him to go to the *Chabad* campus rabbi for an explanation.

Shulamit left for Israel shortly after and returned to her roots. She started to keep *Shabbos* and eat *kosher* and now looks forward to building her own Jewish home. Shulamit says today, that my father's voice was guiding her from Above. She could hear the pain in his voice and realized the pain she would cause her family if she intermarried. By Divine Providence, she had visited me the day before her boyfriend proposed. My father said these words so long ago, but they gave her the strength to say "No." Just like my father's words touched so many in his lifetime, his influence continues to impact lives even today.[25]

A SONG OF SORROW THAT STRUCK A CHORD

"I allowed myself to feel the grief as it came over me."

Never Alone Journal, December 12, 2013

Today, I chanced upon a song by Chanale Fellig called, "Don't Ever Leave," which uncovered buried emotions that I had suppressed for years. As I listened to the song several times, the trapped feelings in me rose to the surface. I cried as I remembered how my father had kissed me and hugged me tightly before he boarded his flight to California. I would have never let go of his hand had I known that it would be the last time I would ever see him. I didn't know that he was battling a life-threatening illness. He took each of us aside and spoke to us before the flight. I wish I could remember what he said to me. I relived the painful memories expressed in the song and experienced a deep sense of loss. I cried buckets of tears and allowed myself to feel the grief as it came over me. I prayed to Hashem for emotional freedom from the pain of loss.

---

25 Years later, in the summer of 2018, the Jewish Girls Retreat campers wrote and produced a movie about this story. The movie is called *At the Breaking Point*. It is available for purchase in the JGU Shop.

Don't Ever Leave

As I walk in Yerushalayim
I don't want to be here no longer, since Abba had to go
Taken away, never given the chance to say goodbye
If only I told him I loved him before he left me to cry.

Now I need a favor from my Father Above
Take my hand, hold on tight, guide me with love
'Cause I feel so alone here
No Tatty to be my guide
"Mima'amakim kirasicha[26]*"*
Don't ever leave my side!
When I saw him last, how he kissed me
I felt him squeeze me tight
When the bus drove away, I didn't worry
I knew I'd see him soon.

Why didn't they tell me he was leaving?
I would have never let go of his hand
And G-d, You know that I trust You
But I don't understand.

Now I need a favor from my Father Above
Take my hand, hold on tight, guide me with love
'Cause I feel so alone here
No Tatty to be my guide
"Mima'amakim kirasicha"
Don't ever leave my side.

---

[26] "Out of the depths I call to You." (Tehillim 130:1)

G-d, You know that I trust You
But how much can my heart break?
Oh, G-d, You know that I trust You
But how much can one nation take?

Father in Heaven, Father, can You hear me?
Father in Heaven, Father, can You hear me?

It felt good to cry and sing along to Chanale's song with a powerful message of hope and faith. After replaying the song several more times, I wiped away my tears and wrote this letter.

Dear Tatty,

I remember how you lit your candles with such tremendous joy; then we sat down on the floor and you played guitar, singing and telling us stories by the light of the candles. You were the best storyteller. I miss you! I miss the joy and love that you spread to everyone you met. I deeply yearn to be close to you again. Tatty, I will find another way to hold your hand and feel your love. I will forever shine your light. I miss you, Tatty! May the light of Chanukah bring the light of redemption!

Love, Nechama Dina

In the process of reconnecting to my father's light, I had to face the dark memories of his tragic passing. While opening these memories elicited intense feelings of grief, this journey was vital to my growth as a mother and leader. When grief is not addressed, happy memories can lead us to a sad place. The trauma of losing my father still wielded power over me. It was necessary to mourn the loss to find closure.

When light pushes away darkness, darkness only waits in the corners for its time to return. I had been pushing away the darkness, avoiding

the subject of my painful loss, but now it was time to reach the next level in my healing and transform the darkness itself. The *Zohar* teaches, based on the words of King Solomon, "*Yisron ha'or min hachoshech* — Light that comes from darkness has an advantage.[27]" The light that emerges from transformed darkness is so much more impactful than light that has never been threatened or concealed.

It is not by chance that I discovered and opened my heart to Chanale's song on *Chanukah*. The *Chanukah* menorah, lit after nightfall,

---
27 *Zohar* III, 47b.

gives us the power to face the darkness in order to light up our corner of the world. Every holiday has a unique message for us to apply to our lives. *Chanukah* teaches us that it is vital to acknowledge and validate our pain in order to shine a greater light. At times, I felt like an olive that was being crushed to extract the oil. It was time to kindle my own *Chanukah* menorah; I was ready to transform the darkness of loss into a new and greater light.

I began the journey of working through my emotions and letting go. I spoke to people I trusted and learned to face the feelings rising to the surface. I also wrote in my journal and let my tears flow. Sometimes, it felt as if I had entered a dark tunnel and I wondered, "Is there light at the end of this tunnel?" I discovered that the light isn't at the end of the tunnel... Rather, we **are** the light!

Every Jew is a walking menorah. Based on a verse in *Zechariah* which compares the Jewish people to a golden menorah, the *Alter Rebbe* explains that each of the seven lamps of the menorah correspond to one of the seven holy *middos* (character traits). The menorah is a symbol of the soul, which has the power to be a vessel of light. We have been given the tools to reveal the hidden light of *Hashem* cloaked in every challenge. We must search for the hidden good and never give up, just like the Maccabees who persevered and found the pure oil to kindle the menorah.

My father taught that "the greater the darkness, the greater the purpose to be revealed. If we take positive actions in the darkest moments, we can deepen our awareness more so than in any other time. A dark and difficult time can help us grow and strengthen ourselves. The more a hardship contradicts the goodness of G-d, the more potential it has to reveal *Hashem*'s greatness."

NEVER ALONE

"I am with you, even if you cannot see me!"

I was feeling alone and overwhelmed by the enormous amount of work that had to be accomplished before the Jewish Girls Winter Retreat 2013. I'd been very concerned about low enrollment and recruiting adequate staff. I was feeling the pressure even though I knew everything would fall into place in the end and be amazing.

That night, I had a dream. I was running a Bat Mitzvah Club, and the girls kept pouring in. There were new girls from all backgrounds. Some of them had minimal knowledge of their Jewish heritage. I was thrilled that they were coming because I had been trying to recruit them for months.

Meanwhile, in another room, lay my father. No one could see him. He was ill, but he was there. After the program, I went in to hug him and said to him, "I understand why they are all coming. It's because of YOU!" He smiled at me and said, "I am with you, even if you cannot see me! You are not alone.'"

Thinking about my dream after I awoke, I realized that *Tatty* was reminding me that he is with me and I am not alone. In the end, we ended up with many campers and the program was incredible in so many ways. My father's statement in my dream, "I am with you, even if you cannot see me!" was no longer just a dream. The challenge was for me to internalize this thought and feel it in my heart.

I decided to title my journal *Never Alone*; it became my space to record the moments that showed me that I am never alone. This journal helped me develop more awareness of the constant Divine Providence in each moment by writing down the blessings in my life and expressing gratitude to *Hashem*. It also helped me recognize my father's presence in my life. Journaling is a beneficial tool that helps me focus my mind on the present good, rather than getting stuck in the past or worrying about the future. When I choose to open my eyes to all the good, I see amazing miracles happening everywhere.

The truth is that we are never alone because we always have G-d at our side. G-d loves us unconditionally at every moment and His love is infinite. Our loved ones are always watching and protecting us from on high. When I tap into this love through recognizing the blessings each day, I feel nurtured and whole inside. Through recognizing the Divine Hand that is always with me, I feel secure and never alone. Gratitude pushes away thoughts of worry and lack. When I open my eyes and see G-d in every situation, I can live with the inner peace of knowing that G-d is guiding my every step.

The first step to growth and healing is to focus on and express gratitude for the blessings in our lives. When we do, the blessings grow.

CHAPTER 4
THE POWER OF THOUGHTS

MY SON AZRIEL'S BAR MITZVAH

"Take time to focus on all the good in life."

Never Alone Journal - *Shevat* 5 - January 2013

It's hard to believe that I have an almost-bar-mitzvah boy! In Lubavitch, it is customary for boys to begin putting on tefillin exactly two months before their bar mitzvah. Is it a surprise that two months before my son's bar mitzvah on Nissan 5 is Shevat 5, which is my father's birthday? Wow! My son Azriel, the oldest grandson named after my father, began to perform the mitzvah of tefillin so precious to my father, on his birthday! My father would have turned 65 on the day Azriel began to perform this mitzvah.

On this day, I reflect back to the day I gave birth to our third child, a beautiful 9.8-pound baby boy, after two girls. At an emotional bris celebration, we named our baby Azriel Yitzchok and felt as if my father was now shining a new light through his precious grandson. He was certainly smiling proudly and rejoicing with us!

At the bris, we bless, "L'Torah, l'chuppah, u'l'maasim tovim — May we merit to raise this child to learn Torah, get married, and do good deeds." Praying that my son would follow in the footsteps of his namesake, I answered "Amen" with my heart and soul, as hot tears trickled down my face. I remember my paternal grandmother, Bubby Wasserman, standing at my side. She smiled with tears in her eyes as she told me that my father also weighed 9.8 pounds at birth.

Never Alone Journal - *Adar* - February 2013

Let me take a deep breath; Azriel's bar mitzvah is in almost one month! Okay... that means that in the next three weeks, we are planning a Purim party, a bar mitzvah, a Pesach retreat for 400 guests, a trip to Florida for our nephew's bar mitzvah, and recruiting campers and staff for the JGR Summer Retreat! This is in addition to daily family life!

Help! How do I stay calm?

My father taught, "Take time to focus on all the good in life." Tefillin reminds us to bind the mind to the heart by giving the brain the power to control the heart, instead of being controlled by the heart's negative emotions. Similarly, my father's teachings are about the power of our thoughts. I know that he is part of our simchah by reminding me that I can be the master of my thoughts and "think out of the box." Inspired by his teachings from Dobra's notes, I am empowered to stay calm, joyful throughout the preparations and stay focused on my blessings.

It's going to be a super exciting month. I CAN DO IT! YES, I CAN!

Baruch Hashem, we made it to Azriel's bar mitzvah, while also planning our largest "*Pesach* in Lake George" retreat, thanks to the help of everyone in our family. Our amazing daughters helped order the matching outfits and dressed the younger children.

The bar mitzvah reminded me to appreciate the blessing of my precious family. Sometimes when life is so hectic, we become overwhelmed and forget to count our blessings. On one of the digitized tapes, my father is speaking to his mother and is telling her, "The essentials of life are to be close to G-d, share love with family, and share in

4 Azriels named after my father

Our family at the bar mitzvah

the joy of life. We live from month to month, yet I am so wealthy I can't even begin to count my wealth! Here, sitting on my lap, is Nechamale, such a beautiful child. We played on *Shabbos* and learned *aleph-beis* together. We went to *shul* and she saw the joy of Jews sitting together and singing."

My father lived a short life on earth, yet his spiritual wealth continues sustaining his growing Jewish family who are keeping his legacy alive. I was proud to celebrate this *simchah* with my mother, Daddy, and brothers, who, thank G-d, all have beautiful families of their own. I thank *Hashem* because I am so wealthy, I can't even begin to count my wealth! *Hashem* has given me the family I dreamed for since I was a young girl.

GROWING JEWISH MOTHERS

"We needed a change."

Thank G-d, the Jewish Girls Retreat was growing. We had rented Sage College in Troy for seven years. The dormitories were very hot and we were tired of cooking in other locations and bringing the food each day to camp. We needed a change. Since we couldn't find a suitable campground, we had rented a floor with 45 rooms at the Best Western Hotel in Albany for summer 2013. But there we faced other challenges,

Jewish Girls Retreat, Summer 2012

like bed bugs, a cloudy pool, and noisy guests, though we enjoyed the hotel air conditioning and onsite kitchen.

We needed the stability of a permanent year-round home. We toured numerous properties, but nothing worked out because there was always something wrong, such as being in the wrong location or the price was too high. It felt like a distant dream. In the meantime, we continued to rent for summer, winter and even for *Pesach* retreats.

We needed practical guidance to turn our dream into a physical reality. It was at this time that Coach Susan Axelrod, whose daughter Sarah had been a member of our Bat Mitzvah Club years before, reached out to me with an email:

Dear Nechama,

...I am writing today with an offer that I hope you will consider. For the last few years, I have been giving considerable time, energy, and prayer to honing my work, my gifts, and my legacy. I have made a decision that part of my commitment must be for something Jewish. After further reflection about all the many important things "Jewish," I decided that I would concentrate on Jewish girls. I have Jewish girls, after all, and in my thinking, it's the girls who turn into women who are going to perpetuate Judaism.

I have watched you for so many years and have always been amazed at your spirit, your talents, your dedication, purpose and creativity. It may be a direct connection to G-d or something, I'm not sure, but it's pure power.

When I received the call about the raffle, I went to your website to try to find more information. There was a line somewhere that says that you're "growing Jewish mothers." BOOM! That was it. It's been on my mind ever since, and I knew that was a sign for me. I'd like to offer you support in whatever way you need. If there is, please contact me and let me know if I can help you and support your work to create Jewish mothers. Thank you.

~Susan Axelrod

AN ABUNDANCE MINDSET

"Abundance flows freely to me."

On August 8, 2013, my husband and I met with Coach Susan and she asked us, "What is your long-term vision and what goals do you want to achieve?" We replied, "A permanent home for JGR with year-round programs and financial stability."

"This vision can happen!" Susan told us. "I have full confidence in you, and it is well deserved. You are among the most productive people I know, and you can do it! The place will find you when you are ready. This is in G-d's hands."

We spoke about how to create a financially sustainable organization with multiple income streams. She also advised us on how to launch a building campaign for a property that seemed very promising. We called our campaign 'Building the Future'. Susan explained, "You need resources to make an impact on the world! Your impact is unlike any other and is worthy of support. You are offering programs of great value that perpetuate Judaism. Founders often have trouble asking for funding. They start a non-profit because they have a passion for the mission, not because they wanted to start a business. But you need funding to allow you to continue to give and build a strong future. Find the people who care about this vital mission and offer them meaningful giving opportunities."

Coach Susan guided me to combine my passions and spiritual goals with practical tools based in physical reality. In our weekly strategic planning sessions, she encouraged me to internalize positive thinking to actualize our dreams. She opened her heart to me and listened to my ideas and fears. She reminded me that the words we use are self-fulfilling prophecies, and suggested that I repeat positive affirmations such as, "Abundance flows freely to me."

She taught me how to reframe negative statements into positive ones, especially my thoughts about money. She empowered me to imagine how much more we could do if we were coming from a place of plenty! She said, "There is an old myth that money is bad. If you believe it's bad to receive money, this has to do with the money story you were raised with... What messages about money did you hear as a child?"

These questions moved me to explore my childhood "money story." I recalled that after my father's passing, we became recipients of many

generous donations from the Crown Heights community. Thank G-d, we were fortunate to move into a fully-furnished, brand-new home and received new clothes and gifts. I loved my new white bedroom set, yet I experienced a huge void despite our improved lifestyle. All the materialism could not replace my father's love and light. My soul yearned for the simple lifestyle and joy I had experienced before his passing. I yearned to recreate the spiritual light from the first ten years of my childhood. Material abundance represented loss and so, unknowingly, I developed a scarcity mindset. It was difficult for me to ask for and receive the support I needed to help others.

Working through my old story allowed me to feel and experience the grief that had been limiting my ability to receive the resources I needed to accomplish my mission. This illustrates what can happen when we fail to address grief. When we suppress it, it seeps into other parts of our lives and can inadvertently impact our work and relationships. Susan reminded me about the power of our words and how to write affirmations to create the reality we desire. We wrote this affirmation as a tool to internalize my new story:

> *My soul receives the support to make the impact I am meant to make. I realize that I don't need to live a haggard life in order to fulfill my holy mission. I want to fully support my family in a holy, beautiful environment — with abundance — to have greater impact and bring redemption to our world!*

I learned that a person with a scarcity mindset selects negative thoughts and adopts a victim mentality, those with an abundance mindset are often visionaries and see the limitless possibilities in the world.

I wrote in my journal: *"I am open to receiving... Just imagine!"*

NOTHING STANDS IN THE WAY OF WILL

"With Heaven's help, your dreams will be fulfilled."

As the buses rolled away following our 2014 summer retreat, I waved to the campers and asked myself, "What now?" I returned home to Troy, New York, and felt bereft of our community of girls. The Troy Jewish population had significantly declined over the years, so it felt especially lonely. We had spent the past year working on a building campaign and the property did not materialize. I was very disappointed.

In addition, so much of my energy was drained because of a very difficult hotel management. The last *Shabbos* of camp, we had to leave our dining hall and eat outside, because the owner was having a wild party. Near our tents, there had been a grill with an entire pig cooking! We really needed a permanent home for JGR and a year-round community. I thought about how grateful I was for all our blessings, my family and camp community. Yet, there was a voice in me searching for more. I could not silence this voice. I poured out my heart and fell asleep with tears in my eyes.

The next morning, I awoke to discover an email from Chaya Bracha Rubin, a singer and composer:

Please listen to this song. You embody this in all ways and enable Jewish girls all over the world to learn and do the same, B"H!!!

Hatzlachah rabbah!!!

Chaya Bracha

Attached was her newly-composed song:

Nothing Stands in the Way of Will

There's a voice within you
That will never be silenced
There's a part of who you are
That's searching for more

Don't shut it out, don't turn away
Because it knows the reason
That you're here on this earth
What you have left to do

And the first step on this journey is to silence your fears
Because the question is not if you will succeed, it is only how!

Nothing stands in the way of will
With Heaven's help, your dreams will be fulfilled
Make your cup, it's waiting to be filled

There's a voice within you
That says you can do it
There's a part of who you are
That's cheering you on

So listen close every day,
Remind yourself of your purpose
While you're here on this earth,
You have so much to do

When you feel like you are pushed up to the edge,
weary mind, broken heart
Like Nachshon, jump into the water and the seas will part!

She had no idea how much I needed to hear these words. I cried many tears as I listened to her song and felt that G-d was talking directly to me, telling me not to give up on my big dreams and to listen carefully to the voice inside of me. Our Rabbis say, "G-d has many messengers." Her song was a reminder to silence my fears and remain on the path to grow and turn our vision into reality.

THE WORLD IS OUR POLAR BEAR

"We don't do what is instinctual when the world is our polar bear."

A month after camp, I traveled to Alaska to celebrate the bat mitzvah of a dear JGR camper, Hadassah Conrad. Her mother, Michelle, bought me a ticket, and I was so excited to visit the other side of the world. At the celebration, I was asked to share a few words, and recounted my father's favorite story about his brother Leonard, who had a close encounter with a polar bear in Alaska, connecting it to bat mitzvah.

Celebrating with Hadassah Conrad in Alaska

In 1976, my uncle took a job in Barrow, Alaska, about 500 miles from the North Pole. One beautiful, sunny spring day in May, he and his friend decided to take their snowmobiles out for a ride on the arctic ice (even though it was about 20 degrees outside). Off they went, just having fun gliding around the icebergs, and eventually stopping to enjoy the view and quiet.

When they were ready to move on, my uncle started his snowmobile and waited for his friend to start his. But his machine would not start; it only backfired.

While waiting, my uncle climbed onto one of the icebergs to enjoy the feeling of being on another planet. His friend was still trying to start his snowmobile and was having any success.

Suddenly, my uncle saw something moving in the distance, something that he quickly realized was a polar bear. He slid down the iceberg, running to inform his friend of the danger and to share information he had read in a book about polar bears: If you come across a polar bear, play dead; you cannot out run it. You need to lie down, pull your knees up to your chest, and hold your breath as long as possible. The polar bear will come up to you to smell your breath to determine if you are food or not.

And then they saw the polar bear's head pop up over of the iceberg. The two men sank to the ground.

The bear approached my uncle, putting his snout to his mouth, and it started pushing my uncle with his snout to get him to move. Realizing that if he made one move he would be bear food, my uncle held himself as still as possible. The bear then left him, probably moving on to his friend. Suddenly, there was a gunshot in the distance and the bear ran off. My uncle ran over to his friend and asked if he was okay. Thank G-d, the bear had not harmed him. He had turned his snow machine on its side and tucked himself up against the track for protection.

My uncle told his friend, "Let's get out of here!" and started his machine, hoping his friend's snowmobile would start. It seems that by turning it on its side, the blockage in the fuel line had been dislodged, and it started! In a panic, they rushed off the ice and safely back to their housing.

This was a favorite story my father loved to tell his students. He shared this profound lesson: "The world is our polar bear. We don't do what is instinctual when the world is our polar bear. We must maintain our cool and our connection to G-d in order to survive and thrive. It doesn't come naturally. We were given the manual, the Torah, as our guide; work at it and stick to it." I can imagine that this story spoke to my father as he battled a life-threatening illness; this was his polar bear. He refused to give in to the polar bears in his life. With tremendous trust in G-d, he worked on himself to maintain a positive mindset throughout his illness.

I returned from Alaska with renewed faith and energy to overcome the polar bears in my life: my fears, worries, and self-doubts. I was confident that by setting goals, thinking positive thoughts and following G-d's plan we would succeed in reaching our goals.

IMAGINE: JEWISH GIRLS UNITE

"The world needs more unity."

For years, I'd had a vision to keep our campers united and inspired year-round. In 2010, Leah Larson and I came up with the name, "Jewish Girls Unite." We planted a seed by developing a curriculum for youth leaders to use around the world. We arranged a few conference calls with campers. As technology progressed, there were so many new possibilities to create an online global community. After returning from the bat mitzvah in Alaska, I was ready to "warm up the world" with an online global community connecting and teaching Jewish girls around the world.

"The world needs more unity," Coach Susan empowered me, "You have the ability and power to make this happen right now, at this moment, at this time, in a way that has never been done before. Visualize in more technicolor detail every day. Visualize in real time with real people. Picture the people who are going to be teaching online. Picture thousands of Jewish girls from around the country watching the online programs, feeling their hearts open and their souls being inspired."

I was concerned about finding people to help make this dream happen. Susan replied, "I will support you. The people who will be the implementers of this dream will come to ask you to participate. This amazing team will work together to create something much larger than ourselves."

My next step was to create a program strategy on paper, a plan that included every detail of our vision for Jewish Girls Unite, with the purpose, goals, and outcomes. Susan reviewed the program strategy with me and said, "Your father would be very proud. JGU is a fitting legacy!"

Rabbi Yosef Resnick, a JGR parent, was my tech support and Leah (Larson) Caras updated the website. *Yaldah* had evolved into an online magazine and JGU was the perfect solution to keep the girls connected. We sent out emails and made phone calls, and girls from throughout the USA and Canada began to sign up for the first online JGU classes[28]. BBM - *Bat Mitzvah and Beyond* was launched on November 10, 2014 and a couple dozen girls joined from around the world. The light of my father's legacy — Jewish education with love and joy — was spreading to Jewish girls everywhere.

28 Girls are invited to sign up for our online classes at www.JewishGirlsUnite.com.

ESSAY CONTEST: THE POWER OF THOUGHT

Winner #18

I vividly remember my father standing at the door of my bedroom and sharing his new tools for a positive mindset, learned at a course he took on self-mastery. Through mastering his thoughts, he had hoped to strengthen his physical health as he battled a terrible illness. He planted the seeds in me, so that later I was open to internalize positivity tools to integrate calm and joy in my life. Where there is joy, the Divine Presence dwells, creating a vessel for us to receive the blessings we need and desire.

I entered the Meaningful Life Essay Contest in February 2015, which helped me further internalize my father's precious notes from Dobra about the power of thoughts. My husband helped me research the Torah sources, Mrs. Evelyn Krieger provided editorial assistance, and Susan helped me write a visualization for a permanent home for JGR, as you will read in the following essay.

Baruch Hashem, out of 500 entries, we won eighteenth place! "*Chai*," which means "life" in Hebrew has the numerical value of 18; this was a clear indication that my father's teachings are alive.

My Life Essay

Are the thoughts that enter our mind a natural result of what is happening in our lives? Is negative thinking limiting our success and overshadowing all the good we have in our lives? Is it possible to master control over our thoughts? Are we afraid of failure and criticism? If left unchecked, negative thinking can control our emotions, hold us back from achieving our dreams, and even result in poor mental and physical health, *chas v'shalom*. *Chassidus* guides us with tools to transform our negative perceptions and realize our true reality.

Harnessing the Power of Thought

Chassidus emphasizes that thoughts are real, powerful and eternal. Our positive thoughts even create spiritual angels[29]. Furthermore, since thoughts clothe our soul, and thoughts have no limitations, thoughts rooted in holiness actually place our soul there. In addition, when our thoughts are focused toward helping another, the person will feel it and actually benefit from the positive thoughts. On the other hand, negative thinking traps us like our ancestors stuck in Egypt. We can go out of Egypt when we overcome our narrow perception of ourselves and overcome our personal limitations. The Hebrew word for Egypt, *Mitzrayim*, actually means limitations[30].

The voice of Pharaoh is still with us today, telling us to believe we can't succeed. He wants us to give up hope. The Hebrew letters of Pharaoh are *hei, ayin, reish, fei* – the same letters in the Hebrew word for *oref*, the back of the neck. In order for the mind to control the heart, our thoughts must pass through the back of the neck. Pharaoh's voice causes a blockage between the mind and the heart. It blocks the voice of the soul from reaching us and revealing the unlimited potential of our soul.

How do we push away the negative voices and gain control over our thoughts? How do we stay positive when challenges arise? First, we can recognize that the mind controls the heart, the seat of our emotions, which means we have the power to be the master of our thoughts[31]. Our evaluation of ourselves and who we are is dependent on the quality of our thoughts. Our effort to choose positive thoughts will result in healthy emotions and desirable conduct.

---
29 *Tanya*, Chapter 12 p.51; *Derech Mitzvosecha* 96b; *Ohr Hatorah Tzemach Tzedek* p. 728.
30 *Torah Ohr, Parashas Vayeira*
31 Ibid.

Chassidus explains that thoughts are compared to water because they sustain us and are always in a state of motion[32]. Our thoughts are always flowing. Negative thoughts can "drown" us.

Sometimes, we feel trapped as if there is no way out, just like it happened after the Jews left Egypt by the Reed Sea. The Jews were surrounded by the Egyptians from behind and the sea before them. There were many different opinions, but only one man who knew what to do. His name was Nachshon ben Aminadav. He did not allow negative thoughts to control his emotions or actions. The *Midrash* tells us that Nachshon focused on G-d's command to reach Mount Sinai and so he visualized where he wanted to be. He had the courage to keep moving forward until the waters split. We can follow Nachshon's example by focusing on our direction and keeping our purpose in mind. By moving forward with positivity, that indomitable sea splits and we are open to experience G-d's miracles in our lives.

Our Good Thoughts

Chassidus reminds us that our minds can only hold one thought at a time. What a simple yet profound truth! Therefore, it is crucial to have a mental storehouse of positive Torah thoughts. Phrases and chapters of Torah, *Mishnah*, and *Tanya* should be engraved in our minds so they are available to replace negative thoughts[33]. These engraved thoughts are so powerful that even when we're not consciously thinking them, they help keep away negative thoughts.

How can this be? This is because negative thoughts are attracted to an empty mind, not one armed with holiness. Engraved *Torah*

---

[32] *Mayim Rabim* 5636 p.4
[33] *Likutei Torah, Parashas Vayikra* — "V'hadarta pnei zaken" Hosofos. Rebbe Igros Vol. 5 Letter 1,374; Vol. 18 letter 6,745; and many more.

thoughts connect us to G-d at all times, and that connection pushes away negativity. We can perceive the soul's unlimited potential. We don't stand paralyzed but instead move toward success.

Utilizing Visualization

Another positive thinking tool is visualization. When one is faced with difficult challenges, it is beneficial to relive positive, uplifting and spiritual experiences, such as a wedding, the birth or adoption of a child, or a meeting with the *Rebbe*. With practice, visualization creates a sensory experience bringing us to the sights, sounds, tastes, and feelings of that joyous time. In this way, we can relive the inspiration and joy we felt at the time so that it inspires and moves us now[34].

My father was a true example of being a master of one's thoughts. He once told his students that even if he developed a potentially fatal illness, it wouldn't change him — it would motivate him to work harder to overcome any negative thoughts. He would recognize his even greater need for a positive mindset. His students were unaware that he was suffering from a life-threatening illness at the time. He didn't become depressed; instead, he chose to focus on his purpose in life, teaching Torah and spending time with his family. As a result, it was hard to tell that he was living with an illness because he expressed positivity and joy until his last day on earth.

Practical Steps:

My father, Rabbi Azriel Yitzchok Wasserman, o"bm, taught the following exercises to use each day to create a flow of positive

---

[34] Interesting to see connection in *Toras Chaim, Mitteler, Rebbe Parashas Bereishis* after many chapters about mind control, discusses suffering in chapter 21.

energy and break the pattern of negative thinking and self-doubt, which if not expelled, may lead to sadness and lack of productivity.

1. Fight negativity with self-talk. Ask yourself, "Am I fighting my negative thinking, which is my personal Egypt? Am I putting forth the effort to take charge of my thoughts and choosing to think positively?"

Tell yourself: "I am the boss. I get to decide which thoughts I allow to enter my mind."

2. Think healthy thoughts. Build up a library of positive thoughts, such as, "Everything happens by Divine Providence. My life is perfect for me. What G-d sends me is exactly what I need. I can succeed." Change the negative soundtrack and play positive thoughts. Cling to positive thoughts like life itself and soon, the negative thoughts will diminish.

3. Fill the mind with Torah thoughts. Torah thoughts connect us to G-d at all times, and that connection pushes away negativity.

4. Start your day off right. The first thoughts and words of the day influence the entire day. Recite and feel the one-line prayer of *Modeh Ani*: "I thank you, living and enduring King, for You have graciously returned my soul within me. Great is Your faithfulness." Thank G-d for the power of your soul to overcome negative thinking.

5. Break through Egypt. How do we break through our own *Mitzrayim*?

    a. Demand: "G-d, take me out!"

    b. Once you begin to let go and release, your redemption will come on its own.

    c. Listen to your soul, which is continually guiding you.

d. Remember: You were created with the strengths of our fathers and mothers.

e. Set aside time each day to develop trust in G-d.

6. **Visualize.** Find the time to relax and relive positive, uplifting moments in your life. It is beneficial to relive experiences, such as a wedding, the birth or adoption of a child, or a holiday memory. With practice, visualization creates a sensory experience bringing us to the sights, sounds, tastes, and feelings of that joyous time. In this way, we can relive the inspiration and joy we felt at the time so that it inspires and moves us now.

Visualization enables healing energy to flow through the body and to develop thoughts that are calming. Mental relaxation reprograms how we think, like rebooting a computer.

Here are the steps:

a. Sit comfortably and close your eyes.

b. Deeply inhale and exhale ten times.

c. Envision relaxing images, such as a sunrise or sunset over a lake.

d. Recreate a positive memory.

e. Feel the positive energy and inspiration of the memory.

f. Envision positive results you wish to happen.

Visualization is the process of mentally imagining a goal or desire in a way that feels as if you're already living in that reality. It's one of the most powerful ways to tap into the limitless potential of your soul and fulfill your greatest dreams and desires!

These coping methods take effort but with dedicated practice they can be learned and used to weed out negative thoughts that are not coming from our true reality. We have the power and the tools to overcome challenges and stay positive in every life situation. When we utilize our G-d given gift of thought and follow the practical steps taught to us by our *Chassidic* masters, we will lead happier and healthier lives and achieve our greatest dreams.

OUR VISUALIZATION

"I close my eyes and envision a beautiful home for JGR..."

Here is my visualization that was part of the above essay:

Currently, my husband and I are working toward the goal of purchasing a property to become the permanent home for the Jewish Girls Retreat. We have faced numerous setbacks and challenges in striving for this goal. While I can't control outside circumstances, I do have control over my thoughts. I can fight pessimism, negativity, and self-doubt by applying these teachings to my life. I must stay focused on fulfilling my mission and purpose. I have the power to strengthen my positive thoughts and trust in G-d when I visualize our dream becoming a reality.

I close my eyes and envision a beautiful home for JGR with happy girls. I drive up the long road to the stunning property. I smile and thank G-d for allowing us to co-create this beautiful reality. I picture every detail — the swing set, the flowers, the community garden and swimming pool. I see the inside of the home with an art room, a dance studio, bedrooms, kitchens, and dining hall. I visualize my father, of blessed memory, smiling from Above because he is proud of his beautiful legacy — Jewish girls who are learning Torah at camp and applying it to their lives. These life lessons will give them the confidence and tools to become future Jewish mothers. I feel ease, joy and calm as I walk the path of the new JGR home.

PSALM 23

"I will dwell in the house of the Lord forever.[35]"

Despite our best efforts to establish a permanent home for JGR, it was taking much longer than expected. As the *Chabad Shluchim* appointed to Southern Rensselaer County by Head *Shliach* Rabbi Israel Rubin, we were looking in a small geographical area, with very specific requirements. In the process of searching for properties, we met several Jewish people, and invited them for *Shabbos*. One woman lit her first *Shabbos* candle at my daughter's Friday-evening bat mitzvah dinner and she also contributed a significant gift to the scholarship fund.

Thank G-d, our visualization led us to rent a new JGR summer home on the grounds of a beautiful boarding school for summer 2015, which included a dining hall, commercial kitchen, dormitories, library, indoor pool, playing fields, and basketball and tennis courts. The beautiful mountain views and garden lent themselves to a peaceful summer experience and served as a great temporary home for JGR. The move to the boarding school was a big improvement from our previous hotel accommodations, where there was only an asphalt parking lot in which to play sports. The disadvantage was that the rent was very high, but we had no other choice. This new added financial pressure weighed heavily on me, or was it my pregnancy that made me feel heavy? It all felt very exhausting.

On the fast of Esther, one month before *Pesach*, we were *baruch Hashem* blessed with our tenth child, named Baruch Mordechai, and three weeks later, we directed a massive *Pesach* retreat in Lake George for 500 guests. We had no time to breathe because summer was only weeks away and there was so much to do to plan for the upcoming summer retreat in this new location with 80 campers and 40 staff

---
35 *Tehillim* 23:6

members. I was beset by concerns and questions. Would we adjust to our new summer location? Would we find all the staff needed? Would we have sufficient campers and funds to cover the higher rental costs?

Needing some words of encouragement, I read a letter from the *Lubavitcher Rebbe* on *Shabbos* about faith, one of my go-to sources of inspiration. The *Rebbe* was suggesting a way to relieve worrisome thoughts: to learn chapter 23 of *Tehillim*, which speaks about how G-d took care of King David when he was alone in a desert without provisions. The inherent lessons in this chapter of Divine Providence and that G-d only does good, are the perfect antidote for thoughts of anxious doubt.

I sat down to learn chapter 23, and found the following meditation on one of the verses:

> "Surely goodness and loving-kindness shall follow me all the days of my life, and I will dwell in the house of the Lord forever." There is ample goodness in the world, and goodness is pursuing me at all times. I just need to become aware that abundance and goodness are surrounding me every moment. I am a child in G-d's "home," protected and cared for by my Father in Heaven.[36]

I remembered that this chapter of *Tehillim* was also my father's last prayer on earth. Yoel Seliger, a *Shabbos* guest and friend who was with my father in San Diego during his last days, had told us that my father, very weak and barely able to speak, kept repeating these words from chapter 23 over and over, "I will dwell in the house of G-d forever."

The next day, I attended a women's concert organized by *Chabad* of Clifton Park. The first song performed by

---

36 Rabbi Daniel Shoenbach, LMFT, *Think Good, It Will Be Good*

talented singers, Rivka Leah Popack and Chaya Bracha Rubin, was this verse in *Tehillim*. I sang along with tears of joy and asked G-d to continue giving me the strength to care for my ten children *KA"H*, as well as my spiritual children. I prayed for a successful summer retreat. I knew this song was meant for me! I could hear my father singing his favorite verses of *Tehillim* with us; reminding me once again to trust in *Hashem*.

CHAPTER 5

Shine Your Inner Light

THANK YOU FOR THE CLOSED DOORS

"G-d is one with us, behind the closed doors."

At this time, we created our new JGU motto, "Shine your inner light," inspired by this song composed and introduced at winter retreat 2015 by Rivka Leah Popack (née Cylich).

In those times
When you find
That each door that you try
Is locked, yet again, and it won't let you by

In your heart, lies the key
Look inside and you'll see
Believe

Don't you know, this place in time,
is waiting just for you
To learn, to give, to love, to live
There's so much you can do

So be the miracle we believe in
Be the candle burning bright
You can be the flame, we're reaching for
Light up, light up the night

Shine your inner light
Shadows fall away
Hold your candle high
Night will turn to day.

I now understood why so many doors that I had tried to open had been locked for years. I found the key to my heart and the heart of Jewish girls everywhere. All the closed doors led to opening this new JGU door — a year-round online community for girls and women — that was waiting for me "to learn, to give, to love, to live."

I began writing weekly *Erev Shabbos* messages, which also gave me a place to reflect on my personal healing journey. I wrote the following post before *Yom Kippur* 2015, after almost one year of teaching Jewish girls online.

> *My favorite moment on Yom Kippur is at the very end of the fast. The Neilah prayer, when we ask G-d to seal us in the book of life, granting us a year of health and happiness. In that powerful moment, we recite the Shema together as one people — "Hear O Israel, the Lord is our G-d, the Lord is One." We proclaim in awe — "Blessed be the name of the glory of His kingdom forever and ever." We cry out with joy — "G-d, He is the only G-d!" seven times.*
>
> *The cry of the shofar is heard. It is incredibly uplifting to feel the unity, awe, and joy during the last moments of Yom Kippur.*
>
> *What is the beauty of this Neilah service, if at this time, G-d is closing the Heavenly gates, sealing our future for the coming year?*
>
> *Chassidic teachings explain the "closed doors" in a positive way. The gates lock us in, as opposed to out, as we stand united with our Father in Heaven.*

How many times do we face a closed door in the form of a rejection, a loss, an unanswered prayer, a closed chapter in our lives and we are devastated and enveloped in sadness and loneliness? With a heavy heart, we wonder why G-d closed the door upon us, yet again.

In retrospect, we find that each time the door closed, G-d was closer, guiding and pushing us to grow and reach greater heights. When we view our challenges through the eyes of our Chassidic masters, we see that a closed door means "G-d is one" — G-d is one with us, behind the closed doors.

Personally, for many years, I searched for the vehicle to express my soul's purpose. I struggled with the "closed doors" that I faced in striving to spread more light. There were moments that I felt so alone.

Today, I am thankful to G-d for every door that He closed and for guiding me to fulfill my soul purpose in a unique way. I feel blessed that I can finally understand the reason for all the closed doors and sing with joy, "Hear, O Israel, the Lord is our G-d, the Lord is One...Blessed be the name of the glory of His kingdom forever and ever."

I share this lesson to remind you to thank G-d for every "closed door." It is the closed doors that open up our hearts to new opportunities. The Neilah service tells us that in our most challenging moments, when a door is slammed in our face, we are never alone, but alone with G-d!

I wrote the following poem in my Never Alone Journal:

In those difficult times, G-d was behind each closed door
Guiding and showing me, there was something better in store
G-d was saying, "Find your mission that I need you to fulfill."

Don't give up; there is nothing that stands in the way of your will.
With G-d's help, we will joyfully inspire positivity and unity
Building the Jewish Girls Unite Global Community!

MAKE ALASKA WARM

"I was put on this earth to touch one neshamah at a time."

In November 2015, I traveled once again to Alaska for the bar mitzvah of Jacob Conrad, Hadassah's twin brother. This time I was also traveling with the intention to invite Jewish girls to join the global JGU community.

Michelle, Jacob's mother, picked me up from the airport and as we were driving, she told me that her bar mitzvah boy was distraught. He was concerned that putting on *tefillin* during the winter months was going to be very difficult for him, because when he leaves to school in the morning, it is dark, and by the time he returns home from school, it's dark again. There are only approximately five hours of sun in the winter and *tefillin* is supposed to be worn during daylight.

I smiled thoughtfully to myself. "Wow! This young boy isn't concerned about his party's color scheme or how many gifts he will receive, but his greatest concern is 'How am I going to bring light and do a *mitzvah* in this dark world? How do I overcome my environment? How can I bring light when there is so much darkness?'"

At times, I find myself asking these same questions: "How am I going to bring light and warmth into our cold and dark world despite the obstacles? Am I more concerned about the 'party,' the things that are temporary in life, or am I focused on G-d's mission? Do I value the

big, glamorous events with many people, or my vital work to inspire one soul at a time to take on one more *mitzvah*?"

The *Rebbe* sent emissaries, Rabbi Yosef and Esti Greenberg, to establish *Chabad* of Alaska even before places with many more Jews, like Manhattan. The *Rebbe* cared about every single Jew, especially those in remote locations. Before the *Shluchim* embarked on their mission, the *Rebbe* blessed them, "Warm up Alaska! *Machen varem.*"

It was a watershed moment for me when I realized that success is not defined by numbers. It is not about leading a huge congregation and community or having hundreds of guests around my *Shabbos* table. I was put on this earth to touch one *neshamah* at a time. If the *Rebbe* sent Jews to Alaska for a handful of Jews, I had a purpose living in Troy for now.

This is what we had been accomplishing all along while residing in Troy. We loved the special elderly Jews who became part of our family. I fondly remember Leah Gaies, who showered love on us until her passing at the age of 98. We even called her *Bubby* Leah. Our family would visit Irvine Meyers, who lived alone until he passed away at the ripe old age of 100. Our children baked him a cake and celebrated his 100th birthday!

Our family would visit Mrs. Platt, an elderly Jewish widow and her son every *Shabbos*, and we'd stay to recite the *Havdalah* prayer at the day's conclusion. We blessed her each week and she blessed our lives. I'd meet Jewish women in a doctor's office and give them a *Shabbos* candlestick.

We were once playing in the park and we met a couple, originally from Israel, with a young boy. They had not eaten in a *sukkah* since they lived in Israel. We invited them to our home for holidays and *Shabbos* meals and became friends. There are so many more examples that they could comprise their own book.

Similarly, Jewish Girls Unite reaches girls living in remote places. As Neshama Sari wrote, "I used to feel very alone as a Jewish girl in a small rural town in Oregon. I would see big communities in other places and wonder what it was like to feel a part of something so special. There are no other Jewish girls my age where I live. That changed when I found Jewish Girls Unite."

It is easy to feel that we are not doing enough. But we must remember that it is not about the numbers but about impacting one soul at a time. Yes, it's true, the world is spiritually cold and dark like Alaska, but we can not allow ourselves to be overwhelmed by the darkness. We must ask ourselves each day, "How can I make it warm and bright for just one more person?"

YOU MUST BRING LIGHT!

"You must go down below into the dark and cold world."

The following story gave me encouragement to continue venturing out of my comfort zone to spread more light virtually and reach out to girls around the world. As a young man, Rabbi Zalman Posner, o"bm, was summoned by the previous *Chabad Rebbe* in the year 1949. It was hard to understand all the words the *Rebbe* spoke due to his failing health, so it was crucial to watch his hand gestures. The *Rebbe* requested that Rabbi Zalman travel to a faraway community and become a rabbi there. Rabbi Zalman was hesitant; he didn't want to move to such a remote location with almost no Jewish infrastructure.

The *Rebbe* encouraged him in Yiddish, "When a soul has to come down to earth, it doesn't want to go. Why? Because heaven is warm and comfortable while living on Earth is cold and dark (*kalt un fintzter*). So, what happens? In heaven, the soul is commanded, 'You must descend below'" — and to demonstrate the point, the *Rebbe* took his index finger and repeatedly pointed downward in a deliberate motion — "you must go down below into the dark and cold world, and you must bring light (*machin dort lichtig*)."

The *Rebbe* instructed Rabbi Zalman to travel to Nashville, Tennessee, where he served as a rabbi for over half a century. Indeed, the *Rebbe* validated, the world is challenging, dark and cold, but we were nevertheless sent here to illuminate our surroundings. We have the power to light up the world and ultimately, light prevails over darkness. The key is to always remember our task and take action to fulfill G-d's mission statement for the world: "Let there be light!" It is this purpose that gives us the energy and courage to overcome all obstacles.

This story reminded me that even when I am overwhelmed by fears, sadness, or worry, I can conquer it. When I ask, "Can I overcome the darkness?" I visualize the *Rebbe's* finger pointing downward: "You must go down into the cold and dark world, and there you must bring light."

FROM TZARAH TO TZOHAR

"We can create our own calm in the storm."

My second trip to Alaska helped me absorb so many vital life lessons. I shared the following message connected to *Parashas Noach* with the women at a *Shabbos* class in Alaska.

How do we learn to increase light and overcome the darkness? The answer is in *Parashas Noach*. We learn about the chaos; darkness, evil and corruption of all kinds. The *"mayim rabbim* — great waters" raging around the ark can be understood as a metaphor for all the trials and tribulations we experience in our lives that we sometimes feel are drowning us. Among them are the challenges in our relationships, the challenges of taking care of ourselves, the challenges of juggling all of our responsibilities.

In *Parashas Noach*, we learn how to live in a way that we remain calm, even when we find ourselves in the middle of a raging storm. As the saying goes, "It's not about waiting for the storm to pass but about dancing in the rain." We can create our own calm in the storm. We can transform the waters of destruction into *"mei noach* — waters of comfort."

What is a *mabul* (flood)? "*Mabul*" means "mixed up." A *mabul* is a mixed-up world flooded by waters from below and waters from above, confusing our priorities that we may forget our spiritual mission. The dark depths overwhelm us!

The Torah, our manual for life, gives us the instructions to handle the challenging waters when we feel like we are drowning.

"*Bo atah... el hateivah* — "Come into the ark.[37]" The word "*teivah*" has a dual meaning in Hebrew: the first is "ark" and the second is "word." Through positive words we can build an ark for ourselves: a means of protection against all the raging waters, against all our emotional, intellectual, and physical troubles.[38]

"*Bo*" is made up of the letters *beis* and *aleph*. When you spell it backwards, it spells "*av*," meaning father. Our Heavenly Father is reminding us that He is always protecting us from the dangers of the floods. In my case, I interpret it as my own beloved father's words will always be my ark and protection.

Additionally, on this *teivah*, you must have a *tzohar*, a light. Words infused with light can banish the darkness in our hearts, such as our negative energies, our anxiety, our sadness. Words of light include words

---
[37] Noach 7:1
[38] *Likutei Sichos*, Volume 1 and *Kesser Shem Tov*

of Torah and *tefillah*, positive affirmations, stories about our loved ones, validating words and uplifting songs.

I had already begun my journey of using the power of words infused with light to heal my heart through writing more often in my journal, compiling pictures and stories, and organizing a memorial celebrating my father's life. Instead of focusing on loss, I was learning to reframe it as, "I am so fortunate to have had an incredible father who touched my life for ten years. I have a mission to carry on his legacy and share his teachings with others." When I changed my words, my story, my language, I revealed strength instead of sadness. I was building my ark.

I shared my father's formula for transforming "*tzarah* — sorrow," into a "*tzohar* — light." (I found it in Dobra's notes taken in my father's classes based on teachings from the Baal Shem Tov.) There are three words that have the same letters, and when we shift them, we transform darkness into light. These three words hint to the ways we can deal with challenges that come our way.

צרה *Tzarah* — **Sorrow:** What is your sorrow or darkness? What is your limitation or challenge?

רצה *Ratzah* — **Desire:** What is your soul's desire? When you are faced with a *tzarah*, reveal your soul's desire to come closer to *Hashem* through the song of Torah and prayer. Focus on what you want to improve or create and take action. Allow G-d's will to be channeled through you. Your thoughts are very powerful and will attract the energy you put out.

צהר *Tzohar* — **Light:** When you listen to your soul's desire and connect to G-d, pray, learn Torah, discover the window to your soul, you allow new light to shine. The challenge itself is transformed and becomes your source of illumination.

What kind of light do we shine? *Tzaharayim* is when the sun is shining the brightest and is at the zenith of its strength. From the *tzarah* comes true *tzohar*, a transformation of the negative experience into a source of illumination! From this *tzarah*, we have a new perception of the world and see things differently, transforming the darkness into a tremendous light, thereby revealing the purpose of the darkness.

SPREADING LIGHT: JGU CALIFORNIA LAUNCH

"How wonderful it is that nobody needs to wait a moment before starting to improve the world." -Anne Frank

The JGU light was spreading to California. Linda Schwartz, mother of Meirah, a camper at the Jewish Girls Retreat was excited to launch Jewish Girls Unite in California for her daughter's bat mitzvah project. Linda was moved to honor the seventieth *yahrtzeit* of Anne Frank at this launch. She wanted the impact of her daughter's bat mitzvah to last longer than the celebration itself. She organized a festive concert for women and girls at the *Chabad* Center in Irvine, California. She also sponsored the new JGU website at JewishGirlsUnite.com designed by

Leah Caras (née Larson), with a new logo, and even printed t-shirts for the attendees.

I thought about the fact that I was returning to California, so close to where my father's life on earth ended. I remember waking up one morning with these thoughts that came forth from my soul. I quickly wrote them down and used it in my welcome speech.

> We all have a little girl inside of us with big dreams. No matter how old we are, we are all young girls at heart. There is a young girl in me who is still ten years old; she will never age nor fade away. When I was ten, I watched my father, Rabbi Azriel Yitzchok Wasserman, o"bm, a beloved educator, board a plane to San Diego, California, to receive treatment for an illness he was battling. I had no idea that I would never see him again.

> The launch of the new website and online community for Jewish Girls Unite fulfills my childhood dream to carry on my father's mission to spread Judaism with love and joy. I am comforted because we are launching JGU in California, where his life on this earth ended. His name was Azriel, which means, "G-d will help," and I am confident that in his merit, G-d will bless our efforts to unite our Jewish daughters across the seas!

> I was reminded recently of something I heard my father say on a recording about how the Holocaust had influenced the direction of his life. He explained why he enrolled at Hadar Hatorah, a Rabbinical school, after receiving a university education. I quote my father: "When I went through the process that led me to make the decision to live my life according to the Torah, I started thinking, 'From where do I derive my sense of self? Is it the length of my hair? What if I would cut my long hair and go on campus wearing a suit and tie? I wouldn't know who I was or where I was.' I was thinking about the Holocaust and asked myself, 'What if someone would take away my clothes, my possessions, and even my life? From where would I derive my sense of self?' I realized I needed a sense of self that was independent of anything in this world. I realized that I was basing my identity on things that were

temporary and could be taken away from me. And then who would I be? What would I be? I would have no idea."

King Solomon wrote, "The soul of man is the candle of G-d." A neshamah is an inner flame that is eternal; it makes us who we are. Each soul is placed in a physical body for a certain amount of years with a unique mission to accomplish in this world.

...When the world around us is spiritually darker than ever before, it is time for us to reach deep inside to discover our inner light and let it shine! Every mitzvah is a candle, every time we study Torah, help another, give charity, use our talents to honor G-d, our soul lights up the darkness.

...We are all "Daddy's girls"; G-d considers every one of us His only child. Parents have the most pleasure when they see their children working together and caring for each other. We are making our Father, our G-d, extremely proud when Jewish girls unite to shine our light!

... Let's take time to visualize our candle within. A candle strives upward. Our soul yearns to connect to G-d, to give to others and add light to the world. When one flame lights another, its light doesn't diminish. It gives power to the next candle to light another candle.

Think of one way that you want to make this world a brighter place and think of one step you can take today to make it happen. A candle cannot keep its light to itself. It must shine for others!

At the event, Linda quoted Anne Frank, "How wonderful it is that nobody needs to wait a moment before starting to improve the world." Hilary Buff, an organizer, remarked, "Imagine if Anne Frank would not have been locked away in an attic — what else could she have accomplished? Even a dim candle adds light in a dark room. We hope that girls will think, 'What can I do today to shine my light and improve our world?'" JGU's new motto, "Shine your inner light," was introduced, and Rivka Leah Popack (née Cylich) sang her original song, "Shine Your Inner Light," for the crowd of mothers and daughters.

MY MIDDLE SEAT

"G-d doesn't ask us to choose our challenges; He chooses us."

After a full day of traveling by plane, we were on our way home from a fantastic weekend celebrating Meirah's bat mitzvah. Tired and exhausted from traveling with a baby, I was finally on the last leg of our trip back to Albany, together with my husband, baby, and three daughters.

On our final flight, we were all assigned separate seats. Even worse than being separated, they were all middle seats. Sitting with a one-year-old between two strangers was not my ideal travel plan. The lady on my right was tight-lipped and stared at me as if I was a criminal because I was holding a baby. Baruch tried to communicate in baby talk and babbled to her, but she refused to make any eye contact or respond to my sweet little boy. Then the kind man on my left offered to move if there was another seat, so I could sit together with my husband. However, every seat was full and no one wanted to change to a middle seat.

I felt like complaining to a flight attendant about the unfairness of the situation. Instead, I took a deep breath and told myself: "Just accept the situation and don't complain. You'll survive this three-hour flight. Remember: the seat assigned to you is by Divine Providence."

As I reviewed this dialogue between my two inner voices, I turned to my considerate seat-mate and thanked him for offering to change places to make it easier for me. I asked him if he lives in Albany and he answered that he resides in East Greenbush. As we are the *Chabad* representatives for East Greenbush, I thought, "Wouldn't it be cool if he was Jewish too?" So, I gathered the courage and asked him, "Are you Jewish?"

"Yes," he replied.

Was I surprised? Now it all made sense.

He told me that he had just returned from an interview for a doctorate program and he was asked, "Are you culturally diverse?" He replied that he is proud to be Jewish and embrace his heritage. He hadn't attended synagogue for a while and asked me about *Shabbos* services in the area, as well as where he could find matzah ball chicken soup. He missed his grandmother's delicious chicken soup because unfortunately she was in a nursing home and was unable to cook anymore. I answered, "Well, now you know that G-d loves you! You are more than welcome to join us for matzah ball chicken soup any Friday night!" I also gave him the information for the local synagogues and programs for students at University Heights *Chabad* and *Shabbos* House.

There is never a mistake in G-d's Universe. Everyone is assigned their "seat" in this world for a greater purpose. Everything turns out exactly the way it is meant to be, because everything occurs by Divine Providence. Once I changed my perception and accepted the seat assigned to me, I allowed G-d's plan to unfold and merited the opportunity to shine His light onto another caring Jew.

I would have chosen a different "seat" in life. I didn't choose to lose my father at the young age of ten. I didn't choose the challenges that I face when trying to spread light. G-d doesn't ask us to choose our challenges; He chooses us. He knows what is best for our soul. This is not a hardship; it is a mission. He gave us our soul powers and the ability to choose our response. This is hinted to in the word "responsibility." I may not be able to change my "seat," but I have the *ability* to choose my *response* and uplift others in the process.

CHAPTER 6

Embrace the Inner Child

TELL THE TEN-YEAR-OLD YOU LOVE HER

"You tried to make it all okay, but it never really was."

After a virtual meeting with our JGU global leadership team to report on the beautiful launch in California, I was filled with gratitude to G-d for our founders, Linda and Ory Schwartz, and our global team. I sent out emails thanking everyone for their support:

> For years, I felt alone in my responsibilities. Thank G-d, I don't feel alone anymore. Today, I am grateful to G-d for sending me each of you to support our Jewish daughters worldwide. Thank YOU for caring about our Jewish future.

An hour later, I received this email response from Susan:

> When you can, find a quiet place. Get quiet and breathe deeply. Close your eyes. Breathe again, a few times. Keep your eyes closed and ask G-d for strength. Go inside and find your ten-year-old self. Tell her you love her. Ask her if it's okay to hold her. When she nods "Yes," hold her close and let her feel your heart beating. Tell her she is okay. Tell her that she is a strong and

special girl and that she will grow up and find a wonderful man who will love her for who she is. Tell her she will use her father's strength and kindness and truth to lead others. Tell her that it is okay to be mad that dad left her. And it's okay to be lonely and sad and that she will find strength.

Hold her and feel her in your arms. You may start to cry, and if you do, tell the little girl that you are so happy now and that is why you are crying. That it's okay to cry. She should not worry about you any longer. You are okay. She can be in peace now, knowing that it all turned out well. Tell her that she may visit you anytime she wants.

When you are ready, ask her if it's okay if you go now. Be sure to get her permission and remind her that she can visit whenever she wants. Say goodbye and then come back to consciousness. You have been carrying that sad and scared little girl in you for 30 years. You tried to make it all okay, but it never really was. Use this meditation to make it truly okay now.

All is well, friend. All is well. Sending love!

Hashem puts people into our lives to give us the messages we need at the exact right time. I read Susan's words and cried tears that felt so liberating. My dear husband was there to catch my uncontrollable tears. Susan realized that the JGU launch in California had awakened the brokenhearted and lonely ten-year-old in me. She gave me permission to feel my feelings and mourn my loss. A child doesn't have the tools to process trauma. Since what happened to

A picture taken when I was 10 years, after finding out that my father was very ill.

my father was not okay, there was a part of me that was still not okay! I didn't realize that the sad little girl in me needed love and comfort. She had to learn that it is okay to not feel okay sometimes, and that we can make it okay with *Hashem's* help and support from friends and family.

This experience shed a whole new light on a favorite song that we sing at the *Pesach Seder*, "*Baruch haMakom baruch Hu, baruch Shenasan Torah l'amo Yisrael, baruch Hu. K'neged arbaah banim* — Blessed is the Omnipresent, blessed be He! Blessed is He who gave the Torah to His people Israel, blessed be He! The Torah speaks of four children." The *Haggadah* specifies four types of children to teach us that we also possess all of these "four children" within ourselves. When we address the wise, wicked, simple, and unable-to-ask elements within, we experience freedom from our personal Egypt.[39]

Pesach gives us the power to be truly free from anything that limits the full expression of our soul. If in the past we were angry like the wicked child because of life circumstances, or silent about our pain, this song reminds us to embrace each inner child. We find inner peace when we recognize that we are G-d's precious child and that He still loves us even when we feel sad or mad. The word "*baruch*," "blessed," is repeated four times, once for each son, to remind us that everything we encounter is a blessing. We honor the child in us and free our soul when we accept and embrace every part of ourselves. We find comfort when we recognize that every experience shapes us. Revisiting and healing unresolved pain is a difficult process, but we must remember that this process of transforming our darkness to light is so precious to *Hashem*.

Rabbi Tzvi Freeman writes on Chabad.org, "G-d created bitter and sweet, dark and light. I can take bitterness and turn it sweet, darkness and make it shine. I can create my own life. It will be hard, very hard. But it will be my own light. When it comes time to return it to its

---

39 Based on *The Rebbe's Haggadah* by Rabbi Chaim Miller

Creator, I will say, 'Look what I made with the stuff you gave me!' And He will say, 'That's my child!'"

BOND WITH THE INNER CHILD

"The armor that was once around your heart begins to melt."

6th grade school picture

Shortly after the JGU launch in California, we introduced a new online leadership class for teens. We taught the girls that in order to give to others, we must also give to ourselves. If we want to love others, we must love ourselves. I realized that I, too, needed to replenish and care for my physical and emotional needs. It was perfect timing when Miriam Yerushalmi, author, and psychologist, shared her guided meditation on bonding with one's inner child. This meditation touched me deeply.

> *Put yourself into a comfortable position. Inhale a deep, cleansing breath of all that is positive and healing, and when you exhale, breathe out all that is negative — the stress and the pressure. Breathe out all negative thoughts, especially those about yourself. Begin to breathe in only positive thoughts about yourself, as your whole body becomes more and more relaxed. With every breath you take, feel your eyes begin to close.*
>
> *Now, envision a beautiful place that you enjoy being in, a place that G-d created just for you. The beauty of this place nourishes you. A deep, penetrating warmth surrounds you; you feel safe. A peaceful stillness reaches deep*

within you, to your very center. At this place, you see a child approach you. A child so innocent, so sweet, so lovable — she is YOU!

Give her the attention she deserves, take the time to give her all that she wanted years ago. Be a parent to her now. She needs you. You need YOU!

Reassure her that she's a gift of G-d to the world — a precious soul. Tell her, "You are a gift of G-d to the world. G-d loves you."

You begin to see a bright smile of contentment and security. The feeling of warmth surrounds the two of you. Something very powerful is happening here, a wonderment is in the air. You hold her hand, and the bonding continues to grow. Hand in hand. The waves of nourishing comfort land right on the heaviness of your heart. The armor that was once around your heart begins to melt. Your heart begins to heal, to mend and to soften. The love and the sweetness help you begin anew. You feel more alive. Something is shifting in you, a new, powerful healing from this amazing moment of bonding. You begin to walk together, still holding each other's hands, not letting go. You feel blessed. You feel grace. You feel safe.

This safe, loving place has helped you do important healing work, and you are better for this. You are always together... never alone. You never have to let go. You're always one. This acceptance and love have helped you. You feel free. Free to be you, to feel alive. You say to yourself: G-d loves me! I love me! Again: I. Love. Me. Forever.

A MEMORY, A MISSION, A MOVIE

"Focus on the beautiful drama of your own existence."

As a *Pesach* activity, my family watched the newly-released *Operation: Candlelight*, a feature film for women and girls, directed by Levi and Robin Garbose. The main character of the movie, Sara Wasserman, lost her father as a young girl. I was surprised when they told me that the father of the main character was named Rabbi Azriel Wasserman.

As I watched the following scene, my eyes filled with tears as I felt the agony of being a young girl who never had a chance to say goodbye to her *Tatty*.

In the scene, Sara lives in a boarding school because her mother remarried. She opens up and tells her new friend, Stella, about her father. Stella, a girl who also lost her father, is hiding out in the boarding school because of a dangerous situation at home. Frightened and concerned about her mom and sister, she is unable to sleep.

Sara: There is a G-d Above, Who is running everything. You have to trust, Stella, that everything that happens to you is for a reason. It's all for the good even if it doesn't feel that way.

Stella: [Notices a picture on Sara's night table] Is that your dad?

Sara: Of blessed memory.

Stella: What do you mean? You lost your dad too?

Sara: Three years ago, and my mother just got remarried.

Stella: What happened?

Sara: [Looking at her father's picture] When I was in fifth grade, my father started getting these terrible headaches. And then they found out it was a brain tumor that was inoperable. Ten months later he was gone, just like that.

Stella: That's so sad.

Sara: Rabbi Azriel Wasserman — everyone loved my father. He always knew the right thing to say and the right thing to do.

Stella: Wow, he sounds just like you.

Sara: Gimme a break, I'm nothing like him.

Stella: Maybe you don't see yourself, but I've definitely never met anyone like you, ever.

Sara: All I know is he was a wonderful person, and I miss him every minute of every day.

Stella: But you seem so together. I'm still, like, totally messed up.

Sara: I don't know. Maybe it's something he said to me.

Stella: What was that?

Sara: He was in the hospital, and he looked up at me and said, "Sara, trust in this: Hashem is always guiding you, even when it hurts." He went into a coma after that and I never really got to say goodbye.

This film was a message from my father to remember his last words, empowering me to trust in G-d at all times. I had been focused on the fact that I wasn't given a chance to say goodbye, but my father found a way to remind me to internalize his teachings, "*Hashem is always guiding you, even when it hurts.*" He also used to say, "Every detail of our lives is being orchestrated by a loving, caring G-d, for our good. Focus on the beautiful drama of your existence." I also realized that if a small piece of my story made a great scene in a movie, my story would make a worthwhile read and could even become a book.

After I watched the movie, I received this touching email:

Hi Nechama Dina,

I wanted to let you know that we just returned from seeing Robin Garbose's film, Operation Candlelight. After the movie ended, we asked Robin about the main character's father, mentioned by name as Rabbi Azriel Wasserman. She told us that her husband, Levi, was very close with your father and since they wanted the name of a real person who had been super special, they chose your father's name. Did I ever tell you about the time I asked your father why he said Tehillim nonstop? He answered me, a fourth-grade student, with so much patience, sincerity, and love. He explained that the world stands on the three pillars of Torah, prayer, and acts of kindness, and if even one is not happening at any given instant, the whole world would cease to exist, so he wanted to do his part to "hold it up."

Some people are so special that you will remember them forever. Your father was one such person!

Sorah Shemtov

My father's teachings touched many and I felt his presence so strongly. Layers of pain were melting from around my heart. I could see a bright light emerging from darkness.

WELCOME BACK, NECHAMA DINA

"My deeds brought such joy to my father."

I traveled to Kingston, Pennsylvania in November 2015 for a speaking engagement at the home of Devorah Leah Schulman (née Seliger), who spent several childhood summers with our family and later became a staff member at JGR. Her father had been a *Shabbos* guest at our home while my father was physically alive and we reconnected in Albany when we moved Upstate. She became a big sister to my children and was a huge help while I was growing JGR and had so many young children. Indirectly, this is an example of my father helping me in my mission through the relationships he formed during his life.

At the conclusion of my presentation, Nechama Dena Zweibel, a speaker and psychological kinesiologist, approached me and asked, "Isn't your full name Nechama Dina?" I explained that I had been called Nechama Dina when I was a child but shortened my name to Nechama when I moved upstate.

She said, "You are now ready to take back the name Dina. Nechama means 'comfort' and symbolizes G-d's kindness, and Dina means 'judgment' and represents G-d's *gevurah*, discipline. You are now ready to create balance and harmony in your life with both names." I smiled at her insight and thanked her for sharing.

The following Friday night, my family was asleep and I had some quiet moments to reflect on what Nechama Dena had said. Her words hit me hard when I realized that I had subconsciously rejected the name Dina because of the broken-hearted Nechama Dina who had never stopped crying for her *Tatty*, who had never fully processed or accepted *Hashem*'s *din*, judgment. When I embarked on the new chapter of my life as a newlywed, I let go of the "Dina" — my ties to the painful memories of loss.

When I realized that the root word for the name Dina is the same word as the blessing we recite upon hearing the news of someone's passing, "*Baruch Dayan Ha'emes*[40]," the heavy rain clouds in my mind let loose, and great drops fell from my eyes.

I wiped my tears, but my emotions were still in a state of turmoil. I was not in a frame of mind to fall asleep. The young Nechama Dina Wasserman yearned to find comfort and accept *Hashem*'s plan with a complete heart. I needed some inspiration, so I picked up an old *N'shei Chabad Newsletter* to read. The cover was gone, and lo and behold the first page was an editorial by Rishe Deitsch, with the following story about a girl named Nechama Dina. I was amazed and knew this had been written for me.

> *Back in November of 1987, my niece Nechama Dina Posner was six years old. The Rebbe had announced that this was the year of Hakhel, the seventh year in which, traditionally, the Jewish king would gather all the Jews and read aloud the Torah. Wherever Jews are gathered, said the Rebbe, we should stand up and say words of Torah, with words of inspiration, thus turning it into something holy, a "Hakhel gathering."*
>
> *Nechama Dina, also known as Dina, lived in Skokie, Illinois, where her parents, Rabbi Yosef and Zeesy Posner, were and still are on Shlichus.*

---
40 "Blessed is the true Judge"

In the summer of 1987, Dina rode a minibus to and from day camp. The minibus also drove children going to and from other day camps. So Dina became friends with "Melissa," a Jewish girl who rode the minibus with her, who was attending a non-frum camp.

A few months after day camp ended, Dina received an invitation in the mail to Melissa's birthday party. With fond memories of the summer friendship, Dina wanted to go.

A few days before the party, Dina's father asked her, "Dina, would you like to do something very good, and make the Rebbe very proud of you?"

The little girl thought about it and agreed that she would, indeed, like to do something very good and make the Rebbe very proud of her.

Her father explained to her what the Rebbe had requested regarding Hakhel. She would have to stand up in front of all of the children at the party and say a dvar Torah. Many were not frum at all, and this would be a whole new concept for them.

Father and daughter worked on "the speech." It was very short. It contained a brief description of what took place in ancient times during a Hakhel year, and a conclusion encouraging the children to do mitzvos. Dina practiced a few times.

[...] A tremor of stage fright passed through the little girl, but she stood up and delivered her Hakhel speech.

Her father came to pick her up. In the car on the way home, he asked, "Did you make your speech?" Dina was happy to be able to tell him that she had, indeed, done it!

And later: "Dina, do you want to write a letter to the Rebbe and tell him that you did as he asked?"

So Dina sat down with a pen and paper and wrote the Rebbe a letter. And not long afterward, she received a signed letter from the Rebbe, acknowledging her letter, and thanking her for what she had done.

Says Dina, "My father was very excited by the Rebbe's letter to me. He had real joy from it. Aside from the fact that it made the Rebbe real to me, I probably didn't appreciate it that much myself; but I do recall my happiness that my deeds had brought such joy to my father. My father was so excited about it, in fact, that he made photocopies of the Rebbe's letter to me and gave them to me for me to give out to my class, to inspire them to follow suit.

"Honestly, I never gave out the copies to my classmates. I just carried them to and from school for a few days, in my backpack. I still have all of them."

I had this experience (giving the talk and then reading the editorial) while I was in the middle of preparing for our annual Jewish Girls Winter Retreat.

Our theme that year was *Hakhel*, or "Unite to Ignite," and the message for me was loud and clear: Our mission of uniting Jewish girls of all backgrounds is bringing the *Rebbe* delight and joy to the father of Nechama Dina (first the Posner father, and now mine). This was one of those pivotal moments in my life when I accepted *Hashem*'s judgment with my mind and heart as one. I once again embraced the name "Nechama Dina" and welcomed her back into my life with a whole heart. I found a new youthful energy and spirit to continue my *Shlichus* uniting and teaching Jewish girls.

Baruch Hashem, the unity and joy were palpable between the 65 campers and staff at that year's winter retreat, and I knew that my father was so proud of the legacy that he began. I was confident that I, Nechama Dina Wasserman-Laber, also brought joy to my father. My father's happiness replaced another layer of the sadness in the broken heart of young Nechama Dina who longed for her *Tatty*. This was another step in my healing journey to accept the "Dina," *Hashem*'s judgment, and find "Nechama," comfort.

REMOVING THE OBSTACLES

"Once you remove the obstacles, you will be ready for this new level in your mission."

My father taught, "Today, Egypt refers to the obstacles that prevent us from accepting who we are. Our job is to remove the barriers that stand in the way of expressing our true selves. When we remove our blocks to personal growth, we claim what's inherently ours. When we break through these obstacles, the potential within will bear fruit."

I called Nechama Dena Zweibel to let her know how much her comments affected me. We felt a deep soul connection and she offered to stay in touch with me through weekly one-on-one *farbrengens*. Our first *farbrengen* took place on *Chanukah*, and after an initial *niggun*, she said, "May our learning bring us to the next level of personal redemption. Let's visualize what that would look like in our lives." She asked me, "Where do you want to go next with everything that you are doing?" At the time, JGU was taking off and we were also considering another property.

Nechama Dena shared a talk from the *Rebbe* that occurred on my birthday. She called it "my birthday *sichah*." She explained that G-d wants us to create a dwelling for Him where He is fully comfortable. A home is where one can completely be at ease to genuinely express oneself. She brought out the novel realization that when you buy a customized gift for someone's home, you will choose a gift according to their liking. Just like we don't question someone's taste reflected in their abode, *halachah* is G-d's way of saying, "This is how I like to dwell in My home." A gift brings people pleasure; *halachos* bring *Hashem* pleasure.[41]

---
[41] *Sicha Parshas Re'eh* 5751

Every time we do anything according to Jewish law, we are conveying to G-d, "I recognize how I can give You satisfaction through acknowledging and validating Your taste." In this way, we create a relationship with G-d that is filled with pleasure.

One of the goals for our retreats is to create a time and place where we tap into what we truly desire. It is where we feel contentment and calm. This is the type of relationship we want to develop with G-d, and this will be reflected in all of our relationships. Therefore, our retreat location will inspire others to have a pleasure-filled relationship with G-d.

Nechama Dena said, "There may be something that still needs to be completed. And once you remove the obstacles, you will be ready for this new level in your mission. We need a stronger level of *bitachon* to remove obstacles from our path. One way to accomplish this is to thank *Hashem* in advance. When we thank *Hashem* even before something happens, we hasten the process of *Hashem's* response, because we are strengthening the energy of our trust in G-d."

She encouraged me to visualize new technology to accommodate many more people, and a secretary to answer thousands of calls and emails. "Let's also visualize a home for JGU and thank *Hashem* for making this a reality in a miraculous way that is above nature. In a way that you can't even imagine. When we have a yearning and desire to move to a new place, *Hashem* is saying, 'This is where I want you to make a home for Me on earth.'"

We learned some of the meaning of the *Hallel* prayer: "*B'tzeis Yisrael miMitzrayim, Beis Yaakov me'am lo'ez... Hahofchi hatzur agam mayim chalamish l'mayanei mayim.* — When Israel went out of Egypt, the House of Jacob, from a people of a foreign tongue... G-d turns the rock into a pool of water, the flintstone into a fountain of water.[42]"

---
42 *Tehillim* 114: 1, 8

Hashem can transform a rock into a fountain of water. We are all "*maayanos*," wellsprings of wisdom, to reach out and help others. "*Beis Yaakov*" refers to Jewish women. We ask *Hashem* to help us open our hearts so we can receive from the giving fountains, since a heart is hard like a rock when it is blocked from receiving wisdom. Once we open our hearts, we can open the hearts of others to receive the wellsprings.

We continued further in *Hallel*, where we say the words, "Not for us (*lo lanu*), O Lord, not for us, but to give honor to your name, for Your kindness and for Your truthfulness.[43]"

When we have desires, we must ask ourselves, "Why do I have this desire?" The answer must be what we say in *Hallel*: "I want it for You, *Hashem*.... *Lo lanu*... This is not for me, it is for YOU! My *neshamah* needs it to accomplish its mission for YOU."

I wondered, could I really achieve my goals to find and purchase a new dream home to accomplish my soul's mission?

Nechama Dena encouraged me to really "see" the vision; to remember at that moment, "*lo lanu*"; to visualize myself in the house for *Hashem*, celebrating *Pesach* and other happy times there; and, to thank *Hashem* for it in advance!

So, I thanked *Hashem* in advance for granting me the most beautiful, abundant home. If it was meant for me, it would work out or *Hashem* would show me something even better.

"*Lo lanu*..."

We agreed to thank *Hashem* every day for three things we already had. This brings more blessings into our lives. *I thank You, Hashem, for my children, for my JGU community, and for my health.*

---

[43] *Tehillim* 115:1

RELEASE THE PAIN

"I release anyone who has caused me pain."

Nechama Dena helped me to remove the blocks to my growth by letting go of limiting beliefs. In another one-on-one *farbrengen*, we learned how to focus on something that we want to heal.

Here are the steps:

a. Focus on something that we want to change or heal

b. Add either prayer or Torah learning, while having the intention to heal the situation

c. Anticipate the full healing with joy

When earlier pain caused by others or limiting beliefs rise to the surface, it is an opportunity to heal and transform the pain into the pleasure of fulfilling our purpose. This is a gift from *Hashem* because *exposure brings closure*. Nechama Dena used a parable to depict her powerful message. Those who have used harmful words or actions toward us, at any time, have attached a subliminal, emotional IV containing toxic energy. Holding resentment toward someone is like keeping the IV attached and receiving a constant infusion of toxicity. We definitely want to detach.

When we release the needle that is stuck inside, we can work on healing. As long as the needle is attached, a person will experience all kinds of negative thoughts that can be triggered by someone else. However, we can erase the harm and pain that happened to us in this life, or any other incarnation, with a few powerful words.

"Sherai l'chol mahn di tza'aron."

(Translation: **I release anyone who has caused me pain.**)

We say it three times.

Nechama Dena applied this to the trauma I experienced as a child.

She explained, "After your father's passing, there was silence and so many people faded from your life because they didn't have the capacity to deal with the loss. They didn't know what to say or how to help you. You will now release all the people who didn't reach out to you in your pain.

"You asked for a *refuah sheleimah* for your father — and the pain remains. You can release your feelings of betrayal by G-d for what felt like your unanswered prayers."

My eyes filled with tears as I recalled the many hours that I prayed for my father's recovery. I had even dared to stand alone outside the *Rebbe's* home several times, waiting for him to proceed to his car so I could beg him to bless my father with good health. The *Rebbe* gave his blessing and said, "He should be *gezunt*."

As a child, it appeared to me that G-d didn't answer my prayers. I felt abandoned and alone. I felt a disconnect. My heart closed.

Receiving a coin from the Rebbe

Nechama Dena said, "When you cry, you can release the pain and you are now ready for deeper healing with the *cheshbon tzedek*.[44]"

We entreat G-d to heal the pain through the following prayer, which is the first paragraph in the recital of the bedtime *Shema*.

Ribbono shel olam — Master of the universe

Hareini mochel — behold I forgive (neutralize the effect)

L'chol mi — anyone (having in mind the particular individual or group)

Shehich'is vhiknit osi — who angered or antagonized me, etc.

Within this paragraph, we pay special attention to the words "*bein b'gilgul zeh bein b'gilgul acher* — whether (this occurred) in this lifetime or another lifetime." There may be a deeper soul connection that needs closure from past lifetimes, as well.

In continuation of this paragraph, we take responsibility for our actions:

Umah shechatasi — and where I have been inadequate in my actions

Mechok berachamecha harabim — erase with Your great compassion.

When G-d erases, there are no traces.

We think, say or do positive things that will strengthen us at a deeper level and help restore balance.

I understood that I have the power to create more love and connection with people who may have unintentionally caused me pain. This is how the inner light shines in ourselves and others.

---

[44] Nechama Dena further explains the steps for a *cheshbon tzedek* in her "My Life Essay" contest submission (www.MeaningfulLife.com).

I OPENED MY HEART

"I wanted to connect to his light."

Through the process of resurrecting my father's legacy and dedicating my life's mission fully to Jewish girls, I also faced the sad little girl in me who longed for her father's love and needed care and compassion.

I felt alone.
I felt loss.
I felt pain.

Many years had passed...
I forgot his loving words to me
I forgot his love and joy
I forgot how lucky I was that he fathered me for ten years

I wanted to talk about his life
I wanted to learn about his positivity
I wanted to connect to his light

I began to heal my broken heart
I began to feel his incredible joy
I began to see his shining light

I opened my heart to Hashem's guidance
I opened my heart to Hashem's love,
I opened my heart to Hashem's comfort

I live to carry on Tatty's legacy and fulfill my soul purpose
I live to comfort souls crying to connect to Hashem
I live to bring nechamah to all Jewish girls

Today, I share my journey to finding "Nechama"
Today, I share the power of turning tears into growth
Today, I share the message of SEEING THROUGH THE THORNS!

CHAPTER 7

FROM ROSES TO PEARLS

MY PRAYERS WERE NOT ANSWERED

*"I don't **have to** daven — I **want** to daven!"*

> Never Alone Journal
>
> Chanukah - December 2015
>
> I composed an affirmation today: "I am growing in my relationship with Hashem."
>
> What inspired me? Recently, I started to dance and then daven to Chanukah music. I was inspired to dance before praying as a result of my one on one learning with Nechama Dena Zweibel and Miriam Yerushalmi. I began to feel joy in my davening. I danced with baby Baruch to a favorite song, "Hakadosh Baruch Hu, Anachnu Ohavim Otcha,[45]" and then recited my morning prayers. I felt my love for Hashem blossom. I thought about all the things I am grateful for in my life today... I felt love for G-d seep into my heart like a fountain of water flowing from great heights.

---
45 "The Holy One, Blessed be He, we love you."

While I was praying, I had a flashback to a subconscious memory that came to the surface from my childhood. I must have been seven years old. It was early Rosh Hashanah morning, and I awoke startled, still fully dressed. I realized that I had fallen asleep without reciting the nightly Shema. Inspired by my father, I had taken upon myself to recite the full Shema prayer from a siddur. I approached my father while he was studying with tears in my eyes and cried that I forgot to recite the Shema on the holiest day of the year. I felt so terrible. He smiled and said, "These are holy tears," and he placed them on my forehead. Why did my father place the tears on my forehead? Perhaps he was training me to use the power of my mind to turn my tears into a springboard for growth. Another message that came to me was that he was teaching me to not only recite the Shema, but to meditate on its meaning and say it with intention.

As I was saying *Shema* on that cold *Chanukah* morning, I began to cry those same tears. I felt my heart open and my soul reconnect with G-d. I suddenly realized why *davening* had become a difficult *mitzvah* for me. I had *davened* for my father to get well. My prayers were unanswered, and then he left me. I felt abandoned and alone. I subconsciously felt a disconnect, and prayer was no longer natural for me. As a teenager, I would *daven* because my mother and teachers told me I had to. As an adult, there were days that I took time to pray and there were other days that I couldn't find the time as a busy mom.

I yearned to appreciate prayer and truly connect to my Creator. As I *davened*, I cried more tears, but they weren't tears of sadness. They were helping to wash away the pain in my heart. I felt my soul ignite and my heart open to my Father in heaven. I felt love for *Hashem* in a way I had never experienced before and gained a new appreciation of the gift of prayer.

I don't **have to** *daven* — I **want** to *daven*! I **want** to ignite my soul each day so I can shine my light for my family and global community.

I need to connect to *Hashem*; He is truly my Partner in everything I do. Would I go to work and ignore members on my team? Of course not! G-d is the One leading my team. I must talk to Him because He wants me to succeed. All of *Hashem's* blessings are waiting for me. All I need to do is **ask** and **pray**!

The same week that I had this prayer breakthrough, I was asked to give a prayer class by a woman yearning to feel the connection with *Hashem* through understanding the prayers. Prayer is called "*avodah shebalev* — work of the heart." When my heart, which had become like a rock, opened to receive the wellsprings of wisdom, it also opened the hearts of others. A month later, we launched our online prayer class, *Roses to Pearls*.[46] It's amazing that a couple of the women who attend the class were my father's students years ago.

Many people tell me that they struggle with prayer. Our prayers begin with *Pesukei D'Zimra*; while the word *zimra* means "song," it also comes from the phrase, "*l'zamer aritzim* — to cut away thorns.[47]" The "thorns" are obstacles that prevent us from feeling an inner connection to G-d. These obstacles affect our concentration in prayer. The purpose of *Pesukei D'Zimra* is to clear our minds and hearts of all these "thorns," enabling us to connect to G-d by focusing on His greatness and the beauty of His creations. Through singing songs of praise about the wonders of nature, we witness G-d in every detail of life: the leaves, branches, and even the delayed bus.

Roses to Pearls symbolizes the journey to opening my heart. Prayer with intention is a powerful tool to see through the thorns and transform life's irritations into pearls. Meditating on the meaning of the prayers creates a connection between the mind and heart. Filling our minds with thoughts about G-d's greatness gives birth to love and joy,

---

46 Women can sign up for our weekly class at www.jewishgirlsunite.com.
47 *Likutei Torah Bechukosai* 47d, *Nitzavim* 51d

instead of sadness and grief. The thorns are eliminated and love of G-d can flow in our hearts. My father imparted this message to me through placing tears on my forehead. I only comprehended and received his wisdom many years later. Through reconnecting to G-d, I also discovered a renewed spiritual connection with my father.

RECORD MY STORY FOR GENERATIONS

"Everything in our lives is 'baruch Mordechai' – truly good!"

My son Baruch turned one in March 2015 on the Fast of Esther. I was rocking him to sleep on *Purim* night to music playing from my computer. We'd had a quieter *Purim* than usual. I remembered the joyous *Purim* celebrations we had when I was a child. I recalled the large *Purim* celebrations in the synagogue in Troy. These happy memories led me to a place of sadness because I missed those days. Unexpectedly, one of the *Purim* recordings that I had digitized of my father speaking on Purim 1982 began to play. My father was singing and sharing holiday lessons with the *Purim* guests. It's unbelievable how my father always finds ways to speak to me!

He said:

"It is a mitzvah on Purim to drink to the point where one no longer recognizes the distinction between 'cursed is Haman' and 'blessed is Mordechai.' What does this mean? We tend to evaluate our lives as good, symbolized by the phrase 'baruch Mordechai,' or bad, as referred to by the phrase, 'arur Haman.' On Purim, we receive the power to see everything in our lives as all coming from the goodness of the Infinite One above. So instead of allowing ourselves to become sad or depressed, angry or consumed by negative emotions, we can become uplifted by all of the good in our lives. We get a glimpse into the true reality of our existence — that all is good. We break the small-mindedness and perceive the underlying reality. Deep down, every Jew knows in

his heart that nothing exists but G-d, because He is the only reality, and that everything in our lives is 'baruch Mordechai' — truly good!"

My sweet baby, Baruch Mordechai, was sitting on my lap smiling instead of sleeping. I knew that my father was smiling down at us. I made a *l'chaim* to my father and felt the joy of *Purim* that comes from seeing everything in our lives as "*baruch Mordechai*"—a blessing.

Upon reflection, it was following Baruch Mordechai's birth that my efforts to see the good and transform darkness into light shifted into high gear through writing blogs and telling my story to audiences. It is not by chance that he was born on the Fast of Esther, a day that overturned the decree of annihilation into the greatest salvation of our nation. Each child is a channel for new blessings and healing.

Queen Esther's story resonates strongly with me. Queen Esther was an orphan, yet she did not become a victim to her life circumstances. When she faced a crisis, she leapt over the obstacles into action and saved her people. I can relate to her upbringing as an orphan and how easy it is to fall into a victim mindset. Yet, we see the same life experiences strengthened her resilience and molded her to become the *Purim* heroine who brought light, joy, and salvation to her People. And today, we are still learning from her courage and faith; we are still telling her story, called *Megillas Esther*. *Megillah* means 'to reveal' and Esther means 'hidden'. Through telling the story, we reveal the hidden hand of *Hashem* and the hidden good in every situation. When we share our story, we connect, support and uplift each other. The truth is, we all have a story. Yours will inspire others, too.

We are telling Esther's story because she requested that her story be recorded for generations. The *Lubavitcher Rebbe* asks why Esther insisted that her role be recorded. Was she looking for fame? Rather, she wanted to teach future generations of Jewish women and girls, that the endurance and continuity of our people depends on **them**. By standing strong in all matters of *Yiddishkeit*, they fortify the Jewish family — and ultimately, the entire Jewish nation.

I love the idea that the evil Haman is now a cookie, thanks to Queen Esther. What a total transformation! A *hamantash* is sweet and brings joy to others. There is a profound joy in transforming pain through finding meaning in our struggles, especially when our experiences can provide healing for others. I'm so grateful to *Hashem* for the guidance and support I received to record my story for generations. I hope the life lessons that I impart through my journey will empower women and girls to overcome any challenge they may face with faith in *Hashem*, whether it is physical, emotional or spiritual.

For years, I used to carry my story alone until I discovered the power of sharing. I feel joy when I empower JGU girls to find meaning in their struggles and share their stories. I want every Jewish girl to know that they are not alone.

BEAUTY IN THE THORNS

"I choose to see the beauty in the thorns each day."

My initial idea for the title of this book was *From Roses to Pearls*, because in my over 30 year journey to find comfort and true acceptance of the Divine plan, I have learned to see through the thorns (acknowledge and grow from the pain), to appreciate my roses (focus on my blessings) and continually transform into a pearl (turn the irritations into 'pearls' and live with constant trust in G-d, as sea creatures are always aware of their source of life).

The first step in healing is to validate the pain — the thorns. Eventually, we come to an awareness of how the thorns helped us grow. As a result, we begin to notice and appreciate the roses — the blessings in our lives. Once we focus on the good, we have the power to transform the pain into 'pearls', something beautiful and uplifting for others.

Using the rose as a metaphor, I wrote the following poem about my shift in perspective. The rose is compared to the soul, which does not lose its beauty even when surrounded by thorns. The thorns help to preserve and protect the rose. The thorns — my challenges — had served a purpose, helping me grow into the person I am today. When we listen to the voice of our soul, we can find purpose in the thorniest situations of our lives.

A Rose

I used to feel like a rose among thorns
The roses in the garden were hard to see
I focused more on the pain of the sharp thorns
I have learned today how to be free

I learned to appreciate the beauty of each rose
I learned to take the time to nurture each seed
I learned to smile as I watch my garden grow
I learned to thank G-d for the tools to succeed

I view the thorns as a symbol of strength and protection
I accept the thorns in life and say, "It's all okay!"
I see how everything in my life is G-d's perfection
I choose to see the beauty in the thorns each day.

I was excited for my trip in June 2015 to share the above message with girls at the Hillel High School in Milwaukee. Some of these girls were our JGR campers, who were the founding students at the school because they wanted to attend a Jewish high school. I prepared a handout with the following poem and included a

picture of my father to express the point. I wanted to show that we can choose to focus on the thorns in our life or on the beautiful roses in our garden. I chose a random picture that came up on my computer. And when I took a second look at the photo, it hit me: behind my father was a framed picture of roses! I was stunned... I had never noticed the roses before.

I felt my father's holy presence at my side, lovingly communicating to me. "Remember, my child, to view the entire picture. The roses were always there, but you didn't see them. There are times that only G-d can see the bigger picture, however, when you are ready to open your eyes, the goodness will be revealed to you. When you are in pain, I am in pain with you. Thank you for lifting me from the thorns with you. Always remember to focus on the good, the beautiful roses in the garden of your life."

Can we ever understand G-d's master plan? No. But we can choose to see the beauty in each thorn. There is so much beauty and growth awaiting us when we nurture the roses in our garden, and cultivate the positive aspects in our lives. We come to realize how the thorns in our lives helped us grow.

A few months later, Rabbi Mendel Shagalov, a grandfather of a camper, visited the camp. He shared with me that he had been at my father's side in the hospital at the end of his life. He said that my father had the face of an angel, and his lips were constantly moving to the words of prayers; there was no fear in his eyes, and he was at peace. Rabbi Shagalov's eyes brimmed over with tears seeing my father's health deteriorate before him. He was noticeably upset, and my father whispered to him, "Mendel, don't focus on the pain, focus on the health (*gezunt*)!"

Again, my father was sharing a fundamental lesson of faith with me, this time through Rabbi Shagalov, guiding me to focus on the beauty that grows from the thorns.

When faced with an obstacle, my positive affirmation became, "This helps me grow!"

It reminded me of a statement my father shared with his students: "This is a perfect experience from G-d to teach me about myself."

My father taught his students, The literal translation of "*Shivisi Hashem l'negdi samid,*" is, "I place G-d continually before me.[48]" The deeper meaning of this verse is, "Whatever G-d places before me, I accept equally."

I accept the "thorns" and the "roses!"

---

[48] *Tehillim* 16:8

SEE THE ONENESS — THE HIGHS AND LOWS

"I feel G-d's embrace. I feel His oneness."

My son was once sharing with me all the different reasons he didn't like homework. At the time, I was rummaging through my cupboard to find the ingredients to bake a cake for *Shabbos*. As I measured the ingredients, I told him that since he loves cake, he doesn't have to wait for it to come out of the oven — he could have a taste in advance. He was confused until I offered him a sip of oil and a spoonful of flour and a little bit of cinnamon to add flavor. "Ick," he said, "I'll wait till after the ingredients are mixed together and baked in the oven."

My son could hardly wait to taste a piece of steaming hot cake. We sat down to enjoy a cup of tea and cake, as well as to digest the relevant lesson. I explained, "My darling child, do you see how once the ingredients are blended and baked, every ingredient is just right? The same applies to our lives. In life, we face all kinds of encounters and each one on their own can be difficult to understand. Yet, our Creator knows that when we connect the dots — every experience, every struggle, the loads of homework and even the rude comments made by others — it all becomes part of building our character. Each ingredient in our life serves a purpose and will eventually result in a delicious and sweet outcome.

At times, I struggle with the various pieces of my life. My mind is fractured by all the different parts. I tell myself that's okay, I am human. When we remember that in every challenge, there is a G-dly purpose waiting to be revealed, we discover our soul's unique light: strengths and insights that G-d wants us to reveal in order to heal ourselves and the world.

We move to a state of oneness when we serve G-d with every part of who we are: the light and the darkness.

What does it mean to serve G-d with our light and darkness?

Personally, for me it means to use my light; my gifts from G-d to share my story of loss and legacy. This is my responsibility. My childhood doesn't define me as a sad victim of fate, it defines my passion and mission to be a voice for those young girls silently suffering from grief and loneliness. I see the *"aleph,"* the Oneness of G-d within every part of my existence. When I see the Oneness of G-d and insert the *aleph* into my *"golah,"* my challenge, then I experience my *geulah*, personal redemption.

When I am in a low state, I search for the high that I am meant to reach. I breathe and remember that all the pieces of my life are part of my song, my Divine mission. This helps me feel calm, instead of stress, no matter what I face in life, because it is all part of my soul's song.

When I can see all the fragmented parts of my life coming together, the difficulties become easier, the fear and worry become reduced. I realize that *in every difficulty there is an opportunity.* My mission carries me through the challenges and obstacles. My mission fills me with joy. Joy leads to song. And my life is transformed into a song with highs and lows — yet, it is all ONE SONG!

> *I visualize every part of me — my light, my darkness — and mix it all as one. I see how G-d shines through every part of me, what I evaluate as good or bad. I accept it and feel okay with it. I feel oneness with G-d. I experience redemption from pain. I love every part of me — my light, my strengths, my personality, my weaknesses and challenges. It is all from G-d. It's all equally good. As I wrap my arms around myself and hug every part of me, I feel G-d's love. I feel G-d's embrace. I feel His oneness.*

When I combine the darkness of loss with my light through teaching lessons learned from my journey with others, I feel oneness in my soul. My soul sings her unique song.

FROM PAIN TO PEARLS

"What if I could transform my sadness completely into joy?"

I'd like to take you to a meeting in summer 2015 with counselors at JGR, where I learned an important life lesson. One night, after our counselors experienced a long and tiring day of shepherding their campers from one activity to the next, we had a staff meeting to unwind from the day, to tell stories, share advice. There were moments of laughter and moments of tears, moments of self-reflection and self-discovery.

I shared my story with the staff, telling them about my journey to see beyond the pain, sharing the message of "seeing through the thorns." Bryndel, a wonderful counselor from Montreal, asked me, "Nechama, why does there have to be thorns? I believe that all is good. There are only roses in my world and no thorns at all." My first response to her was that we are not living in a world of only roses; there will always be thorns, since there is so much pain around us. Upon further reflection, though, I took her words to heart and asked myself, "What if I aspire to reach a level where I don't see the thorns anymore? What if I turn my sadness completely into joy?"

This led to a discussion with the counselors about the teachings of Rabbi Akiva and Rabbi *Nachum Ish Gamzu*.

Rabbi Akiva used to say, "*Kol man d'avid Rachmana l'tav avid,*" which in Aramaic (the language most widely spoken by the Jewish People at that time, while Hebrew was spoken by the scholars) meant, "All that the Merciful One does, He does for good." In other words, even the bad will lead to good.

Rabbi Nachum said, "*Gam zu l'tovah,*" which in Hebrew means, "This is also for the good." In fact, it is believed that because he often repeated this saying, he was called "*Gamzu.*" He lived in a world where all is completely good at every moment, where even pain is good.

The Talmud relates many fascinating stories about Rabbi Akiva and *Nachum Ish Gamzu*. Here are two of them that illustrate their mottos, as told by Nissan Mindel on Chabad.org:

> *Rabbi Akiva had a narrow escape from death. He was once on his way to a city when the sun set and he had to take shelter in the woods. It was a dark night. He lit the only candle he had. He also had a rooster with him to wake him early in the morning, and a donkey on which he rode. Now, a strong wind blew out his candle and he remained in darkness. The next moment, the rooster was snatched by an animal of prey and a similar fate befell his donkey. Each time, Rabbi Akiva said, "All that the Merciful One does is for good."*
>
> *In the morning, when Rabbi Akiva arrived in the city, he learned that a band of vicious robbers had passed through the forest and attacked the city. Had they known of Rabbi Akiva's presence, he would have suffered violence at their hands! So it was good that the candle's light was blown out, that the rooster was not there to crow, nor the donkey to bray!*

And now the story about Rabbi Nachum:

> *Rabbi Nachum was once sent to Rome to try to persuade the Roman Emperor to be more kind to the Jews. He was carrying a precious box filled with gold and diamonds, a gift for the Emperor. On the way, he stopped at an inn, where he stayed for the night. On the following morning, he continued his journey, not knowing that the innkeeper had stolen the treasures from the box and filled it with sand and soil. When Rabbi Nachum finally reached Rome, he presented himself to the Emperor and handed him the box. On opening it, the box was found to contain nothing but earth. The Emperor was filled with anger, thinking that the Jews wanted to mock him. Nachum was thrown into prison and certain death awaited him. However, Nachum was not dismayed and said, as usual, "Gam zu l'tovah — This is also for the good."*

At his trial, one of the Emperor's advisers said that the Jews would certainly not have dared to mock the Emperor. He suggested, therefore, that perhaps this was no ordinary dirt. The adviser said he had heard that when Avraham, the first Jew, went to battle against Chedarlaomer and his confederate kings, he threw sand and soil at them, which G-d turned into arrows and deadly weapons. In this way, Avraham won the battle against the mighty kings. Maybe this sand and soil were of the same kind! Now, the Emperor had been at war for some time, but could triumph over his enemy, so he ordered this sand and soil to be used. Indeed, the miracle again occurred, and the enemy was defeated!

Nachum was immediately freed from prison and given many gifts, and the petition of the Jews was granted.

The *Lubavitcher Rebbe* explains that ultimately, even those matters that presently conceal and obscure goodness and holiness are themselves transformed into good; not only in a manner of "All that G-d does, He does for the good," i.e., that goodness will eventually result, but in a manner of "This too is for the good," that the matter itself becomes good.

This difference is to be understood from the story itself of *Nachum Ish Gam Zu*, where the transformation of the earth into weapons served as overtly revealed goodness, as opposed to the expression, "All that G-d does, He does for the good" wherein something was merely "for the good" but not transformed into actual goodness.[49]

Based on the *Rebbe's* explanation above, my staff and I concluded that Rabbi Akiva's teaching is the foundation of faith. We believe that the negative will lead to a good outcome. I agreed with Bryndel that it was possible to learn from Rabbi Nachum's story to have firm belief that all is truly good in every moment, even when it's not apparent. A

---

49 *Igros Kodesh*, Vol. XIV, p. 441.

mindset of *Gam zu l'tovah* — that this too is good — actually causes the negative to be transformed into a revealed good, where there are no longer any thorns. With trust in *Hashem*, that the negative situation itself is also good — the good will be revealed.

PEARLS OF WISDOM

"We have the strength to form pearls out of life's challenges."

On the last Friday night of camp, the JGR staff assembled for a special gathering. We had all grown so much, and watched our campers blossom and mature. It also happened to be the *Shabbos* before my father's thirtieth *yahrtzeit*. After a few songs, Bryndel stood up and said that she had something for me. With a big smile, she presented me with a beautiful pearl necklace, explaining that it was a gift from her grandmother, Mrs. Julie Gniwisch, for all my hard work that summer.

In great surprise, I exclaimed, "Wow! Are you giving me a real pearl necklace? Thank you so much for the beautiful gift."

And there was something I had to say to my staff: "Thank you for another life-changing summer. I will take to heart the pearls of wisdom that I gained from you this summer. These pearls," gesturing to my new necklace, "are formed when an oyster takes an irritating grain and covers it up with layers of nacre until it is transformed into a glowing pearl. I learned from you, Bryndel, that it is possible to live in a state of mind where 'all is good at every moment,' as *Nachum Ish Gamzu* showed us. We have the strength to form pearls out of life's irritants and challenges. We can let go of the pain and transform it into a purpose that creates positive change in the world. We can live with this realization each day and experience revealed goodness in our lives."

I felt that my father was speaking to me through my JGR staff, stretching my faith to the level of *Nachum Ish Gamzu*. My father was an unforgettable teacher who always pushed his students to grow and challenge themselves. He was pushing me to grow in my trust, still guiding and teaching me.

Turning pain into pearls is a process, which differs for each person. Just like time is needed for a pearl to form, a butterfly in the cocoon, and a seed to germinate in the ground, it is vital to give ourselves the time to experience and appreciate the process of creating our own pearl. Transformation happens when our painful experience is transformed into pearls of wisdom for others.

CHAPTER 8

G-d Comfort Me

COMFORT, COMFORT MY PEOPLE[50]

"G-d, please comfort my aching heart. Please help me see the light in the darkness."

I have discovered that in the healing process after loss, there are many layers of grief waiting to be peeled away in order to experience true *nechamah*, comfort. Once we strip one layer away, we face the next one. It may appear to be a setback, yet each time we reveal and heal a deeper part of ourselves.

After summer camp 2016, a staff member suggested I read an article about Rabbi Yaakov Dovid Klar, the Associate Director of Project CHAI, a program of the Chai Lifeline crisis team. The article was about the trauma he experienced when he was 12 years old and his

---
50 *Yeshayahu* 4:1

father was diagnosed with a serious illness. While the adults in his life tried to protect him by withholding details from him, the suspicion only added to his anguish. On his own, he walked to the hospital and shockingly found his father on his deathbed.

Rabbi Klar's story triggered a pain so real and deep within me before my father's thirtieth *yahrtzeit*. I felt angry that I was denied precious parting moments with my beloved father at the end of his life. (Anger is part of the grief cycle so I guess this was a process that needed to happen for my healing.) I remember pleading to visit him in the hospital in San Diego, but it was not meant to be. Over the duration of my father's condition, I was shielded from knowing about the severity of the situation. When my father departed for California to receive treatment, I had no idea that he was facing a life-threatening illness. I remember waving goodbye at the airport and saying to my father, "I can't wait for you to come home." I never entertained the thought that I might never see him again.

That night, I tossed and turned in bed. Sleep eluded me. I got up and wrote down my feelings in my journal. My last thought before I finally fell asleep was a prayer to G-d: *Please show me the purpose of the pain of not having a chance to say goodbye to my father. G-d, please comfort my aching heart. Please help me see the light in the darkness.*

Once again, G-d did not forsake me. The next day, I received a call from Mrs. Rochel (née Schmukler) Lazaroff, who had been my head counselor at Camp Pardes Chana. Today, Rochel is a *Shlucha* who provides spiritual, physical and emotional support services to patients and their families at the Texas Medical Center in Houston. She was calling with a quick question, but before she hung up, I decided to use the opportunity to express my deepest gratitude to her. I told her, "I want to thank you today for being one of those special people who provided me with a listening ear and understanding as a teen in camp."

Rochel remembered every word that I had shared with her as a young girl and she told me that today, in her work with families going through similar tragedies, she advises parents to let the child be part of the grieving process. "People overlook the child's feelings and try to protect the child from pain. The adults already begin the grieving process before the death, but the children are not able to mourn properly."

Rochel continued, "I have to thank you because my interaction with you during that year after camp had a lasting impact on me. Your story has helped me in my work. I only understand the incredible devastation of a child in your situation because you shared your deepest feelings with me years ago. I realized that it took years for you to get to the next step because you never grieved properly at the time of the tragedy. You were denied precious parting moments, and so the pain remained because there was no closure.

"When people in similar situations ask me what to do with their children, I tell them to let the children say goodbye and give them the gift of sharing loving parting words. If not, then BOOM! It's a tremendous shock when suddenly, the parent is gone. I tell parents not to deny their children meaningful parting moments with their loved one. They don't have to expose the children to the horrors of the illness — children don't have to know all the details — but let them create precious memories with their parent. It's crucial to give the child exposure to the reality of the situation so that later on, they can have proper closure."

She suggests that families take pictures together even if the child is very young and won't remember it. The image of the parent with the child validates their connection in the child's mind, allowing the parent to come alive. Adults naturally want to protect children, and no one wants to face the reality of death, but as Rochel says, "Grief is like entering a dark tunnel; until you go through it, you can't reach the light. Many people are afraid of entering the dark tunnel, but it is a crucial experience for comfort later on. The more one grieves in the beginning, the better it is for the person later on."

Rochel encourages parents to allow their child to feel the emotions of the loss itself because once the pain is validated, they can move forward and ask themselves, "Okay, so what am I going to do about it now?" It is like taking a bitter tasting pill, but then one can move on and be healthy. She tells families dealing with tragedy, "Now is the time to mourn and experience the pain. You are allowed to be angry. It's important to validate the pain and beg G-d to take it away, and this will lead you to the light."

I don't blame anyone for protecting me from knowing about the seriousness of my father's situation. I understand that I was shielded from the pain out of pure love and good intentions. And thank G-d, now that I have mourned the loss, I can move forward into the light. Now, it's time to ask myself, "Okay, so what can I do about this?" Today I share my story and the wise words spoken by Rochel, for maybe there will be a family or a child out there who will be helped because I put these words on paper.

G-d sent Rochel to help me see the G-dly purpose in the pain. I felt another layer of grief peeling away, knowing that my story has helped Rochel in her noble work. I see another purpose for my pain knowing that all these years, my story has guided others.

FINDING MY FATHER IN ME

"I cannot see his smile but I can smile for him."

The next day, July 24, 2016, was the fast of the 17th of Tammuz, known as *Shivah Asar B'Tammuz*, the start of a three-week mourning period for the destruction of Jerusalem and the two Holy Temples. While we mourn the Holy Temple in Jerusalem, we find comfort for all the tragedies that befell the Jewish people throughout history.

Greeting #28

Over three thousand years ago, on Av 9, the Beis Hamikdash was destroyed. The Holy Temple was the place where G-d's presence could be felt tangibly. It was the window to G-d, and the Temple was His physical home in Jerusalem.

After the destruction of the second Temple, G-d placed the Temple within us. Instead of traveling to a physical structure in Jerusalem, it is now up to us to find Him in our inner Jerusalem. Our bodies are our Temples, our souls are our windows, our minds are our Kohanim, and our animal instincts are our sacrifices. We don't bring sacrifices today, but we can pray. We don't travel to the Temple, but we can journey into our souls every day. We cannot find the Temple in Jerusalem, but we can discover G-d within us.

On Av 4, my dear father, a beloved teacher, Azriel Yitzchok Wasserman, o"bm, left our physical world at the age of 37. On Shabbos during the shivah week, Shimshon Stock, o"bm (a dear friend who helped our family and called my mother every day), stood up in the 770 synagogue and proclaimed, "This week, we lost two Temples."

My heart mourned the passing of my holy father for years, until one day, I realized that although I cannot visit my father in his home on earth, G-d placed my father in my heart and soul. It is up to me to find him within. I cannot hear my father teach, but I can spread his timeless teachings. I am not able to hold his hand, but I can hold hands in unity with Jewish girls from around the world. I cannot see his smile, but I can smile for him and share his love and joy.

This is G-d's master plan. G-d wants us to reveal the holiness of the Temple in every part of our being. He wants us to transform this entire world into a home for Him. He wants me to reveal my father's deep connection to G-d and his joy and positivity in my heart and soul. He wants me to spread my father's timeless teachings to the entire world. Our efforts to reveal G-d within us leads us to live with pure inner joy and peace. Likewise, when I reveal my beloved father in my heart and soul, I am filled with tremendous inner joy and peace.

As I wrote these words, tears trickled down my cheeks, not from sadness, but from the realization of the great responsibility I carry — to be a voice, hands, and feet for my beloved father. I see new meaning in the words wrote to him in the hospital, *"I'm waiting for you to come home healthy and strong with new strength. I want to see you healthy and strong with new strength like you never had before!"* My father's soul returned home to *Hashem*, and from his heavenly abode he certainly received new strengths that he never had before. When I connect to his soul, I reveal new strengths within that I never had before!

May our efforts bring us to the time when all sadness and tears will be transformed into never-ending joy with the coming of *Moshiach*! May we all come home to our third Holy Temple speedily in our days and be reunited physically with our loved ones.

It is no coincidence that my name is Nechama, which means comfort, and I was born in the month of *Menachem Av*, which means "father comforts." On the day of birth, one is endowed with all the powers one will need to face all of life's challenges. In the same month that I suffered the loss of my father, G-d also gave me the strength I needed to withstand this challenge; my birthday, the 28th of *Av*, is the numerical equivalent of the Hebrew word *"ko'ach,"* which means "strength." And this post was my 28th blog post.

The *Lubavitcher Rebbe* explains the passing of a righteous person:

The death of a righteous person is compared to "the burning of the House of the L-rd." These events (burning of the Beis Hamikdash and death of tzaddikim) are outwardly tragic; from their inner perspective, however, their purpose is to reach yet a higher level — which is attained by the transformation of tragedy into joy, which produces a joy loftier than if there were no tragedy in the first place, just as light that blazes forth from darkness is more intense than ordinary light, especially when the darkness itself gives forth light.

In the words of Rambam: "All these fasts are destined to be abolished in the Messianic era, and, moreover, they are destined to be festivals and days of gladness and joy." These fasts transformed into festivals will be of a level much loftier than the regular festivals today, for the revelations of the future era will be infinitely loftier than those of our times.

For the inner dimension of these tragedies to be manifested also outwardly, in this world, "vessels" are needed in which to absorb their lofty nature. In our case, the proper "vessels" with which to receive the lofty nature of a yahrtzeit are all aspects of Torah and mitzvos. The lesson we derive from a yahrtzeit, then, is to increase in Torah and mitzvos, an increase that transcends all boundaries. We must make many "vessels" — many both qualitatively and quantitatively.[51]

WINDOW TO THE SOUL

"When it is dark, search and find the window to your soul."

Singing the Hebrew *pesukim* of *Tehillim* and even saying them in English has been a source of healing for me. I find the songs of King David so comforting when my heart is aching. He reminds me that no matter what I go through in life, "G-d is my Rock!"

---
[51] Sichos in English

I was overcome with emotion while reading Psalm 27 on the *Shabbos* after my father's thirtieth *yahrtzeit*. The words, "For my father and my mother have forsaken me, but the Lord gathers me[52]" jumped at me while praying, and I burst out crying, unable to stop the tears. Since, I didn't want my children to worry if they saw me crying, I went for a walk and let my tears flow. I cried for those years so long ago when I felt alone and forsaken because I could not see my father physically and I didn't know how to create a soul connection that brought me joy.

I thought about David's words. Does the verse mean that because parents are human, and may not always be there physically, we should be comforted knowing that G-d's love will never forsake us? This didn't comfort me at all. I cried even more because I missed my father's love too. Could it be that when we are connected to the soul of a loved one, which is a piece of G-d Who is infinite and eternal, then their love and spirit remains with us forever? I wiped away my tears and felt the hole in my heart fill with the love I now knew I had never truly lost.

G-d's love is an infinite source of support that connects us to the spirit of our loved ones. We can connect to G-d through prayer, Torah study and *mitzvos*. When one relies on love from external and temporal sources alone, they may feel completely devastated when that limited source fades along with the love they received from it. When I recite this verse, I remind myself to tap into the infinite love of G-d, as well as the eternal love of my dear father's soul.

In the most challenging moments of his life, when King David's life was in danger, he turned to G-d with a song while playing his harp. These songs in *Tehillim* light up our darkness today. In my most challenging moments, I too have the power to reveal my light, and sing my song in the sorrow to bring a new tomorrow, just like King David. My father certainly internalized this truth.

---

52 *Tehillim* 27:10

Our talents are a window to the soul. They provide us with a healthy outlet to express the pain and allow the soul to shine through the darkness; through our gifts, we can heal wounds and overcome obstacles. We learn this lesson from King David who composed *Tehillim*, the book of Psalms, throughout all the trials and tribulations that he endured in his life. He would wake up at midnight to take out his harp and sing. He faced many struggles, including escaping the clutches of ten enemies who wanted his life, being chased by Saul, being captured by the Philistines, his family's abduction, the death of his baby and being driven from his throne by his son. Nevertheless, he consistently placed his trust in G-d, prayed for help, and thanked and praised Him in times of salvation.

Let's remember our gifts from G-d are the exact tools that we need to overcome life's challenges. As it says, "G-d doesn't give us anything we can't handle; along with the challenge, we are given the inner strength."[53] We don't need to look outside ourselves for the solution; the strength is within the recesses of our soul if we only take the time to search and find it.

COMFORTING HEARTS IN CALIFORNIA

"I will keep going and create a happy home for my children!"

My journey to comfort others and spread Jewish Girls Unite brought me back to California in January 2016. Miriam Rav-Noy, who had been a student of mine at the Maimonides Hebrew Day School, lost her husband, Ariel, at the young age of 36, leaving her with seven children. When I heard the unfortunate news, I stayed in contact with her, supporting her throughout that first, very challenging year. Dobra's notes from my father's classes were a source of inspiration for her. As the *yahrtzeit* approached, we felt that in addition to the traditional *seudah*,

---
[53] Talmud Avodah Zara 3a

it would be beneficial for Miriam's healing to organize a *yahrtzeit* gathering exclusively for women. She asked me to travel to Los Angeles to be the guest speaker.

With Miriam Rav-Noy in California.

I thought about my presentation for many days and nights. As a teacher, I learned to be comfortable speaking before a crowd; however, this was different. What was there to say to a family facing such an enormous loss? I was concerned about comforting the family with the right words. Susan was very encouraging, and assisted me in organizing my thoughts and suggested that I focus on three key points. I also prepared myself by learning with Nechama Dena Zweibel and we created this affirmation for my trip: "I create open and comforted hearts!" It really wasn't about the words I would say, but more about touching the audience with words of *nechamah* from my heart.

We were created in the image of G-d. When a family is in pain, there are no answers. However, we can emulate G-d by being there with them in their pain, share empathy, listen, love, and pray. G-d appeared to Moshe in the burning bush and reassured him, *"I shall be with you in your present distress, and I shall be with you in future exiles and persecutions.*[54]*"* We can use similar language to comfort another, "I am with you in your pain. I am here for you. I am holding space for you. I am praying for you. My heart is with you."

When I travel to be a guest speaker, I come to inspire women and girls, but I am even more inspired by the people I meet. At the *yahrtzeit* gathering, Miriam spoke from her heart, thanking the Los Angeles

---
54 Exodus 3:14

community for all the support she'd received and explaining her secret for survival. She shared, "I ask myself every day, 'Where am I needed now? What does G-d want from me now? Who can I help because of what I went through? Who can I comfort?' G-d chose me to go through this to fulfill my mission. My mission right now is to be the most supportive mother to my children. I therefore started weekly parenting classes in Ariel's memory."

On the way home from the cemetery with Miriam and her mom, I listened to their stories about their family members who had survived the Holocaust and lost most of their family members. With love in their hearts, they spoke about one of their dear aunts, who had decided that she was not going to allow herself to be depressed following the Holocaust. She made a firm decision to nurture happy children in a joyful home. *Baruch Hashem*, she raised a beautiful family that gives her much joy and *nachas*.

Miriam mentioned that her first reaction to the shocking passing of her husband was the same. She told herself, "I am not going to allow this tragedy to pull me down. I will keep going and create a happy home for my children!"

I had packed inspiration, comfort, and love in my suitcase to give; however, I returned home with so much more than I could have ever given. Miriam Rav-Noy, my student, became my teacher, showing me that we can all discover the "Miriam" within and sing the song of our souls even through the most difficult times.

COMING FULL CIRCLE IN SAN DIEGO

"Allow the beauty of the person's life to return through sharing memories."

As I worked on writing my speech for my next speaking trip to San Diego, California in March 2016 — a place associated with tremendous loss for me — I cried through the intense emotions that were rising to the surface and Susan supported me through the process. Painful memories about accompanying my father to the airport when I was ten years old resurfaced. He told me he was going on a trip to get better. I had no idea that he was fighting for his life. The flight was delayed, and I ran around with my brother, playing games. Little did I know it would be the last time I would ever see him.

I realize now that I was not meant to see my father in pain because he didn't want to cause me the pain of seeing him suffer. I wasn't meant to say goodbye because my destiny was to return to California multiple times for happy occasions to shine his legacy and light.

I shared these points with the women at *Chabad* of San Diego in connection to *Pesach*.

Our experiences of pain often become a barrier between the past and present and can limit our ability to connect to the precious memories of our past. In the *Shabbos* evening *Kiddush*, we say, "*Zecher l'Yetziyas Mitzrayim* — A remembrance of the Exodus from Egypt"; in remembrance, lies the secret key to redemption. We begin to heal and turn grief into joy when we allow the beauty of the person's life to return through sharing memories. When we say, "May the person's memory be a blessing," we are also implying that upon remembering the departed person, we bring blessing for the living.

Every *Pesach*, families gather with children and grandchildren to retell the story of our Exodus, so we don't forget our past and the legacy we must continue. Don't we know it already, and can't we just get to the meal more quickly? Through recounting the story in great detail, we make a connection between the mind and heart. The story includes *maror*, bitterness. Why do we remember this aspect? The bitterness can only go away once we taste it. It takes great strength to remember and face it, and know that G-d is always there with us in the pain. Our story is the precious legacy of a 3,000-year-old history of bitterness and joy. *Pesach* reminds us to share the stories even when they're bittersweet, and to let our children know that they can overcome limitations and rise above life's challenges, just like their ancestors.

If we understand in our mind that G-d is good and has a master plan, why is it difficult to let go of pain buried deep in our hearts from years earlier? It is because the heart doesn't understand time, which is why the holidays, generally a time of great joy, can also cause emotional chaos — because we go back to the place and time when we were children. The joy can be diluted by wounds from the past that never healed.

Is it genuinely possible to heal a wounded heart? We have the incredible capacity to heal. Once we process and validate the grief, we can release the bitterness from the heart. This power sources from our soul, which is not influenced by sorrow, because the soul, a piece of G-d, is always okay and must keep singing her song.

Although intellectually I knew I was okay, my heart retained the pain of my loss which was still taking up space; and every so often, the young and grieving Nechama Dina Wasserman would appear, demanding my attention and love. As mentioned earlier, we need to embrace every type of child on *Pesach*. In my case it was the brokenhearted Nechama Dina who didn't have a chance to say goodbye to *Tatty*, the girl who was struggling with suppressed emotions, the angry teenager who found it difficult to pray. She needed support to heal emotionally and mend her broken heart.

We heal when we show our inner child our matured perspective of the truth; we can help her to become secure in the successful resolution, we now understand, to the painful past, and to trust in *Hashem's* master plan. We can write a letter to our inner child and help her see the purpose in her pain to become a light for the world, just like the Jews in Egypt.

"In every generation, a person is obligated to see himself as if he himself went out of Egypt.[55]" Despair is a form of Egypt. Pharaoh is alive and well today, urging us to believe that we can't overcome our limitations and break through our boundaries. When we heed this voice, we are trapped like our ancestors who were slaves in Egypt."

However, we can ask ourselves, "Do I have the courage to break out of my personal Egypt? Is it possible to let go of my limiting beliefs that keeps me imprisoned in my personal Egypt?" Yes! We thank G-d daily in our prayers for taking us out, remembering how He did in the past "with a strong hand and outstretched arm," and that He does it again every day. We can be liberated by following the path paved for us by those who came before us.

Celebrating *Pesach* grants us the ability to release old pain, sadness, and anger. Pain is power, and with support, we can harness its energy to create positive change in the world. Deep pain is transformed into a deep passion that serves a greater cause, and it's the passion that brings purpose to life.

My trip to San Diego was another piece in my journey to find closure and fill the void in my heart. I had the opportunity to express my thanks to the *Chabad Shluchim* who were at my father's side during his last days on earth and gave a workshop to the girls at the school run by *Chabad*. I returned home to New York imbued with the love and joy of the *Chabad* Jewish community of San Diego. I had come full circle.

---

55 *Talmud, Pesachim* 116B

LOST IN PAIN

"My father knew I needed a "hug" and a listening ear."

"Matching couples together is as difficult as the splitting of the sea[56]," states the Talmud. One day, my oldest daughter, Chaya, expressed a concern to me, "Mommy, how will you find time in your hectic life to focus on researching *shidduchim* for me?" I told her not to worry because *Hashem* is the ultimate matchmaker and that, of course, it was one of my priorities. My mission, after all, is to help Jewish daughters build Jewish homes, including and most importantly, my own Jewish daughter.

Baruch Hashem, not long after that conversation, Mendy Shepherd from Detroit came into Chaya's life through a recommendation from her close friend, Devorah Leah. They dated and were engaged a couple months later. My sea parted. It was a miracle! As I let go of my personal Egypt from within, I was ready to celebrate and dance with my daughter at her wedding.

The wedding was scheduled for June and preparations were very hectic, since at the same time we were preparing for 70 campers and 40 staff members at the Jewish Girls Retreat, which would start just a few days after the wedding. In addition, I also had JGU online classes to teach along with other work to do.

A *simchah* is a very emotional time that can open up old wounds if they never healed. On one of my trips to New York to shop with Chaya for her wig, I met an old friend, Raizy Schwartz. (She was the friend who lost her father when she was five years old.) She brought up many memories, some of which were bittersweet as she reminded me of the challenges we shared while in high school.

After spending two days shopping, I got into my car to drive home. As I started the car, I also turned on a fountain of tears. So many

---
56 *Sotah*

emotions rose to the surface. I remembered how I had cried so hard for my father at my wedding that I ruined my makeup. The pain was real again. I wanted my *Tatty* to be physically present at my daughter's wedding. He loved weddings and was such a great dancer. I cried so much that I could barely see the exit coming up to get onto the highway to Albany. Instead, I just kept driving with tears streaming down my face. I was truly lost in my pain.

I didn't know where I was going, so I continued, figuring I would get off and turn around. I got off at the next exit and found myself on the road that led to my father's burial spot. This was unbelievable! I have a terrible sense of direction and did not know where I was going. Yet someone above really did know. My father knew I needed a "hug" and a listening ear. I made a stop at the cemetery and cried a million tears. I had the invitations in the car, and so I officially invited him to his first granddaughter's wedding. I let all my tears flow; there was still more sadness and grief to let go. I realized my father had been guiding me to come visit him and was truly celebrating with us. Once I wept, I felt so much better. From that point on, I was able to celebrate the joy of my daughter's engagement with all my heart.

Baruch Hashem, I was fully present at the wedding; I barely shed a tear, and my makeup remained intact... I had processed my emotions before and was therefore able to feel pure joy at the celebration.

Sunrises are more intense after a month of gloomy skies. Emotional pain and sorrow, like the sun, eventually sets and gives way to a new tomorrow filled with hope and happiness.

IT'S MY TURN

"When I picture my father, I see joy, not pain, for he turned his life into a song."

On one of my trips to New York in the winter of 2016, Yehudis Cohen asked me to speak to her students in *Machon L'Yahadus*, situated in the very same building where my father had taught over 30 years ago, when it was called *Machon Chana*. This building brought me back to my childhood in Crown Heights. As I walked up the stairs, I could see myself as a young girl gazing through my bedroom window into the window of this school's classroom. From my house across the street, I used to watch my beloved father teach Jewish girls about G-d and His love for them. Now it was my turn.

The office staff greeted me warmly and I asked if they remembered my father. With a sorrowful expression, one of the women nodded that she did. I felt sad that my father's memory evoked painful emotions. I hoped that my presentation would bring his joy back to the walls of this school; I would share the joy of perpetuating my father's legacy of transforming pain into purpose.

As I climbed the stairs to the classroom, I felt as if my father was holding my hand, walking with me into his school to shine his light. I was going to elevate my father's soul with the love and joy with which he had lived his life, and share it with others.

I recalled tossing and turning in my bed one night so many years ago, waiting for my father to come home from teaching night classes. I was proud that he was a beloved teacher to so many, but I wanted my time with him too. He was gentle, warm, and wise and from a young age, I wanted to learn all I could from him. As soon as I heard the key turn and the door open, I jumped out of bed.

"Nechama Dina, you're not sleeping yet?"

"I wanted to say goodnight to you. I missed you! How were your classes?"

"Baruch Hashem, teaching was a joy. The girls have so many questions, and they are thirsty to learn and grow."

"Tatty, I want to become a teacher like you when I grow up."

"Nechama, I will teach you how to teach. And you too will teach others about the joy of Judaism."

"Nechama, are you ready to speak to our students?" asked Rabbi Majesky, the dean of the school, jolting me back to the present.

I looked at the young women eagerly waiting for my words of inspiration. It was time for me to share my father's legacy and let his voice return to this building. I still wasn't sure where to start, so I began by playing my father singing a *niggun* from my computer. As we sang along, I looked out the window to my childhood home across the street, and in my mind's eye, saw my father singing this same *niggun* as he walked up the four flights of stairs to our apartment.

I asked the girls, "In times of challenge, can you serve G-d with joy?" I pointed to the window and said, "I learned the answer from my father, Rabbi Azriel Yitzchok Wasserman, of blessed memory. I remember how he walked up four flights of stairs in terrible pain with a song and a smile. When I picture my father, I see joy, not pain, for he turned his life into a song. He modeled to me that we can rise above life's challenges and illuminate the darkness with love and joy." I went on to explain the *Alter Rebbe's* teaching, that the light that emerges from the night is the greatest light, and we could all feel the room become suffused with my father's radiance. My call for action was to encourage them to sing and smile more and join JGU's One More Light 2016 Campaign, to invite women and girls to light *Shabbos* candles. Every Friday night, we are given the strength to dispel the darkness with our Shabbos candles.

During the long bus ride back to Albany, I reflected on the events of the day. I felt consoled, knowing that from my father's holy resting place in heaven, he had taught me how to teach and imparted to me his legacy of education with love and joy. As I continue to find his voice within and share it with the world, I feel grateful and fortunate for all that he instilled in me in the formative first decade of my life. From the time I was young, I was given the candle to shine through all darkness, and now I am passing it on to all my Jewish sisters.

CHAPTER 9

One More Light

A CANDLE OF MY OWN

"You are a lamplighter. You can conquer the darkness."

As my healing journey continued to transform the darkness of loss into light, I remembered a book published by the *Lubavitch* Women's Organization with a picture of me lighting *Shabbos* candles at five years old. The published book was the second volume of two very special books, initiated by the *Lubavitcher Rebbe*, titled *A Candle of My Own*. They included thoughts on candle-lighting by Jewish girls from all backgrounds. *A Candle of My Own* is about young girls making Judaism personal; each one must have her own unique connection to *Hashem*. Once a girl (or woman) lights her own candle, she is empowered to make her heritage her own and light up the world with *mitzvos*. The *Rebbe* requested that Mrs. Esther Sternberg, director of the *Neshek* candle-lighting campaign, include photographs of young girls lighting candles; I remember posing for a picture while gazing at a *Shabbos* candle. The second *A Candle of My Own*, published in 1979, included my picture. I treasured this book as a child and read it often.

"The candle is mine alone to light"

Today, when I pull out this anthology, I realize that this picture was a gift to remind me of the real me: the bright and confident young girl I had been before I experienced loss. It reminded me of the light, strength, endurance and resilience of my soul that is more powerful than any sadness or darkness. I know it is not by chance that my picture was in the book. I was being given a clear message: "You are a lamplighter. You can conquer the darkness. You have the power to shine a candle of your own." Every Friday night when I kindle my *Shabbos* flames, I remember who I am, and I reignite my soul to carry me through another week until it is *Shabbos* again.

This beautiful book from my childhood led me to further my involvement in the *Shabbos* candle-lighting campaign. In August 2015, I met with Mrs. Esther Sternberg and told her that Jewish Girls Unite would like to support the work of the *Neshek* campaign, putting candle-lighting at the forefront of our efforts to inspire girls and women to grow in their observance of *mitzvos*. With Mrs. Sternberg's guidance and blessing, JGU announced a new *Shabbos* Candle-Lighting writing contest for girls around the globe, with the intention of publishing a third book on candle-lighting. The following year, the third candle lighting book, titled *One More Light*, was launched at a Global JGU Celebration in March 2017 at the Jewish Children's Museum.

The following song was composed by Rivka Leah Cylich for this global celebration:

Did you hear the story told?
As each soul comes to this world
It answers the purpose of creation

Do you believe that it could be?
A single soul, like you or me
Could change the world and all we see forever

Plant a seed and watch it grow
Drop a stone, the ripples flow
Farther than you'd ever know

The sea is vast, the oceans wide
But greater is your will inside
A simple act can change the tide

Yes, I believe like the sunrise each day
You light up the world each time that you pray
I believe like a flame burning bright
You shine through the darkness with each Friday light
A moment the world is waiting for
For you and your one more
Your one more light (4x)

Reach within to find your art
The colors that define your heart
Each of us can paint our part

Inspire me, I'll inspire you
You'll hit a wall, I'll pull you through
Heart and soul in everything we do

A million beats of a million hearts
Flames collide and outshine the stars
One melody with a thousand parts

Chorus

Sheker hachen v'hevel hayofi
Ishah yirat Hashem hi tit'halal
T'nu la mipri yadeha
V'y'haleluka bashe'arim maaseha[57]

Chorus
Your one more light (4x)

I believe like the sunrise each day
We'll light up the world.

At the 2016 celebration, Linda Schwartz was honored as the founding benefactor of Jewish Girls Unite, launched in honor of her oldest daughter Meirah's bat mitzvah in March 2015. She reflected upon her own journey, noting that her inspiration for building a Jewish home was a *Shabbaton* she attended thanks to her *Shlucha*, Rochel Lazaroff.

---

[57] "Charm is deceptive and beauty is naught; a G-d-fearing woman is the one to be praised. Give her praise for her accomplishments, and let her deeds laud her at the gates." (*Mishlei* 31:30-31)

At the *Shabbaton*, Rabbi Manis Friedman had explained the power of candle-lighting, and she began to light candles. This one *mitzvah* led to her marrying her husband, Ory, whose name means "My Light."[58]

It was time to start planning for the bat mitzvah of Linda's second daughter, Sivan. Inspired by Linda's journey to building a Jewish home, we brainstormed and added a new dimension to our One More Light Campaign — The Invite to Light Challenge, encouraging girls to reach out and invite one more girl to light candles. Linda offered to give away 1,000 gold candlesticks (designed in 1974 by the *Lubavitcher Rebbe* for the *Neshek* candle-lighting campaign) with a "One More Light" necklace, to be given to every girl who joined the campaign.

We shared the *Rebbe's* teachings with Jewish girls everywhere from our JGU Virtual room in September 2016 and invited day schools across the country to join. We taught that every girl is an ambassador of light. When a girl lights *Shabbos* candles, she is not just kindling a flame; she is igniting her soul to shine her special light in the world. The *Rebbe* encouraged young girls to light because one is never too young to shine, to be a leader, to illuminate the darkness. Each person has a unique light that no one else has, and we show gratitude to G-d for it when we shine our light. When we share our light with others, our flame is not diminished—it is only brighter for the whole world.

In the midst of planning this meaningful bat mitzvah project, we discussed the idea to invite the *Shlucha* from *Chevron* to speak on our global broadcast for Jewish Day Schools online. Linda enthusiastically said, "Why don't we visit *Chevron* together with our girls in honor of their bat mitzvah?" Sivan and my daughter Rivkah were friends from the Jewish Girls Retreat, and were both preparing for their bat mitzvah by learning about Sarah and Rivkah *Imeinu* and their mitzvos. I had a deep desire to bring my daughter Rivkah to Israel for her bat mitzvah,

---

58 A longer version of the story is included in the book *One More Light*.

and it was a dream that Linda made possible for us. My three daughters, Shaina, Raizel, and Rivkah, all joined me on this unforgettable trip to Israel in September 2016. We met up with my children Chana and Azriel who were both studying in Israel at the time. It could not have happened at a more perfect time.

L'CHAIM IN THE JERUSALEM SUKKAH

"Your father's powerful l'chaim transported the sukkah from New York to Jerusalem."

A few nights before we departed on our trip to Israel, I received a Facebook message from Yitzchok Bloom, an accomplished artist and a friend of my father. He shared with me a beautiful black-and-white drawing he had created over 30 years before, depicting my father's *sukkah*. In the picture, you can see my two brothers and myself. The background of beautiful hills did not look like Brooklyn, though, so I asked him about the location of the *sukkah*. He told me, "In this picture, your father's powerful *l'chaim* transported the *sukkah* from New York to Jerusalem." It was no coincidence that a few days later, I found myself in a beautiful, heavenly *sukkah* in the hills of Jerusalem with my dear children and the wonderful Schwartz family. And on that holy *Sukkos* evening, we were certain that my father was also there with us, blessing us with his enthusiastic, "*L'chaim!*"

When we look for the signs, we may realize that our ancestors are communicating with us in a different form. When I open my eyes, I see this in my life in so many ways.

SIMCHAS TORAH IN CHEVRON

"I am not an orphan. I am the daughter of Sarah Imeinu and Avraham Avinu."

On *Hoshana Rabbah*, we traveled to *Chevron*, where we would be spending *Simchas Torah*. Upon arrival, we were greeted graciously by the *Chabad Shluchim*, Rabbi Danny and Mrs. Batsheva Cohen. As I gazed at the candles set out for the many guests who came to spend *Simchas Torah* in *Chevron*, I thought about Avraham and Sarah and the many guests they hosted. I struck the match, lit my 12 candles for each member of my family, *baruch Hashem*, and covered my eyes. Reciting the *brachah*, a few steps away from Sarah's burial spot, *Me'aras Hamachpelah*, I prayed silently for my daughters and all of our Jewish daughters to become strong links in the chain that began with our Mother Sarah.

Surrounded by my daughters Chana, Shaina, Raizel, and Rivkah, I uncovered my eyes and gazed at the glowing flames. In that precious moment, my heart understood the meaning of legacy. A loss before it's transformed into legacy is like an unlit lump of wax with a central wick. It is very, very dark. Yet, all it takes is one small action, like the strike of a match, to transform darkness into light.

Sarah can no longer physically light her own candle, but we can do it for her! We keep her flame burning. So too, every soul is a candle. We keep the flames of our loved ones burning and eternalize their light with every *mitzvah* in their memory.

After we lit the candles, we prayed, danced and kissed the Torah with so much joy, holding hands in true unity with our Jewish sisters, in the place where our founding mothers and fathers are buried. I cried happy tears when I realized that I am truly at home with our Father Avraham and Mother Sarah, celebrating the joy of our heritage with my Jewish family. I am not an orphan. I am the daughter of Sarah *Imeinu* and Avraham *Avinu*. I am home.

I felt Sarah's embrace.

I felt Sarah's love.

I felt Sarah's light.

I wake up every morning and know that I am not alone. I am working in close partnership with our Mother Sarah. Sarah *Imeinu* is

L: Linda and Sivan Schwartz lighting candles near the burial place of Sarah.
R: Lighting candles with my daughter Rivkah.

the true director of Jewish Girls Unite and our efforts will keep her flame burning eternally. I felt that Sarah was thanking me for sharing her legacy with all of her Jewish daughters. Our mother Sarah inspired my Jewish sister, Linda (or Chana Liba Leah), to invite me home.

SHARING THE STRENGTH OF SARAH

"I found the light of legacy."

I shared the power of candle lighting as our source of strength with seminaries in Israel, with JGU girls online, with women's groups and returned to California to lead a mother daughter program in February 2017. We were getting ready to publish the One More Light anthology for the 2017 JGU March Celebration and I was inspired to write my own thoughts about candle lighting.

On *Shabbos*, we recharge our inner flame — our soul — and remember that we carry on the legacy of our Mother Sarah. As women and girls, we are the ones to carry on the legacy of Sarah *Imeinu*, and share her message with others. All Jewish daughters in all generations, inherit her strengths to dispel darkness and nurture the spark in others as teachers, mentors, mothers, sisters, and friends.

When life engulfs us in darkness
We have a choice: we can get lost in the dark or search for the light
It was very dark when I lost my Tatty at age ten
I searched for my beloved father's concealed light
I knew with effort, I would find the hidden light
I found the light of legacy
I found the light in my soul
I found the light in each day
I found the light in each person
I learned to kindle a candle of my own
I learned to appreciate my unique mission
I learned to share my light and help others shine
I learned to inspire girls to transform darkness into light

Sarah, Matriarch and founder of our Jewish nation
Sarah gives us strength to shine light for the next generation
Sarah's candles illuminate our homes on Friday night
Sarah teaches us how to help others shine their light
Sarah listened to her inner voice; she knew she wasn't wrong
Sarah says: "Listen to your inner voice", you are strong
Sarah's voice taught others with dedication and love
Sarah inspires us to love our Father Above
Sarah prepared challah with great effort for her guests
Let's share our gifts with others and strive to do our very best
Shine your light, the world is waiting for you to dispel the night
Your One More Light will transform darkness into light

Each week, when we light our Shabbos candles
Let us ask ourselves: Where do I want to shine light this week?
Let us ask Hashem: Please give me the strength to transform darkness into light.

The *Lubavitcher Rebbe* teaches that every mother is Sarah and every daughter is Rivkah. I thought about how much I can relate to Sarah's life.

I Am Sarah...

I am married to my husband, Avraham...
I am blessed to name my first son, named Azriel Yitzchok...
I am blessed to light candles with my daughter Rivkah
I will take a firm stand when necessary...
I yearned to be a mother and will do anything for my children...
I keep Sarah's flames burning every Friday night...
I love hosting guests and baking delicious challah.
I am an educator and teach women and girls...
I overcome challenges with faith in one G-d...
I focus on the positives despite the tests in life...
I never give up on my hopes and dreams...
I need my own tent, my oasis, to recharge...
I bring the blessing of abundance to my family...
We wandered from place to place to spread light...
I thank, praise and pray to Hashem and encourage others to do the same...
I am forging a legacy of light every day for future generations...

We are all the daughters of Sarah *Imeinu*.

Let us ask ourselves each day: How am I like Sarah today?

Celebrating the new book with friends at the 2017 Global Celebration

THALIA'S LEGACY OF LIGHT

"Now the world is dark but soon it will be bright for us."

At the JGU Global Celebration of 2017, we launched the *One More Light* book, an anthology of the best entries from the 2015 candle lighting writing contest. I shared with the audience at the Jewish Children's Museum in Brooklyn that my journey to discover my father's legacy led to honoring the legacy of our Matriarch Sarah and so many others, helping others transform loss into a legacy of light. *One More Light*, the third candle lighting book, published by our JGU Press, was filled with beautiful tribute pages and photos honoring women and their light, including the legacy of one special JGU girl, who sent in a submission from Australia.

On January 20, 2017, we were shaken and heartbroken upon hearing the news that five people were killed when a man deliberately drove into a crowd in the heart of Melbourne, Australia. Thalia Hakin, a precious ten-year-old girl, was one of the victims. I was terribly saddened by the tremendous loss of one of our precious Jewish daughters.

Thalia Hakin o"h

A couple of days later, I was working at my dining room table and reading through the 140 poems and essays that had been selected from over 300 submissions for publication in *One More Light*. That morning, I decided to check my email one more time to be sure that we had not overlooked any submissions. Suddenly, I noticed an unopened email with an attachment from Robin Moscow of Beth Rivkah Primary in Australia. A beautiful handwritten poem appeared on my computer screen. I nearly fell out of my chair at the writer's familiar name...

These were Thalia's words—words she had written in September 2015 for the JGU Candle Lighting Writing Contest. We read Thalia's poem, and we could hear the words of an angel. Her soul was speaking to us.

> When you light up a candle you light up your neshamah and you light up the world. And when you light up the world, you make it a better place, for you and me and everybody. Now the world is dark but soon it will be bright for us. And im yirtzeh Hashem, Moshiach will come.

Thalia left us a legacy of light; her words illuminate a dark world! Sarah *Imeinu* and Thalia (whose Hebrew name was also Sarah) are depending on us to keep their eternal flame alive. We have the power to light up their *neshamos* when we cherish the *mitzvos* and light *Shabbos* candles. They are counting on us to take action — to strike the match and turn the darkness into light.

We shared Thalia's legacy with the launch of a new song, sponsored by the Seymour Fox Foundation, at the third JGU Global Celebration in 2017. During this occasion, we sang the JGU theme songs composed for each of these past three celebrations — three steps to lighting up the world — beginning from our launch in California in 2015.

1. "Shine Your Inner Light" (JGU theme song 2015):

The theme of this song is to trust and "shine your inner light." We can all turn "night" into "day." If we have only enough candles to light for either *Shabbos* **or** the *Chanukah* menorah, which takes precedence? The answer is that the *Shabbos* candles do, because **the first step** to spreading light is by lighting up ourselves and our homes from within. We ignite our inner flame each day through prayer, Torah study, and fulfilling *mitzvos*.

2. "One More Light" (JGU theme song 2016):

Next, we must shine "one more light." Focus on one person, to make a personal connection and touch a single soul. Encourage another to shine *her* inner light, because **the second step** is to illuminate our environment. When our soul is lit up, we can illuminate other souls. One person's energy added to one more person's energy generates exponential synergy.

3. "Light Up the World" (JGU theme song 2017):

The third step is when our unique light spreads outward from our immediate surroundings to light up the world at large.

FROM SORROW TO SONG

*"You are Rabbi Wasserman's daughter!
I can see it in your eyes."*

As I described earlier, I missed my *Tatty's Shabbos* melodies and Torah teachings. I wanted to sing with him again! I missed his love, joy, and inspiration that flowed like an ever-gushing waterfall to all. As the years went by, I unfortunately forgot his *Shabbos* songs. The memories were buried deep within me like a seed planted underground. One *Shabbos*, I heard a song that once again evoked bittersweet memories in my heart, and eventually, it led me to discover a new song.

It was the winter of 2016, and I was attending the annual International Conference of *Chabad Shluchos*. I was invited to the home of Rabbi Levy Djian for a *Shabbos* dinner. He began to sing a beautiful *Sephardic* rendition of "Shalom Aleichem," welcoming the *Shabbos* angels. The tune sounded familiar. "Where did I hear this before?" I wondered.

It was as if Rabbi Djian read my thoughts, and he shared, "Over 30 years ago, when I was a young boy, my family stayed at your parents' home for *Sukkos* in Crown Heights, and we heard your father's spirited "Shalom Aleichem." Throughout my childhood in Paris, my father would sing the tune we learned at your father's *Shabbos* table."

I tried to hold back the emotions erupting in my heart. By the end of the meal, I felt heartbroken; I was overcome with longing for my father's light and songs. I remember walking down the stairs of their building alongside my daughter Chaya, with tears streaming down my face.

Shabbos is a time of joy, not a time for tears; yet, it's a time to quiet the chaos of the week and connect to the soul deep within. This cry was my soul, my inner child, who was yearning for complete *shalom* — for peace and comfort, yearning to be free to fully express itself and be redeemed from the sadness and grief. The journey was not over: the many layers of grief in my wounded heart still required healing from all the years that I had suppressed my feelings. My buried emotions were forcing their way to the surface and I was ready to remove another layer of unresolved childhood wounds. It was time to nurture the seeds planted with my tears, and cultivate it into a sprout of hope and healing for myself and others.

I walked down Kingston Avenue with my daughter toward 770. I recalled the song my father composed in Camp Emunah: "Kingston Avenue, Kingston Avenue, where I want to be. It's the best Avenue 'cause it takes you right to 770." I smiled through my tears, picturing my father's joy to be near his beloved teacher and leader, the *Lubavitcher Rebbe*.

When we arrived at the Friday night *oneg*, I found a seat to listen to the excellent speakers. But with so much emotion rising to the surface, I found that I could not concentrate, so I slipped out quietly for a break. I met a friend outside the hall and as we conversed, she mentioned that we were all gathered there as sisters. I shared with her that I was the oldest child and the only girl in my family; as a teen, I had always felt so alone in my pain since I didn't have any sisters. I was in a daze as my tears overflowed.

Several women recognized me and joined our circle congregating outside the hall. They sat with me, hugged me, and listened to me share the pain that I had buried for too long. One woman told me that she had been inspired by my talk at the gathering in Los Angeles honoring the memory of Miriam Rav-Noy's husband, o"bm. My inner child felt comforted and supported, surrounded by soul-sisters who were giving me a shoulder to lean on and a reminder of the light that emerged from the darkness.

Out of over a thousand women in the hall that night, the *Rebbetzin* of a ten-year-old JGR camper bereft of her father walked by our circle of sisters. She stopped to say, "Good *Shabbos*," and mentioned that her student had gained so much, both spiritually and emotionally, from the Jewish Girls Summer Retreat. She had come home happier and much more expressive, having been reassured by the knowledge that I understood her situation. At that moment, G-d was once again revealing to me the purpose of my pain.

A few weeks later, I had the urge to text Rabbi Djian, asking him if he would sing my father's "*Shalom Aleichem*" for me in a voice note. I wanted to sing it at my own *Shabbos* table, but I had forgotten the melody. I didn't receive a response from him. I didn't realize that he had unfortunately just lost his father, and was therefore unready to sing the song for me. Perhaps I was not ready either. I needed more time to nurture the seed of pain, which had already begun to break through the ground, and fortify it.

One year later to the day, in February 2017, I was in Brooklyn again for the annual *Shluchos* Convention. I was invited to manage the crowds of women entering the *Rebbe's* holy room where he had studied and met with people for countless hours, after Friday night services. As we waited for the men to empty out, a middle-aged gentleman who filed past looked at me, and proclaimed, "You are Rabbi Wasserman's daughter! I can see it in your eyes." I was amazed that he recognized me.

After two hours of directing the flow of the hundreds of women who came to pray in the *Rebbe's* room, I left 770 to return to my hosts for the *Shabbos* meal. As I turned the corner, lo and behold, there was Kalman, the man who had recognized my father's eyes in me.

As we walked up Kingston Avenue, Kalman shared his vivid and fond memories of my father's *Shabbos* table. "We used to sing and dance to your father's spirited '*Shalom Aleichem.*' We even stood on the chairs, and your father would say, 'Break through the barriers with joy!'" And then Kalman danced his way up Kingston Avenue, singing my father's "*Shalom Aleichem.*" I was blown away, absorbing the melody that I had yearned to hear once again.

I could hear my father singing with Kalman from heaven. My heart was singing as I connected to his soul shining so brightly on his beloved Kingston Avenue. In that unforgettable moment, I felt the outpouring of my father's love and joy. I knew that he was proud of me for working through the painful emotions, to strengthening my trust in G-d, thus turning sorrow into song.

THE JGR SINGING CONTEST

"See the good, my love, and trust the One above."

Several months later, I was directing my sixteenth summer session at the Jewish Girls Retreat, and I announced an original songwriting contest in conjunction with our theme, "Sing Your Song." I decided that I was going to join the competition and lead by example.

At the same time, my daughter Chaya arrived at camp from the hospital with our first grandson. It was incredibly hectic preparing for a *Shabbos bris*, wrapping up the end of camp, and juggling my roles of camp director and first-time *bubby*. I went to check on my daughter and see how she was managing in her camp apartment. I found her struggling to care for a baby while dealing with recovering from childbirth. I stepped in to help, and I rocked my tiny grandson. As I soothed my precious bundle, I jotted down words for my song for the JGR song contest, choosing to set the lyrics to my father's "*Shalom Aleichem*" melody:

Kuk nisht oif der vei

Kuf oif dee gezunt

See the good, my love

And trust the One above

These were among my father's last words when he was ill. I looked up and noticed a few tears trickle down my daughter's face. I felt my father's voice, speaking and singing through me, bringing healing to his daughters. Chaya told me later that this song gave her strength to focus on her new blessings, rather than the hardships of adjusting to motherhood.

That night, I stood up in front of the camp, a few days before my father's *yahrtzeit* on *Av* 4, and I shared the above story. I even dared to sing my first solo in public, with the encouragement of our JGR Music head, Chaviva Tarlow. On *Shabbos*, we sang and danced to this spirited song, just like we did around my father's *Shabbos* table so many years ago.

For so many years
Tatty, I missed you
I never knew
I could see you
Oh Tatty, I longed for you
With my heart and soul
I yearned to be with you
And hear you sing this song

Chorus:
Kuk nisht oif der vei
Kuf oif dee gezunt
See the good, my love

And trust the One Above
Tatty, you never left me
You were just concealed
Until the day I realized
To open up my eyes

I can truly feel you
I can truly hear you
I can truly love you
I can learn from you

For you are really with me
Each and every moment
You are my guiding light
In the darkest night

Today, we celebrate
Tatty's shining legacy
With our precious family
In total harmony
With your first great-grandson
Your light shines through and through
From generation to generation
He's your continuation

Chorus:

We can truly feel you
We can truly hear you
We can truly love you
We can learn from you

*We're singing your song
And we know it won't be long
When we'll sing our song together, in the Holy Land*

Chorus:

*Tatty, you never left us
You were just concealed
Until the day WE realized
To open up OUR eyes!*

The *Rebbe's* father teaches that the only reason to cry after a *tzaddik's* passing is if there is no one to carry on the teachings. But as long as his children and students follow in his path, his life is perpetuated. The mission of his descendants and students is to ensure that they "keep him alive" in the proper manner, i.e., learning his teachings and following his ways.[59]

YOU ARE MY PEARL!

"Tatty is proud of me."

It was the last *Shabbos* at the Jewish Girls Retreat of 2017, and I was surrounded by the joy and love of my immediate family, as well as my JGR family. Hundreds of candles were being lit by our Jewish daughters, symbolizing the legacy of our Matriarchs; every girl, another candle, keeping the flame of Judaism alive. It was the *Shabbos* before my father's 32nd *yahrtzeit*, and a new light was born to my daughter, our first grandson. After I lit the candles, I didn't only pray and ask for my wishes; behind my covered face, I thanked G-d for all the miracles. As I lifted my hands from over my eyes, I hugged my mother who had

---
59 *Sichas Parashas Va'eira* 5742

come in for the celebration, my daughter (the new mother), my mother-in-law and a host of vibrant campers. "Good *Shabbos*, Good *Shabbos*!" With a smile, my dear mother said she had a gift for me. She handed me a heart-shaped box, and I opened it to find a gold necklace with a pearl. She told me that this had been a gift my father gave her many years ago. He had presented it to her with a card which read, "You are my pearl!"

Tears of joy filled my eyes. I could hear my father speaking to me once again. I knew I had earned this necklace. It is certain that he has been guiding my journey to becoming a pearl. It is a way of life, to see the good in the irritations we experience, and turn negative into positive. I strived to transform *Tatty's* loss into a legacy of light and love.

I understood the message that *Tatty* is proud of me for working on myself to focus on the positive and transform pain into pearls. This pearl necklace was a gift from heaven. Thank you, *Tatty*, for joining our *simchah* in your special way.

MY COMFORTED FAMILY

"His memory is a source of light, love, and inspiration."

The next day, we celebrated the *bris* of my father's first great-grandson. Tears flowed as our first grandchild was named Azriel Yitzchok by my wonderful brother, Azriel Yitzchok ben Azriel Yitzchok, who was born after my father's passing. It was a moment I will never forget. What a joy and comfort to know that my father's children and grandchildren are following in his path and carrying on his name and legacy!

At the meal, the *mohel*, Rabbi Levi Heber, explained that a *bris* on *Shabbos* goes beyond nature since we override all the rules of *Shabbos* for the sake of the bond between a baby boy and G-d. The message I received from this concept on the *Shabbos* before my father's 32nd *yahrtzeit*, was that it was now time for our family to go beyond our nature, and bond with our father's soul with pure joy in our hearts. After all, it was the 32nd *yahrtzeit*, and 32 is the numerical value of "*lev,*" the Hebrew word meaning "heart." As my father would say, "*Simchah* breaks through all barriers." This special *Shabbos simchah* broke through all the barriers to the joy in our hearts!

Today, I am grateful for a deep connection with my father that goes beyond any limits of physical time or space. Instead of deep sadness, his memory is a source of light, love, and inspiration. For years I longed for my father to be at my side. Now I feel at peace, knowing that he never left and is smiling from heaven at the legacy that he began. It is clear that he is guiding our activities every step of the way. He taught Judaism with joy and love, and JGU's methods reflect that, striving to encourage each girl to express her creativity with joy and love of G-d. He continues to guide all who are involved in empowering *Hashem's* precious daughters around the world to carry on the flame of Judaism with joy.

THE CRY OF MY SOUL

"Tatty, you taught me to deeply understand the cry of my soul."

Erev Yom Kippur, I read a Facebook post from a dear friend, Altie Kasowitz (née Green):

This is one of the hardest days of the year for me. Every year, without fail, I call my Mom on Erev Yom Kippur to get a blessing from her. I choke up every time, I know she feels the same way. I wish my Dad were here to give me the blessings with her!

I commented on her Facebook page: "Your father is still blessing you." But then I choked up, and tears filled my eyes. I wiped them away, suppressed the painful feeling, and went to *shul* for *Kol Nidrei*.

The day after *Yom Kippur*, I was speaking to my daughter in Israel, and when she asked me about my *Yom Kippur*, I remembered that feeling again. With tears, I apologized to her for the times I didn't validate her feelings during her teen years because my heart hurt to feel. I just wanted to fix her situation instead of feel her pain.

She said, "Ma, you know how many people never get to where you are today?" I told her that I love her so much and thanked her for understanding me. I said goodbye, but my tears continued to flow.

Since, I have learned that it is okay to feel pain, it is okay to cry, I decided not to suppress, but rather to embrace the feelings bursting their way to the surface of my heart. I used the opportunity to channel my intense emotion for the positive.

Taking a walk to the park, I allowed my tears to flow like a river. I asked myself, "If I know that my father's soul is blessing me from heaven, why do I still feel such deep, intense sadness? Haven't I worked on myself to accept G-d's master plan with all my heart and soul? I understand my beloved father lived his 37 years to the fullest. I am grateful to carry on the legacy he began. If so, why do I cry today? Will I always feel pain?"

Yom Kippur is the day that reveals the deepest levels of our soul. Suddenly, I realized that my inner cry was emanating from my soul longing to be close to my Father in Heaven (G-d).

Dearest Tatty,

The day your soul left this world, you taught me the most significant lesson a father can teach his daughter; you taught me to deeply understand the cry of my soul. The way I long to hear you sing around our table and bless me is the way my pure soul longs to sing her unique song and be close to our Father in Heaven... every single day.

Tatty, although I know you are still blessing me from on high, I cannot be satisfied. I still want to see your smiling face and hear you sing and dance with my eyes and ears. Today, I wipe away my tears and place them on my forehead as you taught me. I turn my eyes toward Heaven with this prayer.

Dear Tatte in Himmel (Father in Heaven),

You are our Light in the darkness. You created the darkness, and even the darkness is good. Still, I beg You, please don't conceal Your face from Your children any longer. This exile is way too long and painful. Please bless us with revealed good. We yearn to see You, G-d, with our eyes of flesh and blood, just like we yearn to be reunited with all of our loved ones once again. Only You can wipe away our tears forever! Until then, we will try not to forget the longing of our soul and keep singing. We await a new day, when we will sing a new song of redemption!

Love always,

Your daughter, Nechama Dina

LETTING GO OF MY DREAM

"I felt my soul yearning for a home where we could share the beauty of Jewish family life."

When another property fell through in August 2017, I began to convince myself that it may be time to let go of our dream to create a physical home for our global community.

I reflected on our journey from JGR to JGU over the last three years: launching the "Home for JGR" campaign and not yet reaching our goal for various reasons.

In an email to Yocheved Daphna, who had made a significant contribution to our 2014 capital campaign, I explained that we were taking a step back from searching for a permanent home for JGR. Instead we would focus on growing the JGU global community through online classes and traveling to bring JGU to educational institutions. Perhaps in the right time, a physical home will happen, but for now we are letting go of this dream and inspiring girls through a variety of JGU global programs on our permanent online platform.

We spent *Sukkos* in Montreal once again because we didn't have a community where we lived, and I was happy to spend time with family. I felt my soul yearning for a home where we could share the beauty of Jewish family life. I met a spiritual mentor, Chana Schmukler (mother of Rochel Schmukler), and mentioned to her that I had given up on finding a permanent location. Instead, I would travel more, teach virtually, and rent venues for our retreats. Perhaps, *Hashem* wants me to spend more time on teaching and writing and doesn't want us to be busy taking care of a property.

She looked at me and with great seriousness responded, "Please don't underestimate the vital need for a permanent home for Jewish girls. *Hashem* wants us to build Him a dwelling place in this physical world. The power of teaching others how to build a Jewish home from your home is unmatched by any other accomplishments. Women are the foundation of the home and usher in the peace and sanctity of *Shabbat* by lighting candles every Friday evening. The candles bring peace into our homes and from the home they spread light and warmth to a dark world. The home provides the core strength for the Jewish family. The home builds the Jewish future. The Jewish future is in the hands of the women. It all begins at home."

I needed to hear her powerful words about the importance of the Jewish home. She reminded me not to give up and that *Hashem* knows the exact the right time.

CHAPTER 10

Hidden Blessings

REWRITING MY STORY

"If I can ease one life the aching, or cool one pain, or help one fainting robin unto his nest again, I shall not live in vain."
~Emily Dickinson

If my story could comfort one aching heart, help one person transform their pain, then I needed to publish my story into a book. For two years, I scheduled time every Saturday night to write and rewrite, reframe and rediscover myself through recording my healing journey from loss to legacy to light.

A painful childhood or young-adult experience often creates a victim-mindset in an otherwise powerful and creative adult. The pain in our aching hearts can overshadow the full picture. How do we forge a connection between the part of us stuck in the old story and the part of us that is strong and wise and can move forward? We begin by retelling the past, painful story. We validate the pain and search for a way the challenge serves us today.

It takes work and courage to break through patterns of childhood to change our personal narrative. When we shatter the limiting beliefs of our old story and retell it with a new realization, reframe it with a new perspective, we choose what we want our next chapters in life to be. This is exactly what happened to me as I wrote this book. I wasn't only rewriting my story from the past, I was actually processing my feelings and searching for the light as we faced an unexpected new challenge. I was living the story that I wanted to write.

My father taught his students, "If we change how we see things, things will change! He would say that we can view each event in our lives in two ways: "This is the most horrible experience without any good," or, "This is the most valuable experience I have ever had."

Every human being struggles in this world; it's part of how we grow spiritually. Spiritual or emotional pain empowers us to help others and become stronger leaders. The moment of self-awareness is transformational. It is when we recognize the inner strength resulting from hardship and ascribe a purpose to the pain. It is when we experience the "Aha!" moment and understand that the challenge was to serve something greater!"

It is when we hear the harmony in the lows and highs of the song of our lives.

The strengths and tools I have acquired over the years support me now in my life on each step of the journey. I feel oneness in seeing how all the low moments were the catalyst to my greatest highs. As I wrote this book, I discovered the strength to redeem myself from an old story and write the remaining chapters with a new lens.

A NEW BOOK

"There was a flame burning inside of me."

We were invited to share our thoughts at the annual *Shluchos* Convention Friday *farbrengen* and I shared my *Shalom Aleichem* story and concluded by singing my father's song, *"Kuk Nisht Oif Der Vei."* I gazed around the room and noticed many women who were teary-eyed and very touched by my story. A smaller crowd of women gathered together and the subsequent discussion continued until 3:00 a.m. One *Shlucha* had lost her husband a year earlier and she spoke to me about her teenage daughter, asking for my advice in how to help her daughter cope emotionally with the loss. Later, this *Shlucha* and I stayed in touch. She even sent me a letter, thanking me for opening her eyes to the emotional needs of a grieving teenager. This was yet another sign for me that my story needed to see the light of day and be published.

Before I left for home, I went to the *Rebbe's Ohel* with Evy Green, a woman who lost her husband and was left to raise 13 children alone. She mentioned how hard it was for her children. I told her about the idea to write my story. She told me, "What a great idea! But writing a book requires a lot of time and focus. It would be ideal to find someone to support the expense of preparing your book for publication." I went to the *Rebbe's* grave and prayed for the financial assistance to support my soul's mission. I had a deep desire and passion to spread my father's message: "Don't focus on the pain, focus on the health." Every *tzarah*, sorrow, can be transformed into your *tzohar*, your light. Every low is the beginning of revealing a higher potential.

Although I had so much to do to prepare for the annual Global JGU Celebration in Brooklyn, I found myself drawn to organizing the chapter titles for my book and compiling my previous writings. There was a flame burning inside of me. I stayed up until the early hours of the morning reading through the writings I had been working on for the last several years. I created a table of contents and knew that my book needed many more hours of work before it was ready for publication. There were missing parts to that still needed to be written.

I was ready to launch this book project. The next day, *Rosh Chodesh Adar*, I received an unexpected call from Micki Massry, who told me she wanted to support our mission in honor of our annual JGU celebration. It had been 18 years since her daughter, Laurie, was in our Bat Mitzvah Club, and we spoke about her upcoming wedding. It was amazing to think that her daughter was one of the founding members of the Capital Region Bat Mitzvah Club.

We spoke about her amazing and loving mother, a Holocaust survivor, and then about her father who passed away when she was 19 and her sister was 16. We discussed how so many people live with sorrow. I shared my experience at the recent Convention, how I had seen the pain of loss in so many of my Jewish sisters, and that I was moved to help uplift others with my story. I told her about my book idea, which I thought could provide comfort. Micki said to me, "It is so important for your voice to be heard and your story to be told. It will free the souls of those who feel pain to live happier lives. What do you need to publish your book?" I said I needed an underwriter and she agreed on the spot, thus began my journey to publishing this book that you are holding in your hands.

It is no coincidence that Micki's Hebrew name is Miriam and the theme for our upcoming JGU celebration was "dancing to redemption with Miriam." I ordered tambourines for all the participants and in the middle of a raging winter storm on March 7, 2018, women and girls danced the night away at the Jewish Children's Museum. We celebrated the power of women, the beacons of light, in the darkest moments of time. We announced the forthcoming JGU Songbook, *Voices in Harmony*, as we hummed along with talented singers and musicians, including Chanie Chanin, Miriam Ilyayev, Tzivia Kay, Mirele Rosenberger, Chaviva Tarlow, and the Tambourine Academy girls' choir.

Writing and editing this book for publication brought me to a whole new level of healing. It was the catalyst that lifted me out of being stuck in my personal Egypt as I faced an unexpected challenge. It reminded me that I am the author of my life story and I can hold on to my vision. Micki is a beacon of light who showed me that the spark of Miriam is within all of us, if we choose to reveal it. And sometimes, it all starts with a phone call to show someone that you truly care and support their mission.

A NEW BABY

"I visualized myself in a new home with a new baby and a new book."

While expecting my eleventh child, *ka'h*, I was in total creation mode. My due date, July 2, coincided with what was originally scheduled to be the first day of JGR camp. I knew I couldn't start a camp session and have a baby on the same day. It was a sign from Heaven to do something different this summer. We found a new place for camp at a Girl Scouts campground in South Rensselaer County, where we were hoping to purchase our permanent home. The only dates available to rent were at the end of August, which would give me a few weeks to recuperate from giving birth. So, instead of our four-week camp session, we planned a one-week summer leadership retreat. In place of all the hours spent on recruiting campers and staff and planning camp activities, I wrote for hours and hours every day, sometimes until past 2:00 a.m. I worked to edit, compile my blogs, fill in the gaps, and write some more. I kept at it for days and nights. There were nights that my story was pouring out of my soul and I slept very little. I visualized myself in a new home with a new baby and a new book.

My mind was also on my pregnancy, which was considered high risk because of my age. An ultrasound at 36 weeks showed that I had low amniotic fluid. At 38 weeks, an induction was scheduled for the next morning. I did not feel ready. I couldn't push away my fears. Was I afraid of the unknown? I had done this before. What was different about this birth? I couldn't understand myself. It had been four years since my last baby. I needed strength so I read a letter from the Rebbe and these words spoke to me: "Allow G-d's will to become your will and everything will be alright."

I called Nechama Dena for guidance to release any limiting beliefs. "We are going to tap into a new belief that will bring the birth of a new baby," she told me. "This baby is drawing a new *ko'ach* into the world; as the mother, you need to feel the *ko'ach* first.

We created a new belief:

I bring this baby into the world with love and joy. I am open and let Hashem truly take care of me. I allow things to happen in their natural state. Birth is bringing a new ko'ach into the world! Birth is bringing geulah into the world! Giving birth is easy, smooth, and fast. The birth of all new projects is smooth, easy, and fast.

That night, I had a dream. I was sitting with several mothers from Brooklyn who had given birth to children over age 40. We were schmoozing and one mother turned to me and said, "You will experience a whole new level of love with the birth of this baby." The dream was so vivid and real.

Throughout the process of labor, I talked to *Hashem* and said, "Your will is my will!" I allowed the contractions to pass through me with full acceptance to bring a new *ko'ach*, a new light, into this world. This reminded me of the greater light that emerges from the darkness. It's all part of the process.

My daughter Chana arrived at the *Ohel* and prayed at the grave of the *Lubavitcher Rebbe* and my father at the time that I checked into the hospital only because her flight from Israel was delayed. She left the *Ohel* at 12:00 a.m., exactly when I received the news that I had made considerable progress in just a few hours. *Baruch Hashem*, Baby Laber was born at 11:45 a.m. on June 21, 2018, 8 *Tammuz*. It was my husband's 48th birthday and my daughter Chana's 20th. Our baby boy was a birthday gift from G-d!

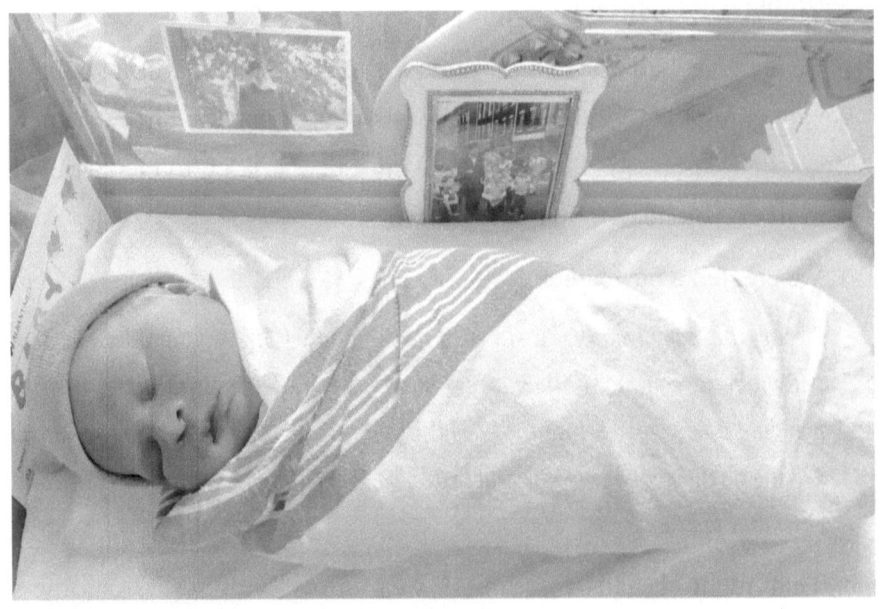

UNEXPECTED NEWS

"We become a leader in the very challenges that we face."

Baby Boy Laber passed all the tests at birth. His Apgar score was nine. That night, my daughter Chana (who stayed with me for the night) took a closer look with her artistic eye and noticed some signs of Down syndrome. We mentioned it to the doctor the next morning, he said they would administer a blood test, but it would take ten days for the results to come in.

I called Nechama Dena and told her that our baby boy may have Down syndrome. Tears welled up in my eyes. I now understood why I had feared the birth. It was very close to *Shabbos*, yet she felt my pain. She offered to sing a song to me with words to soothe my soul. These were her words that she composed to the tune of a *niggun*:

A special neshamah has been given to you,
A unique mission he was chosen to do.
You are the parents Hashem chose for him
So he can fulfill his mission.

It is not what you had planned
Hashem is holding your hand
It's not what you've done wrong
It's what you have done right

You are so brave and courageous, this to undertake
You have all you need — it's for Hashem's sake.
It's really important for both of you to know
Hashem loves you, He cares about you so

Strengthen your bitachon and miracles will come
You are not alone, Hashem is with you
You are being held up by all the good you did do
Hashem is having real nachas from you too

All the souls you've inspired are your advocates
They're davening that you can rise above this
Experience the newborn baby bliss.

Believe that you'll see Hashem's miraculous hand
Even if right now it looks different than planned
And you don't understand

We know Hashem can act beyond limits
Anything's possible, Hashem is infinite
Even if the doctor's diagnosis is definite

It's time for a heartfelt tefillah as the mother of this precious neshamah
Hashem wants you to offer the deepest shirah
Open the door through tefillah with joy
Hashem is giving brachos to this baby boy

Anything is possible in the blink of an eye
Hashem does not expect more than just for you to try
He wants us to glorify His Holy Name
Being present with His will, in your pain.

Take everything you have taught in your class
And absorb it in your own daas
Apply it to your life, especially right now
Be open — Hashem will show you how

Show everyone you're a dugma chaya
In this challenge, to see the brachah
Soon you can even be b'simchah

You just need to be the keli
And use this opportunity
To turn to Hashem with sincerity

To transform this darkness into light
As you've empowered others to shine bright
You can access your own might

You have the tools and the kochos
The understanding and brachos
Derived from your own mitzvos

You have the strength and the support
With bitachon, you can hold the fort
Accept and utilize it the most

When you understand this, you can open up your eyes
This is where transformation lies
To break through this limited guise

As an example, this child came to this world
To show the effect of turning pain into pearls
Ultimately, Hashem's will is fulfilled

The reality can change with bitachon
You can see miracles with your son
Especially after all the good you've done

When you understand this, you can open up your eyes
This is where transformation lies
To break through this limited guise.

We ended our call by creating new beliefs about my baby and myself:

My baby is healthy and fully functional. He has strong capacities. He is intelligent. He reaches milestones on time. He is not what doctors say. He is a miracle unfolding. I am an example, a dugma chaya of bitachon. I am fortunate and blessed. I lead the way to the final Geulah. I show others that our thoughts affect everything in our world. Thank you, Hashem, for the merit to be part of your miracle!

She concluded by sharing: "When we infuse the *aleph* - oneness of *Hashem* into *golah*, we also become an "*aleph*", a leader and experience *geulah*, inner redemption. We become a leader in the very challenges that we face and we empower others because of our challenge."

Nechama Dena's song gave me strength as I processed the pending diagnosis. I shared her comforting words with Chana, who stayed with me for *Shabbos*, while my husband cared for the rest of our children at my in-laws. On *Shabbos*, I decided that we would name the baby Yosef Chaim. Yosef in Egypt overcame so many challenges and was not a victim of life's circumstances. He gives us the strength to be a lamplighter despite the adversity we may face. My family would persevere with any unknown challenges ahead and find the song in the sorrow.

I CHOOSE

"Our little guy was a gift we didn't know we needed."

I put my fears aside and focused on planning for a *bris* celebration. Our family decided that no matter what the results of the tests would be, we were going to celebrate the life *Hashem* gave us and love our baby just the same. It was a whole new level of love.

Yosef Chaim was named at a beautiful *bris* ceremony at the Maimonides Hebrew Day School. I became teary-eyed, as I heard the blessings recited at the *bris* ceremony: "Give thanks to the Lord for

He is good, for His kindness is everlasting. May this little infant Yosef Chaim become great. Just as he has entered the Covenant, so may he enter into Torah, into marriage, and into good deeds."

After the *bris*, the doctor called Avraham and confirmed the diagnosis that changed our world forever. I asked my husband, "So what did the doctor say?" He answered, "What is there to say?"

For the next few days, all I did was cry, while I processed the confirmed diagnosis and researched everything about my baby's extra chromosome 21. It was hard for me to sleep. As I read about it late at night, I held Yosef Chaim in my arms and tears of grief rolled down my cheeks. I feared the unknown. I cried for the challenges my child might face. I cried from worrying that my life would become consumed with caring for this child.

I cried because it felt as if my life's dreams were about to disappear once again. My world seemed very dark.

While reviewing the manuscript for the songbook, *Voices in Harmony*, one last time, I noticed the song "Special Child" by Chanale Fellig. I remembered how I had questioned if I should include this song in the book. I listened to the song as my tears flowed, while internalizing the song's message.

A meeting was held far from earth
With the angels and G-d above
They said it's time again for another birth
This child will need much love
And though his progress may seem slow
And accomplishments he may not show
Let's be careful where he's sent
We want his life to be content

Chorus
Please G-d find someone who
Will do this very special job for You
And let them realize right away
The leading role they're asked to play

And have them show him till the end
They'll always be there as his friend
And share a love so rich and strong
And that's the place where he'll belong

Make sure his parents hold him close
And never miss a smile
And when life gets hard they'll always know
He's a gift to them, this child!

The date of Yosef Chaim's birthday, *Tammuz* 8, held so much meaning. The number eight represents the supernatural. The month of *Tammuz*, according to teacher of *Kabbalah*, Rav Yitzchok Ginsburgh, is the time of the year to rectify our sense of sight. The rectification of sight entails two complementary poles: seeing Divine providence in our lives and seeing the good in each other.

I have a choice to focus on my child's deficiencies and worry about Yosef Chaim's delayed development, or I can choose to see his beautiful angelic face. He is healthy in so many ways, *ka"h*. He passed his hearing test. He has a healthy heart. He is moving and kicking and looks around with his beautiful, sparkling blue eyes.

Now I internalized my father's last words to Rabbi Mendel on a whole new level.

I sang my own song:

Kuk nisht oif der vei,

Kuf oif dee gezunt;

See the good, my love,

And trust the One Above!

I realized *Hashem* was giving me the opportunity to live with my father's teachings each day. Our little guy was a gift we didn't know we needed. Our family was chosen to be the *Shluchim*, G-d's emissaries, to love and care for this precious soul.

And then I repeated the *Rebbe's* words said many years ago to my dear mother, "When you are the *Shluchim* of *Melech Malchei Hamelachim HaKadosh Baruch Hu*, there is no room for sadness."

HASHEM CHOSE YOU!

"The ultimate good is our reaction to it."

Although I intellectually understood that everything from *Hashem* is good even when it hurts, my heart was still not convinced. I was having a hard time accepting my situation. Yet, life needed to move on. I was back to planning my online classes for girls by July 7. I was looking for ideas for a fun and meaningful summer workshop. My answer came in the form of an email invitation to join a five-day creative journaling challenge from Rae Shagalow, an educator and artist.

Challenge Day 1:

Open up any Torah book that you have on your shelf, the Chumash (Bible), Tehillim (Psalms), your siddur (prayer book), or any other Jewish book that inspires you. Choose one word [or phrase] from the text that speaks to you. Write that word in your journal in large letters. Decorate the word or draw and color a decorative border around it. As you decorate the word, let it resonate and fill your soul with the feeling that you want to bring into yourself, into your day, and into your relationships with G-d, yourself, or others. This is called hisbonenus, deeply contemplating a passage in the Torah and learning it so completely that it becomes a part of you.

I encouraged my JGU online students to try this exercise and I joined them. Opening up a prayer book to the morning Torah blessings, my eyes landed on these words: "*Bachar banu... Hashem* chose us." I colored the letters and contemplated that *Hashem* chose me for the mission of being Yosef Chaim's mother. I was chosen — *bachar banu* — for a special mission and when we are G-d's emissaries there is no room for sadness! My sadness was melting. My aching heart was beginning to find *nechamah* and I was ready to forge ahead with joy in my mission.

I knew that Yosef Chaim is a gift much greater than the child that we expected to have but I kept wondering to myself: "What is the hidden blessing that my entire life's purpose has seemingly fallen apart? What is the mission I have been given with Yosef Chaim's birth? What is the lesson I need to learn? How is it possible that my soul's mission would conflict with the birth of this special soul?"

I read these words from my father to his students. It was as if he was talking to me:

When something happens to us that seems to contradict our purpose, we ask, "Why is this happening to me?" We may not see it but if we approach with faith that everything is for the good, then we will see the good. The true good is to be able to lift ourselves above and eventually free ourselves from the definition of what is bad. If I hold by this definition, then I am going to be miserable. The ultimate good is our reaction to it. Be willing to accept that there is a good beyond our definition of good.

I spoke to several people about our unexpected news. I asked Leah Namdar what she thought *Hashem* wanted from me. Her reply was, "You mastered doing. *Hashem* wants you to learn how to be." She happened to mention that she was in the middle of directing her overnight camp for girls, from her property, which has two houses. I hoped that one day we would be able to do the same. I thanked her so much for always being there for me.

My sister-in-law, Leah Wasserman, was jumping for joy when I told her the news. She said that her uncle with Down syndrome is the family's favorite uncle. Chana Cotter, an educator and artist, came over to meet Yosef Chaim. She shared that she worked with many students with Trisomy 21 and that they were her favorite and most lovable students. She told me, "You will see that Yosef Chaim is such a blessing."

I prayed to see the revealed blessing.

SHARING THE DIFFICULT NEWS

"It is essential to reach out to others for support."

Goldie Plotkin called to wish me *mazal tov* because she had heard about the suspected diagnosis from my sister-in-law, Bassie Laber, who is her sister. She told me that when her Zalmy, o"bm, was born with Down syndrome, she only received two *mazal tov* wishes. *Baruch Hashem*, today the world is much more open and accepting. With pride, she said that Zalmy o"bm was her badge of honor and the pride of her family. I was grateful for her moral support.

Life had taught me two vital lessons: 1) A challenge means you are chosen for a G-dly mission, and 2) It is essential to reach out to others for support. I needed support, so I reached out to moms of children with Down syndrome and joined online groups and WhatsApp chats. I learned and read books so I could give Yosef Chaim the best start to life. But I felt uncomfortable sharing the news with my local and global community. My grandson's birthday was approaching, and it would be our first time facing the public since the diagnosis. I wasn't sure if we should let people know or keep the news about Yosef Chaim to ourselves. I emailed Goldie for advice.

Hi Goldie,

I was very inspired by your positive perspective on special children. It helped me truly feel b'simchah at the bris. His name, Yosef Chaim, reminds us that he adds life and joy to our lives. I didn't mention his condition to anyone at the bris because we didn't have the confirmed test results.

We've received the test results and he has regular Trisomy 21. We were at a doctor today who specializes in special needs. Yosef Chaim has low muscle tone and we will start early intervention as soon as possible.

He seems to be nursing well to me... but he lost weight since our last doctor visit. He said it's typical for babies with Down syndrome because they are sleepier. I need to go back for a weight check on Friday.

I am trying to get grounded back into my life... but it's not easy. Do you think I should tell people already? He just looks like a newborn. We are going to a birthday party tomorrow for my grandson. Do I share our news or wait until it's more evident in his development?

Hi Nechama,

I feel that you should share this news with your friends and community as soon as you can. After the birthday celebration, let everyone know that you are proud. You accept this new challenge with simchah, strength, and complete bitachon that Hashem is good and will be there with you. This is an incredible opportunity to teach all your friends and community how a chassid lives. How to connect to Hashem and that you walk the walk.

I'm always here for you. Just call or text anytime. Besuros tovos and a huge mazal tov again.

Your sister Shlucha,

Goldie

We decided to share the news by creating a video about Yosef Chaim. My children and I tweaked the lyrics of a popular children's song and applied it to Yosef Chaim. My talented daughter Shaina produced a video with my boys singing the following song, along with pictures of Yosef Chaim, and then I told the story of Yosef Chaim's birth and diagnosis:

Hashem gave us a present,
Do you know what it was?
He gave us Yosef Chaim, so we could love him so.
He asked some other families, "Do you want this gift of Mine?"
But they said, "No, thank You, for Yosef Chaim there is no time!"
Then to the Laber family, Hashem did go;
They said, "'Na'aseh v'nishmah[60],' 'cause we love Yosef Chaim so."

I received so much love and support from family and friends around the world. So many reached out to me and sent me messages filled with love.

---

60 *We will do and we will hear." (Shemos 24:7)*

Dear Goldie,

Thank you for your advice. I'm in awe of your approach. I am amazed at how you never stopped your activities but only grew in your Shlichus all these years despite the challenges. You are such an inspiration!

It's been a hard week. Since Yosef Chaim's birth, he either lost or maintained his weight. My days are filled with doctor appointments and therapy visits. Summer retreat is in two weeks and I have the upcoming year of JGU to plan.

How do I manage? I know Hashem is taking care of me and loves me but I'm very tired and exhausted...

Love, Nechama

My father's words in Dobra's notes were just what I needed:

Hashem would never create a situation, you couldn't handle. The challenge is tailor-made for each person. We have the capacity to see through the experience. Step out of your limiting beliefs and experience a new level of Hashem without limitations. If we take steps, in the darkest moments we can grow, strengthen ourselves and deepen our awareness more so than in any other time.

A test from Hashem is an opportunity to awaken the strengths and power of the inner soul. Stand firm in this test to flower and blossom into a new self that perceives the world totally differently. It will be growth-inducing and reveal a deeper self. Through revealing our potential, Hashem gives us greater potential to reveal.

PLEASE SUSTAIN THIS CHILD

"He gives food to all flesh, for His kindness is everlasting."

At five weeks old, Yosef Chaim still weighed less than he weighed at birth. I was frustrated. Babies typically lose weight after they are born, but they usually gain it back within a few days.

I'd prayed for his health before his birth and I continued to pray for him. I had lost count of my prayers. Sometimes I prayed with a prayer book and other times I just spoke to G-d, beseeching Him with all my heart. I knew He was listening. I knew He was waiting for my prayers. I gazed at the angelic face of my newborn baby, Yosef Chaim, and prayed to G-d to bless my child that he should grow strong. I had been up with him for many nights and I prayed for strength. I prayed for everything I needed to care for this precious soul entrusted to me. I prayed for the strength to pray, to sing, to cry, to appeal even when I felt drained.

I asked for the clarity to appreciate how every challenge is a blessing from Above. I prayed to recognize the blessings in my life. I prayed and sang with gratitude to G-d for all my beautiful blessings even in my sorrow.

"You should eat and be satisfied and bless G-d.[61]" We are commanded to thank *Hashem* for our sustenance. *Hashem*, our Father, is involved in every detail of our lives. We are grateful to Him for providing us with our food and caring for us at every step.

How many times have I said the Grace After Meals without thinking about the meaning? Do I notice the miracles taking place at every moment to sustain my family and myself?

My baby, Yosef Chaim, reminds me to appreciate all that G-d provides for us, His children. My precious infant has low muscle tone,

---
61 *Devarim* 8:10

so he was sometimes too sleepy to eat. As a result, he wasn't gaining enough weight, although I had thought he was just the most content baby ever. We visited the doctor often to check his weight gain and after doing my part, I prayed to *Hashem* to help him grow. Thank G-d, at six weeks old, he had finally gained back his birth weight.

As an experienced mom, I have nursed babies before, but it never took this much effort and focus. At the same time, I had never been as grateful to *Hashem* for every ounce the baby gained. We celebrate Yosef Chaim's progress and bless G-d every day for this little miracle. I have faith that if G-d is able to care for all His children, He can care for my teeny tiny infant. When I worry about providing for the needs of our growing family, *bli ayin hara*, I remind myself of the words in the Grace After Meals, "Blessed are You, L-rd our G-d, King of the universe, Who, in His goodness, provides sustenance for the entire world with grace, with kindness, and with mercy. He gives food to all flesh, for His kindness is everlasting."

WE FALL TO RISE

"Frustration is a good thing, it leads to motivation!"

I had Yosef Chaim evaluated for early intervention when he was four weeks old. He receives therapy multiple times per week, and since I have to be home when the therapists come, I realized it would be almost impossible to continue traveling from place to place for retreats and programs, as well. Throughout the years, we had rented and moved everything but the kitchen sink for our programs and retreats in facilities sometimes over an hour from our home. I could not see myself doing this with Yosef Chaim.

I reflected back to November 2017, when I had been the guest for a *Shabbaton* with 25 girls at Beis Chana, a high school in Connecticut.

Our *Shabbaton* theme had been "Dream it Real." After the meal, the table was set with *Shabbos* desserts and the girls gathered for a *farbrengen*. I opened with a question: What is your dream? In the *parashah*, Yosef's dream impacted Jewish history. It all begins with a dream. I shared with the girls how I prayed that one day very soon, I would be able to host them in my own place.

Sitting with these girls, I was able to see my vision more clearly. I loved the size of this group. I could see similar retreats in a large home. As soon as I returned from the *Shabbaton*, I went online and searched for a large home. It was time to dream it real. I found a promising home with four acres and we were in negotiations with the owners. We created our transition plan, obtained bank approval for a mortgage and even started organizing and packing. We waited to hear if our offer was approved.

A couple weeks after Yosef Chaim's birth, we received disappointing news from the lawyer that the owners rejected our offer. After trying so many times to find a permanent location without success, our dream felt as distant as a boat far out into the sea. Would my boat ever reach the shore? I was feeling extremely down. All my dreams seemed to be fading away. I just wanted to cry and curl up in bed with Yosef Chaim.

There was a loud voice shouting inside of me, "GIVE UP! It's not possible to find a home to meet the needs of your family and global community." We received more disappointing news while getting ready for our one-week retreat in August. We had been awaiting approval for a significant grant that we had received the previous three years for the summer retreat. We received a letter from the board stating that we would not receive the grant this year.

"WHAT?! *Hashem*, another blow? It's too much," I cried. "*Hashem*, help me see the disguised blessings." My child is struggling, our finances have hit rock bottom, and I feel purposeless and isolated in Troy. I was frustrated beyond anything I had ever experienced. It really hurt. And then I heard my baby's therapist say, "Frustration is a good thing, it leads to motivation!"

My home in Troy felt smaller with Yosef Chaim's therapists. My baby needed a new home with more space. I needed a home where I could care for my baby, while also fulfilling my purpose. We had found campgrounds to rent in Southern Rensselaer County only available for one-week in August, which wasn't the best timing, therefore we had lower enrollment. Everything seemed to be waning. I felt like the moon as it gets smaller and smaller in the night. I remembered that the Jewish calendar follows the moon and *Rosh Chodesh*; a new month takes place when the moon is barely visible. While it felt dark, I prayed that this was not the end but a new beginning.

I read words from the *Rebbe* that uplifted my spirits:

You must know that there would be no falling, without the true goal of rising. G-d creates no negative phenomenon unless there is the ultimate goal of a positive result. If there is an illness, then the possibility for a cure must be here. 'The cure precedes the illness.[62]*"*

Not only does the cure come before the sickness, but the purpose of the decline is to reach higher, for the route to reaching loftier heights is by first descending to the depths. To make a dwelling place for the Shechinah in the lower worlds, there must first be a descent. Only then can one be transformed and elevated to become an abode for G-dliness.

An example of this concept would be the story of the Tanna, Nachum Ish Gamzu. The precious stones and pearls he bore as a gift to the Emperor were switched for sand. It later turned out that the sand was the "sand of Avraham, our father" (which brought miraculous results). Not only was there a way found to remedy the loss of precious stones, but the loss also brought a much greater miracle. The effect of this gift of sand was much greater than the gift precious stones would have been.[63]

---

[62] Megillah 13b
[63] Sichos in English

CHAPTER 11

Lighthouse on the Hill

THE TURNING POINT

"My help comes from Hashem."

As I wrote and re-read the draft of my book, I realized it was filled with messages that I needed to internalize. I was experiencing grief again because I was mourning the child I'd thought I was going to have. I wrote to Micki Massry:

> While nursing, I have been spending time revising the book. The ideas I wrote about while waiting for this precious baby to be born are helping me to rise above the challenges at this time. It is actually quite ironic.

I really needed this book's messages to transform my *tzarah* into *tzohar*. I read my own words, written months before: "*Hashem* doesn't give you a challenge you can't handle because with the challenge, He gives you new strengths." This calmed my heart.

I was so thankful that I had listened to my inner voice, my soul's yearning to write this book, when I had a window of opportunity. I was thankful that *Hashem* had sent me his angels to support this endeavor. This book was truly the cure that preceded the illness.

My book was ready for editing. I had been trying to reach the editor who had revised an excerpt to publish in a magazine for LINKS, an organization that provides support to girls who have lost a parent. I reached out to her and we totally clicked. On my father's *yahrtzeit*, she accepted to take my book on as her project.

My father's *yahrtzeit* precedes *Tishah B'Av*, and for most of my life this was a week of sadness. While fasting for the destruction of the Holy Temple, I reflected, "Will I allow my life's mission to be destroyed like the Holy Temple?" In frustration I asked myself, "If there was only one thing I could still do, what would it be?" Yosef Chaim forced me to prioritize. He anchored me down. I wanted to teach and have retreats. We couldn't continue to wander from place to place anymore with our programs. I was searching for the lighthouse to guide my boat to the shore. The sea was stormy but I would not let myself drown in a sea of negativity.

My father taught his students:

Re-energize with good, healthy thoughts. Harmful thought robs us of life-energy. Every test is a challenge to uplift us. Challenge necessitates change, so goodness can come forth. It's our choice to either make the necessary changes or give up.

I looked up and noticed the dream board I had created during a JGU Creative Online Club earlier in the year. I had cut out pictures of a beautiful home and wrote what I wanted for our family and community: "An oasis of peace, pool, leadership retreats, fireplace, Jewish home, large office, *mazal tovs*." My vision board helped me refocus on this dream.

I prayed with all my heart. "*Hashem*, bless us with a home where we could create a dwelling place for You on Earth. *Tatty*, please help us carry on your legacy in the most beautiful way."

I would stay on the path of our dreams, pray and take action. On my baby's crib, there was a card with the psalm *Shir Hamaalos*, and I slowly read King David's famous words: "I lift my eyes to the hills, from where will my help come? My help will come from the Creator of heaven and Earth!" I tried to absorb these words. My father's name is Azriel, meaning "my help comes from *Hashem*." This was the lesson he taught me and so many others.

HELP COMES IN MIRACULOUS WAYS!

"It was the dawn of a new day."

A couple of days later, on *Av* 13, an unexpected gift arrived in the mail, with the return address of 770 Eastern Parkway. Inside the envelope there were ten crisp $100 bills. I was in shock. I took it as a clear sign that the *Rebbe* was encouraging me and sending me the beginning of a down payment. In addition, we received another unexpected contribution from Sruly Richler, who sent it because Rosh Lowe asked him to support us. These moments reinforced my faith with hope for the future. It was a message that I shouldn't give up but keep on fighting. It showed me that just like I never expected to open my mail and find these gifts, help will come from our Creator in miraculous ways!

After the excitement passed, I felt sad and frustrated once again. I guess the lows and highs were coming more frequently. I was fighting for my son's sustenance and health. I was pumping, giving him formula, and also nursing. This was not an easy routine, but there was nothing that I wouldn't do for my child. In addition, the formula we used was causing Yosef Chaim terrible stomach pains. I didn't know what to do. I felt like a new mom all over again. I complained to my husband that it was becoming too difficult; I was exhausted and feeling very depleted.

My husband noticed my frustration and remarked, "Don't worry, Nechama. Good things are happening. We received the envelope with $1000 in the mail." My husband has so much faith in *Hashem*. I just laughed.

I read a saying in a support group for moms on Facebook: "A child with Down syndrome doesn't come with a manual, but he comes with a mom who doesn't give up!" I was this kind of mom now! Just as I was fighting to sustain my child and help him grow, I had the power to sustain my spiritual children. Anyone I teach is considered like a child. I would fight to continue my work with our Jewish daughters. I would keep searching for a home in order to expand our work without the challenges of renting and schlepping from location to location. We would find a home where Yosef Chaim and my children would be surrounded by a loving community.

On *Tu B'Av*, *Av* 15, as I was up feeding Yosef Chaim late at night, I did an online search on Zillow. There must be a home waiting for us, I thought. We had seen dozens of properties over the past ten years that hadn't worked out. This time, I was determined. I searched for a home with a pool, a couple of acres, and guest bedrooms. I found one that fit my criteria. I noticed that the price had been lowered on July 16... *Av* 4... my father's *yahrtzeit*! This was another good sign from Heaven. I emailed our realtor a link to the property at 1:00 a.m.

On August 1, *Av* 20, we toured the property. It was made for us. It was only once we went to view the property that we realized that it was literally across the street from two hotels. This two-acre property with a pool and a three-story house could accommodate retreat participants in the nearby hotels. We would serve meals at our home cooked in our *kosher* kitchen. It felt like an oasis of peace surrounded by many trees, yet it was right off the highway and in the center of town near stores. We placed the offer the next day. I was breathing through each step as

if I was having a baby all over again. On August 3, *Av* 22, with thanks to *Hashem*, the offer was accepted. On August 9, *Av* 28 — my birthday! — we signed a contract with the sellers.

"From where will our help come?" Throughout the process, we noticed that the help we needed was coming to us from the most unexpected places! Thank You, *Hashem*. Just when I had reached my breaking point and the world felt so dark to me, it was the dawn of a new day. A new chapter of my life was beginning. I was blossoming into a new self and revealing a deeper self. It was time to sing a new song!

HAPPY BIRTHDAY - SEE THE BLESSING

"I experienced the truth that every soul is created with a unique purpose."

On my 44th birthday, I gained a deeper understanding of the meaning of my name: Nechama Dina. A classmate of mine with the name Nechama Dina messaged me that her mother used to bless her, "May you find comfort, *nechamah*, in the *middas hadin* — the seemingly bad." She explained to me that one is comforted when we see how the *middas hadin*, our test, is transformed into a purpose and is the *nechamah* itself.

Wow! I never realized how much my name defines me. When parents name a child, they receive Divine Inspiration. It is certainly not by chance that my name is Nechama Dina!

Yosef Chaim turned seven weeks old on my birthday. I reflected on those seven weeks with the following post, which received hundreds of supportive comments.

> *Victor Frankl said, "Man's main concern is not to gain pleasure or to avoid pain, but rather to see a meaning in his life." When our precious son, Yosef Chaim, was ten days old, he was diagnosed with Down syndrome. My initial reaction was self-pity. "What a terrible thing. This was not in the plan. How will my life go on?" I was overcome with fear of the unknown. I cried many tears. After speaking to several wonderful people, I heard them say to me, "Mazal Tov! He is a blessing from above. You are AMAZING! You were chosen for an incredible mission. It is not what you did wrong, but what you did right." I was elated and so grateful to Hashem.*
>
> *A couple of weeks later, I found myself feeling very down. I wondered why I was NOT SEEING the blessing. I was exhausted and tired of trying to figure out why Yosef Chaim wasn't gaining weight. I was tired of spending days at the doctor. I was not living up to being the amazing, joyful mother I wanted to be. This was plain hard. After ten children, ka"h, I felt like a novice. I begged Hashem for the strength to accept my situation with joy. I wanted to SEE the blessing.*
>
> *The opening verse in Parashas Re'eh [my birthday parashah] says, "SEE, I [G-D] put before you today a blessing and a curse." It contains 49 curses that will befall the Jews. Our sages explain that a Divine curse is actually a blessing that is too great to be revealed within our limited world and must therefore be disguised as a curse. When we trust in G-d and believe that everything that happens is for our good, we SEE revealed blessings.*

I reframed my thoughts and began to adjust to our family's new reality. I experienced the truth that every soul is created with a unique purpose. It's okay if Yosef Chaim is different from my other children. I am grateful for all the good. He is a beautiful baby, ka"h, who needs my love just like the others. My love overflows with joy.

It is our hardest moments that lead to our greatest joy. A joy that is derived from seeing the beauty of each soul. A joy that emerges from being a conduit to fulfill G-d's will. A joy that comes from finding the joy in the journey.

May we find "nechamah," comfort, from the "dinah," challenge, itself. The [din] challenge itself becomes the catalyst to bring about the greatest [nechamah] comfort and blessings in our lives. The real challenge is to open our eyes and SEE how the hardship is a blessing. It takes work to reveal the blessing. In the process we learn, we grow, create new friendships and spread light.

I AM CARRYING YOU

"I was flying high on Hashem's protective cloud."

Now that we had an accepted offer on a house, we desperately needed the remaining funds for the down payment. It was right before *Rosh Hashanah* and we were scheduled for a closing after *Sukkos*. I called my brother Azriel to update him. He advised putting up a website with a building campaign goal. We had some funds in savings from the initial stages of our capital campaign in 2014. This campaign "baby" also needed to gain more weight. Nothing was going to stop me now! There was nothing I wouldn't do for my spiritual children. I prayed that everything would go smoothly.

I knew we weren't doing this alone. And then we received a clear sign from Above.

I received an email from Rabbi Shmuel Metzger, who was my father's second-grade student, with a picture of my father carrying my brother Mendy and me. I was six years old at the time. I had never seen this picture before and felt sure there was a Divine message for me. And after a couple days of reflection, I got it! Although it may have appeared that my father left us 33 years before, he had been carrying his children all along. Children include his students because they are a teacher's spiritual children. My father was still carrying his children and students and blessing us with a sweet year.

I shared the picture and this message with my JGU email list, announcing the launching of our "Build the Future" campaign. Leah Caras designed a beautiful brochure and website, inviting people to "invest today in the future confident Jewish mothers and leaders of tomorrow!"

Over Sukkos, I felt my father's presence so strongly as quite a few donations were given in his memory. He felt so alive! *Tatty* was certainly helping us to create our dream, a dream he had planted in me when I was a young girl.

We spent the holiday in Montreal, where we bought Yosef Chaim a new formula from Israel. It was very expensive, but we didn't think twice because we'd heard great reviews on this Israeli product. He loved it and we hoped that he would start gaining weight. At three months he was only 12 ounces above his birth weight. If a baby doesn't grow, it affects brain development too. Just like I was doing everything in my power to sustain my baby, Yosef Chaim, I used the same power and energy to "Yosef Chaim — add life," to our campaign. We prayed and made phone calls to let people know about this exciting opportunity.

As Yosef Chaim gained weight, our campaign gained momentum. This was no coincidence. As I overcame obstacles with Yosef Chaim, I was also building my inner strength to overcome obstacles along the path to realizing our dream.

On *Chol Hamoed*, I received a call from a very dear friend named Hannah. "How is the campaign going?" she asked. I told her that we were making progress. "How much more do you need in order to purchase the property?" she inquired. I told her where we were holding in the campaign. She responded that she would put a check for a large amount in the mail to help us reach our goal before the end of *Sukkos*. I was blown away by her generosity. I was flying high on *Hashem*'s protective cloud. The cloud that carried the Jews in the desert became real for me.

THANK HASHEM IN ADVANCE

"This itself will bring the ultimate Geulah."

We were ready for the closing on the Wednesday after *Sukkos*. We had miraculously raised the funds needed. Yet *Hashem* had other plans. The closing was canceled the day before it was supposed to take place. I couldn't breathe. There were unexpected complications that had to be resolved first. My first thought was, "What if the worst happens and it falls through?" I refused to think about it. I spoke to Susan and we reframed the thought, "What if everything goes smoothly?" We had to do our part to help clarify the issues. Avraham and I were up very late putting together the information needed. We would not get an answer until Friday. With bated breath, we awaited the news that things were cleared for closing.

Thursday is the day I teach a prayer class for women online. I had already invited women to bring *l'chaims* to celebrate the purchase of the property. I felt like canceling my class because I couldn't think straight. I thought to myself, "If I don't have peace of mind, how can I inspire others? I was planning to celebrate with the participants; now, what will I say?" I picked up a book of Psalms and sang in my sorrow just like King David did in times of distress.

I called Nechama Dena for help breaking through any barriers by releasing limiting beliefs. We realized that one of my limiting beliefs is that I feel responsible for too much. Perhaps fear of a whole new responsibility was holding me back? When my father passed away, I took on a lot of responsibility. Nechama Dena said, "As you embrace this new reality in this new location, you will experience a new level of release from the grief you experienced in the past. Instead of feeling responsible, give *Hashem* the responsibility and allow Him to send the blessings through you. *Hashem* is responsible for everything. *Hashem* creates loss, and He fills the void. He is responsible to provide for all of our needs."

I mentioned to Nechama Dena that I was embarrassed to give my online class because everyone expected us to have closed on the house. She encouraged me to say *l'chaim* in advance during the online class and thank *Hashem* for His salvation.

That night, my class participants and I thanked *Hashem* ahead of time for granting our wishes, as if they happened already. I said, "Thank You, *Hashem*, for granting us a new home for JGU, where we will create a dwelling place for You."

I shared that if King Chizkiyahu would not have waited to sing *shirah* until after the Jews were saved from the army of Sancherev, he would have become *Moshiach* and brought the complete Redemption. The *Shelah* states that the Redemption will come when we begin the *shir chadash*, new song of thanks, for the incredible miracles of Redemption — before it actually takes place — out of our tremendous trust and joy. This itself will bring the ultimate *Geulah*.

At the end of the class, I randomly played a *niggun* and it turned out to be "*Ki B'Simchah Seitzeiu* — You will go out with joy, and be led forth in peace. The mountains and the hills will burst into song and the trees will clap their hands.[64]" I knew these words would be fulfilled. It was time to sing and dance, not only ourselves but with the hills (the property is on Thompson Hill Road) bursting into song, and the many trees on the property clapping their hands!

The *Rebbe's* deeper explanation of this *pasuk* is that the mountains and hills are the obstacles in life. The trees are barren at times. At times, we wonder why we have to go through a certain challenge. This song is the promise that the trees will bud and we will sing and dance above the obstacles. I was certain that the trees and hills will celebrate *Hashem*'s new home to glorify His name.

---

64 Isaiah 55:12

DANCING WITH DAD

"My father was already dancing with joy in heaven."

It was Friday morning, and we had not yet received the okay to close on our new property. I took a deep breath and remained confident in *Hashem's* miracles. I had seen so many miracles unfold until now; I knew the next miracle was on its way. I prayed with all my heart and soul that morning. After my morning prayers, I sat down for my coffee. I had a few moments to check my email and I remembered that my father's second-grade student, Rabbi Eli Abramowitz, had sent me an email a few days before, but I hadn't had a moment to open it. He had sent me a link to *"Tishrei* with the *Rebbe"* on YouTube.

In complete amazement, I saw my father dancing in 770 with my brother Mendy and me in his arms to the song *"V'samachta B'chagecha -* And you shall rejoice in your festival.[65]" The picture I received earlier was from this video! I was 100 percent certain that today we would receive the final approval for closing. I was overcome with emotion and found myself laughing with tears in my eyes.

We still had to resolve one more issue, but it was with renewed strength, knowing that my father was already dancing with joy in heaven. Shortly thereafter, we received the okay and the closing was rescheduled for *Cheshvan* 8. Yosef Chaim was born on *Tammuz* 8. Is this a coincidence? The number eight represents that which is above nature. Our lives are certainly beyond nature. We are a miracle!

Baruch Hashem, on Wednesday morning, *Cheshvan* 8, we closed and received a golden key to our new home for JGU. We gathered and made a *l'chaim* with our children and my in-laws, who continuously researched potential properties and moved to Albany in order to be part of our vision. Their support helped keep our vision alive over so many years.

---

65 Devarim 16:14

We were so grateful to the 150 supporters[66] who made it happen, including very generous gifts from my sister, Racheli and Avrohom Jacks, my brother Azriel and Chana Wasserman, my mother, Uncle Lenny Wasserman, Hannah and Yehudah, Eli Nash, Yocheved and Yehudah Daphna, Tzivia Chaya and Yakov Rosenthal, and Linda and Ory Schwartz . We thanked *Hashem* for guiding us to create a dwelling place to glorify His name. And of course, when we danced a happy dance and toasted *l'chaim*, we knew my father was dancing and saying *l'chaim* with us.

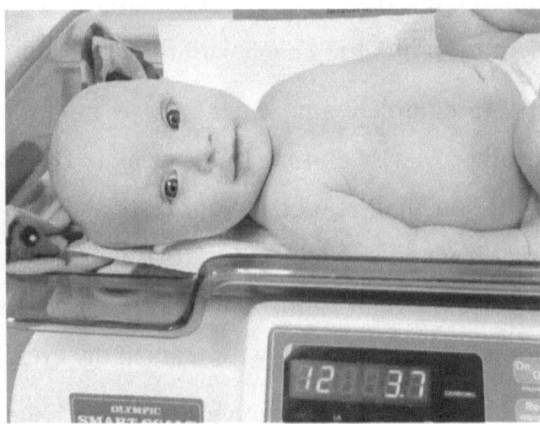

TWELVE: THE LUCKY NUMBER

"Change location, change your fortune."

It was moving day at last and in the middle of everything, I took Yosef Chaim to the doctor for his four-month check-up. We weighed him, and lo and behold, to our tremendous joy, he was 12 pounds! He had exceeded all of our expectations and gained over three pounds in one month. This was no coincidence. The saying goes, "*Meshaneh makom, meshaneh mazal* — Change location, change your fortune.[67]"

---
66 All donors are recognized at www.jewishgirlsunite.com/building-campaign
67 Talmud, *Rosh Hashanah* 16b; *Bava Metzia* 75b

Our new address is 12 Thomson Hill, Yosef Chaim was 12 pounds the day we moved into the home, and my Bat Mitzvah Club girls preparing for their twelfth birthday started this whole journey. We taught our girls for years that bat mitzvah is not a one day celebration, but a life long goal. It is important to become a bat mitzvah, rather than just celebrating the birthday. This is my life long goal to empower girls and women to be proud Jewish daughters.

As we drove our children to our new home that night, in a car packed with blankets and clothes that the movers couldn't take, we sang together, "*Mimitzrayim ge'altanu....* We are leaving our Egypt!"

MY THANKSGIVING IN THE HOSPITAL

"I can feel sorry for myself or look for the pearl in life's irritations."

Shortly after we were settled in our new location, Yosef Chaim had to go to the emergency room for RSV (Respiratory Syncytial Virus). I wrote the following message during my eight-day stay in the hospital:

> As I sit here in the hospital with little Yosef Chaim on the weekend of Thanksgiving, I have so many thoughts to share. I have two options: I can feel sorry for myself or look for the pearl in life's irritations. I can be upset that I missed celebrating my oldest daughter's birthday with her and that I'm not home with my children during their vacation. But instead, I choose to reflect, thank Hashem, and find the good.
>
> I reflect on how it's so easy to take our health for granted. When we have health, we have the strength to take action. While walking through the hospital hallways, I realize how many people have it much worse. I meet the mom of a child who needs a tube for feedings, and is also deaf and blind. This mom loves her child unconditionally. I am even more thankful for the

unconditional love and support that I receive from my family and friends. I am grateful for the nourishing food they bring me.

This is my Thanksgiving.

I met so many caring nurses. One nurse shared that she would love to be at her family's Thanksgiving dinner. She's grateful she has a job and can help Yosef Chaim get better. I tell her that she is a pearl. She says, "What do you mean?" I share with her that in the opening of King Solomon's song, "Eishes Chayil," a woman is compared to pearls: "A Woman of Valor [Eishes Chayil], who can find? Her worth is beyond pearls." Just like an oyster transforms an irritating grain into a lustrous pearl, the woman of valor transforms life's irritations into pearls. She smiled and said, "Thank you for your inspiration." We are both seeing the pearl in spending this time at the hospital. I am ever so grateful for the caring hospital staff.

This is my Thanksgiving.

My dear children pile in to visit us, and the staff at the desk ask them in wonderment, "Are you all Yosef Chaim's siblings?" Now the secret is out: Yosef Chaim is not my only child, and I'm not 25 years old. Yehudah, age nine, sees his precious brother with a blue tube providing "high flow" attached to him. He says, "He looks like a scuba diver." I hug him and respond, "Yes, Yosef Chaim is a deep-sea diver, helping us find the pearls in life. Sometimes, the good is hidden but we will never stop searching for the beautiful pearls." I embrace each of my children as they hug me like never before. I am grateful for their love that fills my heart.

This is my Thanksgiving.

Dear Yosef Chaim, your little body needs support to breathe right now. You remind us to appreciate every breath of life, and that every day is Thanksgiving. Every morning, we say Modeh Ani together, and you smile at me. It's been harder for you to smile these days, but you still do when you can. We thank Hashem in advance for your recovery and say, "Thank You,

Hashem, for our little 'Chayal's[68]' complete recovery!" I am grateful to have a home to return to with my precious baby boy very soon!

This is my Thanksgiving!

I returned home after a week in the hospital, elated that Yosef Chaim pulled through miraculously but also overwhelmed by all of my responsibilities. I was physically and emotionally drained. Someone encouraged me to connect with Sarah Kranz-Ciment, a physical therapist and project director for the Ruderman *Chabad* Inclusion Initiative (RCII). She was so caring and understanding and gave me advice for coping with a child with special needs. We also discovered that we both lost our father at the same age. As a result of our new friendship, her daughter Nava joined the JGR winter retreat.

A few days after I brought Yosef Chaim home from the hospital, it was *Chanukah*. It was the first time that all of our children were together in our new home. We lit our menorah surrounded by family and friends. I watched my children's smiling faces glow like the flames; children who had grown up yearning for this day, children who now see with their own eyes that G-d does answer our prayers. And I realized that no darkness can dim the lights of my father's menorah, nor the "menorah" within each of us.

---
68 *Chayal* means soldier and the initials of Yosef Chaim Laber in Hebrew spell *Chayal*.

RETREATS IN A NEW HOME

"We unearthed the treasured pearl within ourselves."

One week after leaving the hospital, we hosted our first winter leadership retreat in our new home for 30 girls. The theme was "Creating Pearls: Transformation." The girls were given two random objects that they had to use to present how we can transform a bad situation into one where we can find the pearl. We had a heartfelt *farbrengen* where we shared our personal struggles of revealing the pearl in our challenges. We painted clay pearls and a shell with guest artist, Chana Cotter. While working, we watched videos of how an oyster forms a pearl from its own irritating discomfort, as well as people who found their own pearls in challenging life-situations.

After a yummy breakfast, we drew pearls on paper, which we then filled with compliments for one another. Following *davening*, we went shopping to buy a gift for our secret admirer-partner, to continue the theme of finding pearls in each other. We also bought ingredients in order to transform them into delicious treats for the banquet, like we transform our hardships into pearls. When we came back, we had a blast beading our very own pearl earrings. At the banquet we enthralled each other with our writings, stories, and song-dance. We unearthed the treasured pearl within ourselves, and bravely expressed our challenges and our breakthroughs.

Following our JGU winter retreat in December, I spent a *Shabbos* as a staff member at the LINKS *Shabbaton*. I was comforted to get a glimpse of an organization that is supporting girls through their grief. I met my editor and so many wonderful staff members and girls. We all had one thing in common — we all suffered loss at a young age. It was so healing to be in a community where everyone understood each other. At my *Shabbos* table, I turned to the girls at my table and asked them their names. I was amazed to find out that sitting near me was the daughter of the *Shlucha* I had spoken to at the *Shluchim* Convention! Our conversation had been the catalyst that inspired me to focus on publishing my story. I was delighted to meet her personally. It felt like a complete circle.

FIRST LEADERSHIP RETREAT FOR WOMEN

"Shabbos in my home was magical."

It was time to plan JGU's fifth global celebration, which was combined with the very first Women's *Shabbos* Leadership Retreat. For so many years, the mothers of our campers had wished there would be a retreat for women too. I was so elated to host our first retreat to unite and celebrate the collective power of Jewish women.

As excited as I was, the preparations felt endless, and I wondered, "Why did I choose this life? Why do I take these projects upon myself? Why do I find joy in filling the rooms of our home with guests? What is the root of my desire to share my love for *Shabbos* and Judaism with others?"

I thought back to my childhood. *Shabbos* in my home was magical. A table filled with guests from all backgrounds. My mother serving delicious food, and my father passionately sharing words of wisdom on the *parashah*. His love for *Shabbos*, each Jew, and G-d spread around the table like the heavenly aromas of my mother's *challah* and chicken soup. As my mother's *Shabbos* candles glowed, so did the souls of each participant. The singing, the inspiration, and the unity inspired so many to observe *Shabbos* and become lamplighters.

It was heaven on earth.

For so many years, I missed my father's table filled with guests, I yearned for my father's heartfelt kiddush and joyful *Shabbos* and holiday meals. There was a gaping hole in my heart that followed me into adulthood. *Baruch Hashem*, for ten years we served a congregation in Troy and hosted numerous guests, but then the community changed. We spent many *Shabbosos* without guests and the void that I felt as a child returned. My children never complained, and they even enjoyed our restful weekends. But my heart could not rest. I could not take the easy path.

Now, our table is filled with family and guests from around the world. I feel my father's love. I see my mother's light. It feels magical to me, just like it was in my childhood. The work may not be easy, but I sense a joy in my soul that words can not describe. It's the joy of being *Shluchim* of *Melech Malchei Hamelachim Hakadosh Baruch Hu*.

It is heaven on earth.

This is the purpose of creation to bring heaven down to earth by creating a dwelling place for *Hashem* filled with love and light.

IT ALL TURNED AROUND

"For the Jews there was light and joy! [69]*"*

We went straight from the Women's Leadership Retreat into *Purim*, which fell out on March 21, which is also Down Syndrome Awareness Day. Yosef Chaim was born on June 21 and turned nine months on *Purim*! When Yosef Chaim was diagnosed with Down syndrome, we had feared the worst. Personally, I had wondered if I would have to decrease my activities to spread the light of Torah. Then we realized that we were chosen and given a very special mission… just like Queen Esther in the palace.

In the *Purim* story we find that just when things appear the worst, the Jews were saved with a complete turnaround — *"v'nahafoch hu.*[70]*"* There are so many examples, including the gallows Haman originally built for Mordechai but upon which he was himself was hung; Esther being taken as queen against her will, which allowed her to bring about the Jewish people's salvation; and *Adar* was transformed from the most tragic month of the year to the most joyous.

"V'nahafoch hu," it all turned around, and "for the Jews there was light and joy![71]"

It's not by chance that March 21 (3/21, like trisomy 21) coincided with *Purim* this year! Our family experienced our own *Purim* story. The diagnosis that had caused us pain now brought us the purest joy and light. Yosef Chaim's birth brought the blessing of a new home, a place to gather to celebrate our light, our Torah, with joy! I would never have imagined when Yosef Chaim was born the love and light he would bring into our home and the world. May *Hashem* keep him healthy always.

---

69 Esther 8:16
70 Esther 9:1
71 Esther 8:16

Our life experiences often feel like disjointed events. But when we open our eyes, we can see the thread that connects them all. We can appreciate the beautiful tapestry that we have created for our family and our global Jewish family. Through sharing our stories, like Queen Esther, we can support each other with love and empathy.

PESACH ON THE HILL

"It felt like my father had sent an angel to sing for me."

From *Purim* we went right into preparations for *Pesach*. *Baruch Hashem*, we had our first "*Pesach* on the Hill" retreat, and it was a beautiful experience.

Tzirel Liba Mitzman, a singer and one of our Pesach staff members performed her original songs and played guitar for the women. I felt like many of her original songs mirrored my journey. It felt like my father had sent an angel to sing for me, just like he may have done while strumming on his guitar.

During *Pesach* she composed this song about our new home, "Lighthouse on the Hill":

When you search but the light is dim
When the storm clouds come rolling in
When the waves crash on the shore
When you try but you need more

Chorus
There's a lighthouse on the hill
Where your soul can drink its fill — of love
When your searching becomes real
You can grow and you can heal
Oh, the caring is for real

At the lighthouse on the hill

When your thoughts are so fragmented
And you are feeling disconnected
Trying to hold onto the storm
And trying to make it to the dawn

Chorus

The light will guide you home
Cause you're right
The beam of light
That illuminates your night

LETTING GO OF OLD BAGGAGE

"Our outer world is truly a mirror of our inner world."

Although we moved into our house in October and we held two retreats for girls, one for women, and one for *Pesach*, it took approximately six months to sell our old house.

It was a process, filling loads and loads of garbage bags and focusing on only taking the things that would serve us in our new dwelling for *Hashem*. The work was enormous. I had accumulated so much stuff over the years — I still had papers from the time I was in grade six, the year my father passed away. Perhaps, I was trying to hold on to the past in the only way I knew back then? Over the years, I kept papers from every class I took or taught, supplies and records from so many programs, and just loads of miscellaneous "stuff."

While letting go of my physical excess, I realized how much emotional baggage I had held onto from the past. I was so grateful that I was given the opportunity to clear my mind and heart and let go of the old story. For years, my sadness and grief took up so much space, just like all the stuff I didn't need anymore because it didn't serve me. It was time to purge and let it all go. It was time to say goodbye to anything from the past that I didn't need. It was time to fully embrace the new light that had emerged from my loss.

As I went through my stuff, I looked at my things one by one and asked myself, "Does this serve me anymore? Is this part of my soul's song?" As I said goodbye, I thanked each thing that shaped me. I realized they all made me who I am, just like every life experience. And they are all part of my soul's song.

I am letting go like a leaf falling from a tree

I am letting go of grief

I am letting go of self-judgment

I am letting go of any hurt that I absorbed into my heart

I am letting go of all the memories that held me back

I am letting go of worry that keeps me from moving forward.

I am letting go of darkness to create space for the brightest light

Today I know that I can hold onto my rich past with joy, I can hold onto my memories with love. I can carry on my father's legacy with pride and shine a greater light created from the darkness!

Our space in our beautiful new home is clutter-free and filled with love and light. Together with my wonderful husband, children, and global family, we are creating a healing "Lighthouse on the Hill" to support other people's journeys to *nechamah* and healing.

How does one let go of unwanted emotional baggage?

It begins with self-awareness — when you get to know yourself and find out who you really are. When you do that, you will realize that most of the things that you thought you knew about yourself are really just old stories. When you can live and appreciate the present moment, you can let go of a painful past and create the future that you envision.

Throughout my journey, I asked myself:

Do I want to live with the limiting beliefs I accumulated in the past, or let them go?

Do I want to see the limitations in others, or their greatness?

Do I want to open my heart to welcome in this present moment with all of its glory, or focus on what I lack?

I remember when I began to appreciate welcoming in the *Shabbos*, despite the fact that I felt isolated from a Jewish community. Instead of feeling lonely, I chose to create space to be alone with G-d, my Father in Heaven, and my beautiful family. Every *Shabbos* was healing, a time to reflect on the past week and a time to pray for the future, while truly appreciating all the blessings from *Hashem* in the present.

Our outer world is truly a mirror of our inner world. I know that letting go of my internal baggage brought the blessing of releasing the home I wanted to move from and opened the doors to a new JGU home. When we fully accept and recognize that every experience shapes us, we allow *Hashem's* will to become our will. As a result, there is no separation between our will and *Hashem's* will. His physical world supports our mission. This is the reality that manifested in our new home; a *dirah b'tachtonim*, a dwelling place, a mini sanctuary for *Hashem* and a lighthouse for all.

TREASURES FOUND

"I am the main character, the author, and the storyteller."

While going through all my old stuff, I saved these heartwarming messages from my children:

Chaya wrote this letter when she was 12 years old:

Dear Mommy & Tatty,

Words cannot express your devotion, dedication, love, and commitment to JGR and your family. Starting as a small day camp, then to Bat Mitzvah Camp and finally, JGR. So much in ten years! The seeds you planted back then are blooming now.

Year after year, camp got better and better. I remember thinking, "If this year was so much fun, I can't imagine what next year will be like!" Indeed, it was true. The hours of work that you put into camp cannot be counted.

May we merit to be in camp next year in Yerushalayim with Moshiach now!

Love,

Chaya

I found Chana's graduation poem from grade 12 with a beautiful message as I said goodbye to our home of 19 years.

Our lives are all but one interwoven journey
Each separate path guided by Hashem's hand
Our choices, and our nurture
Yet truly we are all on the same journey
We are the prince searching for the king
Will the king lift me up and escort me into his innermost chambers?
Or will I invite him into my humble home?
Will I take the long-short way, or the short-long way to reach him?
Will I be a swimmer or a climber, a soldier or a sailor?

The journey stands before me
And it's hard to walk away without looking back
Yet I know that I am standing on a foundation beneath my feet
My roots run deep into the soil, and now my branches can reach infinity
With Hashem's help, I know I'll find my way
Because I am the main character, the author, and the storyteller.

On Mother's Day, I received this email from Tzipporah, a devoted JGU teen student:

Dear Mrs. Laber,

Happy Mothers' Day! Wishing you a year of only brachos, simchos, and revealed good from Above. Also, may you merit to see the fruits of your "Labers" — your children, students, and many holy projects (a.k.a. "brain-children") in whom you've invested so much — that they should go mei'chayil el chayil, in the ways of Torah, mitzvos, and Chassidus, and bring unbounded light into the world!

Thank you for being such an incredible dugma chaya for me and for all the other girls you've taken under your wing! Your living lessons, especially of unconditional love, gentle nurturing, and passion for Yiddishkeit, have transformed me. B'ezrat Hashem, I will try to carry them on and make them a part of me all my life — no matter where in the world I might be — and share this light of yours with anyone whom I meet, to have a positive impact on them.

"Teach with joy... Be a living example of the values you wish to transmit... Speak with words from the heart, and they will enter their hearts..." It's astounding how precisely you live and guide us by these three simple and pure directives; anyone can see and feel it! Rabbi Wasserman lives on through you so clearly, and you are such a nachas to him! Thank you for showing me how to pass on the flame of Judaism and Jewish education with love and joy. I

want to join this chain, too, and give others what you've given me, and what your father taught.

May you be blessed by Hashem in every way imaginable, and beyond.

With admiration, appreciation, and lots of love,

Your JGU Student

The breathtaking pond view

A DREAM COME TRUE - JEWISH LEADERSHIP CAMPUS

"Open for Me an opening the size of the eye of a needle, and I will open for you an opening the size of a hall.[72]"

We received a call from our new neighbors one month after Pesach, offering to sell us their property — a total of 12½ acres, with a house overlooking a four-acre pond. This was our five-year vision, which I had just written down five days earlier! Our programs were growing so fast and needed more space. *Hashem* was presenting us with this incredible opportunity to expand our vision and live the dream that we had envisioned for so many years. As we concluded this book, we were

---
72 Midrash Rabba Shir Hashirim

already working on our next chapter — to acquire the new property and establish the Jewish Leadership Campus.

We prayed to *Hashem* that we would have the ability and assistance needed to expand our vision with peace of mind and abundance. We took action and prepared a presentation for potential partners. We made many phone calls and wrote emails to let our friends know about this miraculous, once-in-a-lifetime opportunity. Our first goal in our *Building the Jewish Future* campaign was to raise the down payment to close on the property in time for the book launch and our August retreat.

Baruch Hashem, on 8 *Tammuz*, while we were getting ready for a triple birthday party barbecue for Avraham, Chana, and Yosef Chaim, Micki came to visit to speak about her book dedication. We also toured the new property and she immediately saw the vision and was inspired. Thanks to Micki and Norman's significant gift, combined with that of Linda and Ory Schwartz, and several other generous partners, we were able to close on the property at 5 Mannix Rd. We closed on *Erev Rosh Chodesh Menachem Av*, the beginning of the fifth month of the Jewish calendar, a month associated with mourning and loss, as well as my birthday month, the day that I was given my mission on this earth. It was only four days before my father's 34th yahrtzeit. This gave us time to prepare for the inaugural summer retreat on a beautiful campus and celebrate the book launch. There is something very heavenly about all this, and we know my father is celebrating too.

Opening the door to the new property.

I called Mushky Gurary (née Greenwald), a previous JGR counselor, and told her about the latest updates on our miraculous expansion. With great excitement she remarked, "Nechama, this is unbelievable. This is beyond. Someone is holding your hand!" I knowingly nodded my head, "Yes I know. Someone is holding my hand."

As I was preparing for the book launch, I was listening to the audio clips of my father, I hear him saying these words, "You take things little by little. You make changes slowly and (pretty soon) after a while, you realize that you accomplished something BIG!"

The Lighthouse on the Hill has expanded into the 12 acre Jewish Leadership Campus. I now understand why G-d says: "Open for Me an opening the size of the eye of a needle, and I will open for you an opening the size of a hall." The right way to advance in achieving our goals is to open a small opening, to take one step powerfully, and G-d will advance us forward and open openings the size of a hall. What connection is there to a needle? It would have been more appropriate to refer to a narrow opening such as a crack or hole in the wall. These few words impart a very important message. A needle is used for sewing, for connecting things. G-d is asking us to create an opening of connec-

My daughter Chaya, son-in-law Mendy, and grandchildren Azriel Yitzchok and Aaron at the Jewish Leadership Campus.

tion to Him, connection to the chain of generations, connection to our people. When we create these connections, G-d opens for us a wide opening, the size of a hall.

We are excited to grow our summer and winter Jewish girls retreats, JGU leadership retreats, *Shabbatons*, and holiday family retreats, all while enjoying the magnificent nature of *Hashem*'s wondrous world. This is just the beginning of establishing and building the Jewish Leadership Campus. Thanks to our partners, Jewish girls worldwide have a home away from home.

Thanks to Micki, this story is recorded so all who read this book will understand that when we trust in G-d and take positive action, our *tzarah* will become our *tzohar*. It is clear that the legacy of our fathers is shining bright, and together with our partners, we will empower future proud and confident Jewish leaders to ensure that the legacy of our ancestors continues from generation to generation!

JOIN THE GLOBAL COMMUNITY!

Join the legacy of love by helping us expand and build the Jewish Leadership Campus! Contact nechamalaber@gmail.com or 518-727-9581.

I hope you will join our global family by participating in our retreats and online classes for girls and women at
www.jewishgirlsunite.com
Be a part of an empowering community of girls and women who are spreading light!

You can also listen to recordings of the songs referenced in this book at
www.jewishgirlsunite.com/songinsorrow

Follow us on facebook.com/jewishgirlsunite
and @jewishgirlsunite

EPILOGUE

Weaving the Tapestry

While editing this book, I became more aware of how much has changed since I began sharing my story. When we share our stories with others, we create community and we impact others with our life experiences. Each person impacted from my story can impact someone else thus weaving a beautiful and colorful tapestry.

It is no coincidence that the Jewish Girls Unite theme for 2019 is "*Weaving the Tapestry, Connecting Women Past, Present and Future.*" It seems that the JGU theme for each year is an expression of my soul's journey. Since we are all connected, my journey affects others in more ways than I can imagine.

We are all part of a much bigger story, those who came before us paved the way and we do the same for future generations. My life has been illuminated by incredible women who have supported and guided me on my journey. *Hashem* brought each one of them into my life at the exact perfect moment. In the process, we have become soul sisters and part of something much greater than ourselves. I have been told by those who supported me that their lives have been enriched because when we give, we also receive. We can all be a *mashpia* (giver) and a *mekabel (receiver)*. Each sister is a leader and has a unique light to add to the glorious tapestry of our people.

I would never be where I am today without the loving support and guidance that I have been so lucky to receive. I strive to give back from the gifts *Hashem* has given to me. I asked my supportive soul sisters what have they received from being part of my journey from loss to legacy and light.

SUSAN AXELROD, CONFIDENCE COACH:

I am elated to see this book now completed. I cannot wait to read it in its entirety and am delighted to let you know that I have already begun to find my own rhythm in referring to it with clients and friends to begin to teach your thesis, that you can overcome grief by bringing to life the legacy of your loved one, that you can feel again, that you can find joy again precisely in the blessing of bringing to life the departed soul as a guide for your own life. I hereby reserve two copies to share with my dear friends who lost their precious jewels and pray with all of my heart that your words will provide comfort in their personal tragedy, that they may learn to feel the soul-teaching of their children and share that teaching widely such that the souls of the departed children will be able to impact others in the way they intend. (Amen)

I remember the first time we wondered at my words to you. I remember wondering, "Where are these words coming from?" It seems so easy and natural now to realize that your father, your *Tatty* o"bm, Rabbi Azriel Wasserman chose me to speak to you, but at that time, it seemed so unlikely, no? In the early days of our loving friendship and partnership, you would look at me with curiosity as if I was saying something familiar, but you couldn't exactly place it. I remember, too, the dawning of awareness. Words would come out of me and while perhaps they challenged, you could easily receive and accept without irritation, defense or resentment. By then, you knew that everything I said was from a place of love for you and utter respect for your work, but still, it was not easy. No one will ever know the personal commitment, the deeply held desire you must have had to listen daily to me and 'hear,' to break through, grow, and break out of the old binds.

I remember sometimes, that I felt elation in your growth, even exultation; and I remember not knowing where such deep feelings came from or why I was feeling them. But by then, in my own journey, I had already started living a life of accepting what was, of 'open and allow.' Through my own work over decades, I yearned for, strived and glimpsed the beauty of living life in awe, on purpose, opening and allowing whatever *Hashem* intended for me. In an ironic twist of blessed fate, part of my core learning on that came from you! The very student I was teaching; later I realized we were never a teacher/student, but always soul-connected on a purposeful journey to heal, to help, to show others what 'living' can be. I believe Rabbi Wasserman (as I call him) was involved. You broke through to now, through this book, to show others that in spite of loss, in spite of sadness, you can find song. Remember how Rivka Leah Cylich's song *Silent Prayer* became my silent prayer? It served us both.

I remember, then, when you received the notes from our friend Dobra, extensive notes she took from your father's classes. You called me and said, "You're not going to believe this." But, of course, I believed. So much of what 'I' had been saying was there in the notes from your father. I remember the day it finally dawned on us. Rabbi Wasserman, your *Tatty*, had found a 'way' to speak to you, to let you know he was always there, he always intended to fulfill your deepest desire of his teaching you how to be a teacher. And today, you honor and share his legacy; you are a teacher extraordinaire for all time. This is not hyperbole, not an exaggeration as you know from students going back 20 years now coming forth and sharing your impact on them. Jewish Girls Unite is now the premier online global community for our Jewish daughters; a safe, loving, sacred space for Jewish girls of all backgrounds to learn, to grow; and sometimes, just to be. As your *Tatty* did, you now share your love (I learned from you and Rabbi Wasserman that all teaching starts first with love of the student) and lessons with total devotion, commitment, and consistency.

If anyone wants to find you anytime, they have but to go to JewishGirlsUnite.com and find you. Always there, always ready with love, with open acceptance. The way you were with me. So, Rabbi Wasserman, through you, is still teaching! I believe it was his partnership with you that helped me find the song of my Jewish soul, something about which I had my own deep sorrow. And, through our honesty with each other, you know how precious that has been for me. Together, we found song in sorrow.

I wish you endless moments of love and impact. Your courage and fortitude is extraordinary. I pray that every reader throughout the generations will receive the Divine 'share' of their own connection to *Hashem*, to Rabbi Wasserman and especially to their own soul.

CATHLEEN BELLISARIO, SPEECH THERAPIST:

I have been a practicing Speech-Language Pathologist working with infants and children for over 25 years. Becoming involved at the beginning of a child's journey to hone their communication and feeding skills is so impactful, both for me and for those I serve! In order to best meet the needs of the children and families I work with, it is imperative to really get to know the strengths and areas of need each family presents. This is accomplished best by simply listening as caregivers share their hopes and fears, successes and failures.

I first met Yosef Chaim when he was four weeks old. He was a tiny slip of an infant, struggling to find the strength to take in nourishment throughout the day. His family was struggling as well, to accept the diagnosis that had been unexpectedly conferred at his birth. I counseled and comforted both Yosef and his parents. The sense of mourning for what was imagined and hoped for was palpable. Miraculously, as Yosef gained strength and fortitude, those around him seemed to as well. His mother in particular began to see his diagnosis and skill sets not as a hindrance but rather as a conduit for good things to come. Her grace and optimism was, and is, refreshing and serves as a reminder to look past the surface to see the beauty that may be hidden upon first glance.

Never has this lesson hit home more soundly than when my own son experienced ongoing medical issues. It was easy to let myself become bogged down in the overwhelming minutiae of caring for a loved one. Whenever I felt at my lowest, I thought of Yosef and his family, and how they actively and continually seek to see the silver lining inherent in any situation. Yosef is seen as a miracle baby whose love and light encourage more positivity to grow. I believe that this outlook is self-fulfilling: the more optimistic and positive a person is, the more good things come their way. We can dwell on the superficial negatives life hands us, or look for the more meaningful, less overt message in any given situation. Yosef is and always will be a reminder that there is so much good around us, if we're only willing to see what is truly being offered.

LEAH CARAS, GRAPHIC DESIGNER & YALDAH MAGAZINE FOUNDER:

When I first came to Bat Mitzvah Camp as a teen camper, I wasn't expecting much more than a fun and inspiring experience. Yet after experiencing the "magic" of BMC—the hands-on learning through every activity, the total love and acceptance of every girl, and the lifelong friendships formed between campers and staff—I knew that I wanted to join the team to ensure more girls would have this incredible experience.

Although Nechama was much older and more experienced than I was, I am so grateful that she took me seriously as a partner. I gained so much from my involvement in JGR: friendships with campers and staff, spiritual inspiration, and so many leadership and organizational skills which I use until today.

In fact, it was my connection to Nechama which brought us to move to Albany seven years ago, a community we are so happy to be a part of. It's a bit surreal that now my children are playing together with her children, B"H!

Throughout all of her ups and downs, it was inspiring for me to see how Nechama always recognized the Divine plan and looked for the good. If camp was small one year, she talked about how much extra personal attention each girl was able to receive; if a project was delayed, then there must be something important that needed to be edited or added.

It has been wonderful to watch the dream of a property miraculously unfold, and I'm looking forward to seeing JGU flourish in its year-round location.

AHUVAH COATES, EDUCATOR & JGU ART COACH:

When I first met Nechama Laber, she was giving her workshop "From Darkness to Light." Nechama herself seemed like such a light. Her story was a start to my own healing process after losing my mom. Nechama and I immediately connected on a neshamah level, and I began to learn and integrate some of her healing tools and affirmations. I started to want to live more of my mother's active legacy. My mother's care, creativity, and compassion began to emerge from within. As Nechama teaches, the person who passed away lives through you. You allow them to keep on living with you and through you, by being a channel of light for them to continue to express themselves through you in this world.

Becoming an art coach for JGU has been a spiritually satiating experience two-fold; helping girls connect to their *neshamos* and deep Torah concepts through art, as well as incorporating my mom's legacy of creativity, love, compassion, in a judgment-free zone. The closeness and creativity of weaving one another into each other's life has been an experience of light and love!

CHANA COTTER, EDUCATOR & ARTIST:

I first met Nechama through a phone call back in the early 2000's. She was looking for a teacher to guide her campers that summer in art. In the beginning, I was reluctant; I had taught summer school before and really did not enjoy the experience. But something inside me coaxed me to say yes. Thinking back to it now, it was most likely that I'd be meeting young Jewish girls from all parts of the US, who were looking to grow spiritually and have some fun. I had been working a lot on Jewish papercuts at that period of time. I spoke with Nechama about my skills and what I could offer the girls in her camp, and she totally embraced it because the art form was in keeping with Jewish tradition.

The camp was in part stationed at a historic synagogue on the banks of the Hudson River in Troy, New York. I was immediately impressed by how various groups of girls, divided by ages, were so engaged in their activities. I remember Nechama was teaching some of them to knead and bake *challah* according to Jewish law. Some of the others were singing, and still others were learning prayer with counselors. I was struck by the relaxed atmosphere. The campers weren't resisting their studies, like I had witnessed in public school. They were smiling and laughing and enjoying their tasks.

In speaking with her briefly each day and watching her and the trained counselors, it was so apparent that this was a place where girls were learning how to be leaders themselves. They were learning by example that Jewish women are valuable and respected in Judaism. I loved my experience there and learned so much from Nechama. Most important, I learned that in order to keep Judaism thriving, we must teach our daughters their incredible roles as Jewesses and to continue the legacy of the faith. It is because of rare "lamplighters" like Nechama Laber who persist and take a stake in this treasure called Judaism that we continue — and will continue on until the end of days.

YOCHEVED DAPHNA, FOUNDING BENEFACTOR & ENTREPRENEUR:

The Jewish Girls Retreat was a very positive experience for my daughter, Golda. It is something that fills a vacuum and a great need because it provides girls with a feeling of wholeness, happiness, and self love. My daughter is very intellectual, but she needed an outlet to express her creativity through art, song and writing. She felt embraced and loved at JGR and the impact is hard to quantify and measure.

It gives me great pleasure to give and to especially help girls and young women explore their creativity. We are blessed to have been founders. I am thrilled that JGR has a permanent home that will impact so many. We can see that Nechama's father is still holding her hand and guiding her to carry on his legacy in such a beautiful way.

ROBIN & LEVI GARBOSE, FILM DIRECTORS:

When my wife, Robin, was writing the screenplay for Operation: Candlelight, a feature film for women and girls, she was looking to create a young heroine with an overwhelming emotional challenge. In the narrative Robin was constructing, the girl's father, a great teacher and tzaddik, had passed away from cancer a few years before and her mother had recently remarried. The young woman's pain was further exacerbated by her mother's decision to send her away to Torah Academy, a fictional boarding school for Jewish girls in Hidden Hills, California.

Realizing an opportunity to memorialize my dearest friend, Azriel Yitzhak Wasserman o"bm, I suggested to my wife that we name the character 'Sara Wasserman', and Sara's late father 'Azriel'. I also suggested we imbue the fictional father with certain attributes of my late friend, the character's namesake.

I thought it was simply the name we were using, and a general likeness. Little did we know that the entire story was being channeled, replicating the events that impacted Nechama Dina Laber's life. Nechama Dina never had the chance to say goodbye to her father, but she found resolution unexpectedly through the film. Her father was sending her a message, "Nechama Dina, trust in this; *Hashem* is always guiding you, even when it hurts." (See page 134 for full story.)

Robin and I are delighted and inspired by the work Nechama Dina is doing, carrying on the legacy and teachings that her holy father, Azriel, imparted to our world.

RACHELI JACKS
EDUCATOR & FOUNDING BENEFACTOR:

"Racheli, you speak first, you're the oldest." My sisters nudged the large, clunky phone into my hand.

"Hello?" I said gingerly. I had no clue who I was speaking to, but apparently this girl miles away in another city was going to become our new sister.

"Hi! I can't believe I'm speaking to you!" The voice replied almost instantly. "Hold on a moment." Amidst the noise on the other side of the line, this voice called out to the people around, "Guys, be quiet, I'm speaking to my sisters!"

I was a bit confused. We had been told she didn't have any sisters, it was just three brothers and her. Who were the sisters she was speaking about?

Suddenly, it dawned on me—we were the sisters! Yes, we were now becoming one family...

I didn't know what our new sister would be like, but her voice sounded incredibly cheerful.

I glanced as my darling sisters listened and watched my every move. The three of us had stuck together through thick and thin, encouraging and supporting one another, never fighting but always being there for each other. We had gone through a lot that past year, and we understood the value of a sister. And we guessed that she must also understand the value of a sister, because she had a similar background to ours, we had been told—both of our families had lost a parent. We also figured that just like our courage-filled journey from the depths of despair to eventually finding the special inner strength lying within us, she must have experienced her own similar journey. This knowledge made us feel somehow connected, although we had never met in person yet.

"Hello?" the voice was back on the line.

"Hi, we're all here by the phone," I answered, motioning to my sisters to squish even closer to the phone. "We're all here. We are all sisters!"

Thus began a deep and cherished relationship in my adolescent years, which continues on until today. As it turned out, we graduated in the same year, in two different cities, which meant that we got to go to sem together. We had the same schedule and did all of our homework and studying together. We shared ideas, and helped each other with model lessons. We got very close at that time, traveling together to be head-counselors in summer camp and then teaching the same grade, departmentalized. When we each got married and lived in different places, we still kept in touch. We would discuss ideas, and I would compose songs based on the year's JGU camp theme which was to be sung by the campers.

Now, when we all get together, we look around and admire our beautiful huge family, which has b"h now multiplied as each of us sisters (and brothers too) has a family of their own. Each of us has a special strength or talent, which we all celebrate, and deep inside we all know that from our challenges there has arisen light.

EVELYN KRIEGER, EDUCATOR & AUTHOR:

I first met Nechama at the inaugural Jewish Girls Winter Retreat in Lake George, New York. I had been hearing about the planning of the event for weeks from my 15-year-old daughter, then Leah Larson, founder and editor of *Yaldah* Magazine.

Nechama recognized Leah's talents, creativity, maturity, and ambition. Together, they conceived JGR. I remember how astonished I was to see Nechama's energy and passion in action at the winter retreat. When I saw my fifteen-year-old daughter confidently present a slideshow about *Yaldah* to the group of young girls, I knew that this dynamic duo would go far to inspire Jewish girls to embrace their heritage and shine their inner light through creativity and leadership.

Since our meeting, Nechama and I have shared many wonderful conversations about education, raising girls, marriage and family, and working through grief and loss. Today, I consider Nechama both a friend and mentor.

TZIREL LIBA MITZMAN, SINGER & SPEECH THERAPIST:

I came to Pesach on the Hill without too many expectations. I thought it might be a nice opportunity to have Pesach away in exchange for contributing to cooking. What I got was far beyond anything I could've ever imagined! Firstly, I found a soul sister. An utterly amazing woman who lives with Torah in everything she does. I barely went out of the house during Pesach but I traveled through the land of emunah and Torah with every meal we cooked. We were a small and extremely diverse group of people and somehow, the magical healing energy brought us all together.

Hashem poured beautiful music through me relating to each aspect of my experience and hence three beautiful songs were born. The first a tribute to the Lighthouse on the Hill, the second is Nechama Dina's story and the impact on her life and the third about Jewish Girls Unite. I feel honored, privileged, and blessed to have entered the "Laber of Love" now known as The Lighthouse on the Hill!

Tzarah* will be your *Tzohar
Music & Lyrics by Tzirel Liba Mitzman

Tatty, why'd you leave me?
I feel so alone
Tatty, can you hear me?
Without you it doesn't feel like home
Everywhere I see your face, how you taught me aleph-beis
It's in my soul
Everywhere I go, I feel you
Your Torah and your songs reveal you
I feel you beside me.

You said:
Your tzarah will be your tzohar
And like drops of spring rain
I'll be here to guide you through your pain
Your tzarah will be your tzohar
And through the darkness of night
Hashem will guide you to your light.

Tatty, you said everything is good even if it hurts
How did you know my life would be guided by your words?
I live my days teaching to trust in Hashem
I live my days reaching to Jewish daughters...
All of them!
Everything I say and do has been instilled in me by you!

You said:
Your tzarah will be your tzohar
And like drops of spring rain
I'll be here to guide you through your pain
Your tzarah will be your tzohar
And through the darkness of night
Hashem will guide you to your light.

I have found my song in the sorrow
Now I see a beautiful tomorrow, right at hand
Tatty, when you gaze down at me
You'll see the legacy that you began

You said:
Your tzarah will be your tzohar
And like drops of spring rain
I'll be here to guide you through your pain

Your tzarah will be your tzohar
And through the darkness of night
Hashem will guide you to your light.

My tzarah was my tzohar
And likes drops of spring rain
You've been there to guide me through the pain
My tzarah was my tzohar
And through the darkness of night
Hashem guides me to my light!

Jewish Girls Unite

Music & Lyrics by Tzirel Liba Mitzman

There's a place you can call home,
You never need to feel alone
Together hand-in-hand,
We will grow and understand
Learning more each day,
The Torah lights our way

Chorus
We are the keepers of the flame
We are the lamplighters
No two of us the same
Yet together we burn brighter
Jewish Girls Unite
We are walking into our light
Together we grow strong,
Our journey is our song

So many highs and lows
And through it all we grow
Our strength we are refining
We're each a facet of the diamond
Our voices carry through the air
HINEINI. I AM HERE!

Chorus

Jewish Girls Unite
We are the keepers of the flame
Jewish Girls Unite
We are the lamplighters
Jewish Girls Unite
No two of us the same
Jewish Girls Unite
Together we burn brighter!

LEAH NAMDAR, EDUCATOR & SHLUCHA:

Talking to Nechama is always an inspiration! She is like a flame, always full of warmth and light and ever striving higher. Her real vision and the courage to make it happen have touched thousands of lives. It's so uplifting and an honor to know this incredible woman, who is a legend in her lifetime.

RIVKIE PIEKARSKI, ASSISTANT PRINCPIAL:

Mrs. Rivka Piekarski, attended the JGU Global Launch in NY, because Mrs. Sternberg, a teacher in Beis Rivkah, was honored. We reconnected and later she sent a gift with this letter.

Enclosed is an additional contribution towards the amazing movement you've begun, uniting girls worldwide and getting young ladies to blossom and grow in their Judaism. This innovative creative "web design" is a true representation and tribute to your father of blessed memory.

As an educator, he was most successful because of his *Emet* — truth and trait of *Pnimiyut* —(to be genuine to the core and to put one's entire self into the moment.) When Rabbi Wasserman saw a child, he saw him in his purest state, he saw his true potential and the generations until Moshiach that will come from this child and so he did all he could to bring out the best in everyone.

You, too, are doing this with Jewish Girls Unite! You are doing your father proud!

May your father move from one *Aliyah*, elevation, to the next - to the ultimate *Aliya*—a soul in a body with the redemption that will take place in the merit of the Jewish women!

RIVKA LEAH POPACK, SINGER:

It has been humbling to play even a small part in Nechama Dina's larger-than-life vision to connect women and girls across the world through JGU. I know that our musical partnership has been part of a greater G-dly orchestration. Thank you, Nechama Dina, for gifting me with this opportunity to add song to the JGU world and connect with sisters across oceans and across time.

DOBRA SPINNER, INTERIOR DESIGNER:

Nechama Dina and I go back. Way back... kinda through a few different lifetimes. Her mother, a soul sister, helped marry me off. Her father, my beloved Chassidus teacher, instilled in me, with his words and his heart, a perspective in dealing with life challenges according to the Rebbe's teachings.

Six years ago, I gave Nechama Dina my class notes imbued with her father's voice, as he battled for his life, unbeknownst to any of us. I think those precious notes played a vital role in helping Nechama Dina internalize much in her own personal healing journey.

She has lived with her father's voice — in overcoming struggle, in transforming and inspiring us through online classes and retreats. Nechama Dina spreads her own light. She sheds light in her actions, constantly endeavoring to empower women and girls. She somehow sees hidden sparks and brings them to the surface. Many of us journey with her, honing our emotional toolboxes, as we apply Chassidus deeply, through soul searching, art, and song. As we travel through our own lives, developing emunah, healing and transforming, we pray our ripple effect will bring personal and global *geulah* to the world.

CHANA WASSERMAN, INTERIOR DESIGNER:

From the first conversation I ever had with my husband, Azriel or Ezzy, as I call him, I always knew his father was a very important person in his life. It's amazing that everyone who ever met him only has the most amazing things to say. Learning about him and hearing the audio recordings gave us a glimpse into his noble personality. On the recordings, Azriel heard the way his father sang with his children and spoke to them with so much love. He learned about cherishing his children and the importance of valuing family connection over materialism. This advice came into his life at the exact right time before our first child, Eliana, was born. He was able to take what he heard and bring it into his life and it gave him direction as a new father. Azriel makes a special effort to sing and spend time with his children, despite a rigorous work schedule.

It feels so lofty and special to be a part of *Tatty*'s legacy. He is very much alive in our home. We have many pictures of him on the wall and we speak to our children about their *Zaidy Tatty* in heaven and their *Zaidy Daddy* in Montreal. It really tells us a lot about him that his children and grandchildren make a conscious effort to bring him into their lives.

I believe in the work that Nechama is doing and I'm amazed at the effort and thought that is put into growing *Zaidy Tatty*'s legacy in such a beautiful way.

MIRIAM YERUSHALMI, AUTHOR & COUNSELOR:

For 15 years, I volunteered to present kids with my "preventative care" information through various artistic activities (dance, drama, art, singing to name a few). One day, my daughter came home and announced that she wanted to join the JGR winter program. I replied, "We'll go together and I'll ask if I can be part of the staff there!"

In the past, I ran a museum in Israel with activities for children. I was sad when I had to give it up. I questioned G-d and thought I wasn't worthy, and I felt depressed. I felt defeated by G-d and my light wasn't shining for a while. I began to study Chassidus and understand that everything that happens is by a Divine plan and it's all for the best. When, Nechama accepted me and invited me to come and share, my light was re-ignited.

NECHAMA DENA ZWEIBEL, INTUITIVE HEALER:

Having the same namesake as Nechama Dina, and being on the same wavelength, with even our modus operandi being quite similar, this has been a special journey together.

Our deep, meaningful, and transformational sessions aimed at maximizing JGU's potential helped me access wisdom that was dormant and emerged through Nechama Dina drawing it out of me. Each time we "farbrenged," whatever obstacle or opportunity that Nechama Dina was being presented with to transform, I found similarities to what I was contending with, with small variations. As doors opened for her, I also saw openings in my life. We even both moved locations around the same time!

Our energies complemented each other very well. It was exciting to travel this journey with her and I anticipated the gift we would discover for her and for the world every time we connected. I was always left with a sense of gratitude for her father's love and compassion and awe for her and her fortitude, humbled by the role I merited to play in her global mission.

I look forward to continuing to support her goals and dreams in creating the Lighthouse on the Hill - Jewish Leadership Campus as the epicenter of Jewish girls and women being empowered to shine their light, under Nechama Dina's warm, loving and capable leadership.

This book is filled with many songs that led my way. Song is the language of the soul. These songs spoke to my soul and gave me the strength to persevere. After finding my song in sorrow, *Hashem* transformed my sorrow into a light that will illuminate other souls. I pray that my story will comfort hearts and bring the ultimate *nechamah* with the redemption.

Thank you dear reader for joining me on my journey. I encourage you to never, ever give up searching for your soul's song, even in your sorrow, because this song will bring a new tomorrow. If you open your eyes, you will realize that every low in life leads to your high and reveals your light. I encourage you to write your story and compose your song about your unique journey with the ups and downs. One day very soon, we will combine all of our songs that have emerged from our sorrows to compose the most beautiful song of redemption, a new song, *shir chadash*. And on that day we will all come home to our third Holy Temple in Jerusalem, G-d's dwelling-place that will last forever.

As King David sings:

רַנְּנוּ צַדִּיקִים בַּה'. לַיְשָׁרִים נָאוָה תְהִלָּה:
הוֹדוּ לַה' בְּכִנּוֹר. בְּנֵבֶל עָשׂוֹר זַמְּרוּ לוֹ:
שִׁירוּ לוֹ שִׁיר חָדָשׁ. הֵיטִיבוּ נַגֵּן בִּתְרוּעָה:

> "Sing praises to the Lord, O you righteous ones; for the upright,
> praise is fitting. Give thanks to the Lord with a harp;
> with a lyre of ten melodies make music to Him.
> Sing for Him a new song.[73]"

---

[73] Tehillim 33:1-3

Acknowledgments

Thank you, *Hashem*, for all Your blessings.

...for choosing me to teach Your precious children.

...for blessing me with my supportive husband and incredible children, and for providing us daily with all we need to fulfill our mission as Your *Shluchim*.

...for all the helpers You send my way to guide me to find *nechamah*.

...for all the angels You send my way to support our mission.

...for taking me out of my emotional and physical Egypt.

...for keeping Your promise: "Just as in the days of your going out of Egypt, I will show you wonders!"[74]

"*Hodu l'Hashem ki tov* - Give thanks to the Lord[75]..." I bless **Hashem** for it is all good.

---

74 Michah 7:15
75 *Tehillim* 118:1

I would also like to pay tribute to:

The *Lubavitcher Rebbe*, zt"l, whose teachings guide my path in life. Thank you, *Rebbe*, for guiding us with your wisdom and empowering us to be leaders to bring redemption to ourselves and the world.

My beloved *Tatty*, **Rabbi Azriel Yitzchok ben Yisroel and Pesha Leah Wasserman** o"bm, who laid a firm foundation of faith and love and still finds a way to teach me. Thank you, *Tatty*, for teaching me how to teach and for continuing to guide me through your messengers.

I am eternally grateful for all the people *Hashem* sent my way to help me keep singing my song in the sorrow until it was transformed into a song of joy. I list the people in the order that they came into my life:

My dear mother, **Daniella Katzenberg,** for rising above the challenges and for raising us with the inner strength to follow the path of our dear father o"bm. She brought me into this world with tremendous sacrifice. She was in the hospital for a month before my birth due to complications. My parents named me Nechama Dina, which means comfort on the judgement, because my healthy birth was a comfort to my parents after a trying situation. I remember how she always woke up early in the morning to prepare us for school. We had home-cooked food and a well-maintained abode. I learned from her how to run a Jewish home and accept help from others when necessary.

I look back with fond memories on the special trip to Israel we took as a family in honor of my bat mitzvah. My mother traveled with four children, including a nine-month-old baby to Israel, so I could have the excitement of celebrating my bat mitzvah in a special way, which helped me forget that *Tatty* wasn't physically with us. She is a living example to me of faith, fortitude, and finding creative solutions in every tough situation.

My maternal grandmother, *Même* **Rachel Bouskila**, o"bm, whose sincere joy and open heart nurtured me and my children until her passing at 93 years old. *Même* would visit often from her home in France and helped us before each family celebration.

My paternal grandmother, **Bubby Lillian (Leah) Wasserman**, o"bm, who personified unconditional love and kindness and never failed to remind me how much I meant to her. She told me that in one of her last conversations with my father, he whispered to her, "Nechama is going to need you. Please take care of her." Her presence in my life was a huge comfort, and her loving nature was a link to my father's loving heart. We lived far apart, yet I always knew that she was just a phone call away. She would pick up the phone with overflowing joy every time I called. I once asked her, "What is your greatest joy in life?" Without hesitation, she exclaimed, "My beautiful children and grandchildren." My Bubby and father had a very special bond and it's not a surprise that she passed away, at 97 years old, on my father's birthday.

My **Uncle Lenny Wasserman**, who encouraged me to write this book, and helped review the manuscript. Thank you for supporting my dreams.

My brothers and their wives, **Mendy and Leah, Shalom and Tzivia, Azriel and Chana,** for their support and friendship. Thank you, Chana, for motivating me to shine *Tatty*'s legacy. Thank you, Chana and Azriel, for helping to found and support the Rabbi Wasserman Legacy Fund.

My **Daddy Katzenberg**, for treating me as his own daughter and for elevating our lives with your beautiful davening and singing.

My sisters, **Racheli, Ziva, and Dina Tova** for welcoming me into their life like a true sister.

My sister **Racheli and Avrohom Jacks**, for being the first to contribute a major gift to our building campaign in 2014. Thank you, Racheli, for composing songs for numerous retreats since the very start.

My husband and soulmate, **Rabbi Avraham Laber**, for his endless love, patience, and support throughout my journey and for being my devoted partner in life, as well as helping to edit this book. Thank you for being the most loving father to our children and for helping me juggle all of my responsibilities.

Ema and Abba Laber, for sharing in our vision and for being loving grandparents to our children

My Laber sisters-in-law for their friendship and for all the good times we share. Thank you, Dena and Nechama, for being counselors at our camp and for helping us in the early years.

My beloved children, Chaya Mushka, Chana, Azriel Yitzchok, Shaina, Raizel, Rivkah, Menachem Mendel, Yehudah Leib, Shneur Zalman, Baruch Mordechai, Yosef Chaim, son in law, Menachem Mendel Shepherd, and grandchildren, Azriel Yitzchok and Aharon. You have taught me to stretch myself beyond my limits. Thank you to my wonderful daughters for helping me at home while I wrote this book. I could never have done it without your assistance.

The Jewish Girls Retreat staff, who teach me so much and help me grow. There are too many staff members to list. You were all a huge part of my journey. Your impact on our campers is everlasting.

Thank you to **my campers and students** throughout the years who have taught me more then I could ever teach you. Thank you to the mothers and fathers who entrust their daughters in our care.

Leah Caras, my partner whose talent and devotion to connecting Jewish girls has created Jewish Girls Unite and designed this book.

Soul sister, **Linda Schwartz and Ory**, for being the founding benefactors for Jewish Girls Unite and the new campus, which created the vessel for more light to shine worldwide.

Coach **Susan Axelrod**, who became our JGU global strategy advisor, for teaching me helpful tools to lead an organization that is a fitting legacy for my father. Thank you for being available for me whenever I need you. Thank you for the numerous hours you spent speaking and brainstorming to create JGU since 2013. I have eternal gratitude to you for supporting my healing journey that lead to writing this book.

The JGU global leadership team of donors, artists, teachers, and singers, who share their skills with our Jewish daughters, spreading light and love.

With tremendous thanks to the generous underwriters of this book, and one of the founders of the Jewish Leadership Campus,

MICKI AND NORMAN MASSRY

whose support turned an idea into a reality and will inspire generations for all times.

GLOSSARY

Heb. = Hebrew | *Yid.* = Yiddish | *Ara.* = Aramaic | *Rus.* = Russian

A"h - *Heb.* This is an abbreviation of "*aleha/alav/aleihem hashalom* - peace be upon her/him/them."

Abba - *Heb.* Father

Adar - *Heb.* The twelfth Hebrew month of the (lunar) calendar; the month in which *Purim* is celebrated

Aleph-beis - *Heb.* The Hebrew alphabet

Alter Rebbe - *Yid.* Literally, "Elder Master," referring to Rabbi Schneur Zalman of Liadi (1745-1812), founder of the *Chabad Chassidic* movement and the first of the dynasty's seven *Rebbeim*

Amen - *Heb.* Literally, "so be it"; a response to a prayer or blessing, signifying acceptance of and belief in the words just stated

Am Yisrael - *Heb.* The Nation of Israel

Av (also, Menachem Av) - Literally, "father" (also, "father comforts"); the fifth Hebrew month of the (lunar) calendar; the month in which we mourn the destruction of Jerusalem and the Holy Temple

B'ezrat Hashem - *Heb.* With G-d's help

B'simchah - *Heb.* Joyful

Baal Shem Tov - *Heb.* Literally, "Master of the Good Name," referring to Rabbi Yisrael ben Eliezer (1698-1760), founder of the *Chassidic* movement

Bar/Bat Mitzvah - *Heb.* Literally, "Son/Daughter of the Commandment"; a Jewish boy who has reached the age of thirteen and a Jewish girl who has reached the age of twelve, becoming an adult in terms of Jewish Law and Divinely responsible for their own conduct; also refers to the celebration marking this occasion

Baruch Hashem - *Heb.* Literally, "Blessed is G-d," but also commonly used to mean, "Thank G-d"

Beis Hamikdash - *Heb.* The Holy Temple in Jerusalem

Bereishis - *Heb.* Literally, "in the beginning"; Genesis, the first of the *Five Books of Moses*

Bitachon - *Heb.* Trust (in G-d)

Bli ayin hara - *Heb.* Literally, "no evil eye"; a phrase customarily appended to mentioning another's praise or good fortune, to indicate the wish that no "evil eye" (i.e. envy, resentment) should affect the individual(s) discussed

Brachah [pl. Brachos] - *Heb.* Blessing

Bris - *Heb.* Literally, "covenant"; a shortened form of the expression "*bris milah* - the covenant of [ritual] circumcision" performed on a Jewish boy, usually at eight days old; the celebration marking this occasion

Bubby - *Yid.* Grandmother

Chabad (or Chabad-Lubavitch) - *Heb.* Acronym for "*chochmah* [wisdom]," "*binah* [understanding]" and "*daas* [knowledge]," the three intellectual faculties of the soul; a *Chassidic* movement established by Rabbi Shneur Zalman of Liadi in the later 1800s, centered in the Russian village of *Lubavitch* for over a century, emphasizing application of one's intellect in apprehending the One True G-d and His relationship with the world, the Divine purpose of every creation, and how to suffuse and elevate our every experience with this consciousness; of or relating to the *Chabad-Lubavitch* movement, a network of emissaries with centers stationed around the globe to disseminate Judaism

Challah - *Heb.* Literally, "loaf;" the traditional, often-braided bread blessed and partaken of at Jewish celebrations and festive meals; originally the portion separated from the dough and given to the priest as a gift in Temple times

Chanukah - *Heb.* Literally, "[re]dedication"; the eight-day winter holiday beginning on *Kislev* 25, celebrated with thanksgiving and kindling the *menorah's* lights in commemoration of two miracles: the recapture and rededication of the second Holy Temple by the Maccabee Jewish legion after its defilement by the Syrian-Greeks, and the final small jar of ritually pure oil which lasted eight whole days to keep the Temple *menorah* lit until new oil was produced

Chas v'shalom - *Heb.* Literally, "mercy and peace"; often appended to a mention or illustration of adversity as an expression of one's fervent wish that the feared negativity should be replaced with G-d's compassion and peace

Chassid [pl. Chassidim] - *Heb.* Literally, "pious one"; a Jew who goes beyond the letter of the law in his *Torah* observance and service of G-d and does everything with vitality and joy; one who adheres to the ways of *Chassidus* and studies its teachings; a member of the *Chassidic* community, or a follower of a *Chassidic Rebbe*

Chassidic - Of or relating to *Chassidus*

Chassidus - *Heb.* Literally, "piety"; Hasidism; the eighteenth-century movement founded in Eastern Europe by the *Baal Shem Tov* which revived Judaism at a physically and spiritually adverse time in history, with strong focuses on the importance of the mystical dimension alongside the practical in serving G-d, the power of joy, love of G-d and one's fellow, and our task to reveal the G-dly spark within all of creation; the teachings and ideology of the movement, which are based upon *Kabbalah*

Chayal - *Heb.* Soldier

Chazzan - *Heb.* Literally, "cantor"; one who leads the congregation in a prayer service

Cheshbon tzedek - *Heb.* Literally, "righteous [i.e. honest] introspection"

Cheshvan - *Heb.* The eighth Hebrew month of the Jewish (lunar) calendar (also called "Marcheshvan"); the month in which no holidays are celebrated, and Jews in Israel begin praying for rain

Chevron - *Heb.* Hebron, a city in southern Israel; one of the "four holy cities" of Israel in Jewish tradition (the other three of which are Jerusalem, Safed and Tiberias)

Chol Hamoed - *Heb.* Literally, the "weekday during the festival"; the semi-festive intermediate days of *Pesach* and *Sukkos*

Chumash - *Heb.* The *Five Books of Moses*, the first section of the Written *Torah*

Chuppah - *Heb.* Canopy beneath which a bride and groom are wed; the marriage ceremony

Daas - *Heb.* Literally, "knowledge"; consciousness; the third of the ten Divine creative energies or attributes (reflected within the human soul); the bridgelike third phase of intellect, at which concepts have developed from a flash of intuition and contemplation, and are now made applicable in one's emotions and actions

Daven - *Yid.* Pray

Devarim - *Heb.* Literally, "words" or "things"; the fifth of the *Five Books of Moses*

Din - *Heb.* Judgement; law or ruling

Dirah b'tachtonim - *Heb.* Literally, "a dwelling-place [for G-d] in the lower realms"; the essential Jewish concept (emphasized by *A"h* - *Heb.* This is an abbreviation of "*aleha/alav/aleihem hashalom* - peace be upon her/him/them."

Abba - *Heb.* Father

Adar - *Heb.* The twelfth Hebrew month of the (lunar) calendar; the month in which *Purim* is celebrated

Aleph-beis - *Heb.* The Hebrew alphabet

Alter Rebbe - *Yid.* Literally, "Elder Master," referring to Rabbi Schneur Zalman of Liadi (1745-1812), founder of the *Chabad Chassidic* movement and the first of the dynasty's seven *Rebbeim*

Amen - *Heb.* Literally, "so be it"; a response to a prayer or blessing, signifying acceptance of and belief in the words just stated

Am Yisrael - *Heb.* The Nation of Israel

Av (also, Menachem Av) - Literally, "father" (also, "father comforts"); the fifth Hebrew month of the (lunar) calendar; the month in which we mourn the destruction of Jerusalem and the Holy Temple

B'ezrat Hashem - *Heb.* With G-d's help

B'simchah - *Heb.* Joyful

Baal Shem Tov - *Heb.* Literally, "Master of the Good Name," referring to Rabbi Yisrael ben Eliezer (1698-1760), founder of the *Chassidic* movement

Bar/Bat Mitzvah - *Heb.* Literally, "Son/Daughter of the Commandment"; a Jewish boy who has reached the age of thirteen and a Jewish girl who has reached the age of twelve, becoming an adult in terms of Jewish Law and Divinely responsible for their own conduct; also refers to the celebration marking this occasion

Baruch Hashem - *Heb.* Literally, "Blessed is G-d," but also commonly used to mean, "Thank G-d"

Beis Hamikdash - *Heb.* The Holy Temple in Jerusalem

Bereishis - *Heb.* Literally, "in the beginning"; Genesis, the first of the *Five Books of Moses*

Bitachon - *Heb.* Trust (in G-d)

Bli ayin hara - *Heb.* Literally, "no evil eye"; a phrase customarily appended to mentioning another's praise or good fortune, to indicate the wish that no "evil eye" (i.e. envy, resentment) should affect the individual(s) discussed

Brachah [pl. Brachos] - *Heb.* Blessing

Bris - *Heb.* Literally, "covenant"; a shortened form of the expression "*bris milah* - the covenant of [ritual] circumcision" performed on a Jewish boy, usually at eight days old; the celebration marking this occasion

Bubby - *Yid.* Grandmother

Chabad (or Chabad-Lubavitch) - *Heb.* Acronym for "*chochmah* [wisdom]," "*binah* [understanding]" and "*daas* [knowledge]," the three intellectual faculties of the soul; a *Chassidic* movement established by Rabbi Shneur Zalman of Liadi in the later 1800s, centered in the Russian village of *Lubavitch* for over a century, emphasizing application of one's intellect in apprehending the One True G-d and His relationship with the world, the Divine purpose of every creation, and how to suffuse and elevate our every experience with this consciousness; of or relating to the *Chabad-Lubavitch* movement, a network of emissaries with centers stationed around the globe to disseminate Judaism

Challah - *Heb.* Literally, "loaf;" the traditional, often-braided bread blessed and partaken of at Jewish celebrations and festive meals; originally the portion separated from the dough and given to the priest as a gift in Temple times

Chanukah - *Heb.* Literally, "[re]dedication"; the eight-day winter holiday beginning on *Kislev* 25, celebrated with thanksgiving and kindling the *menorah's* lights in commemoration of two miracles: the recapture and rededication of the second Holy Temple by the Maccabee Jewish legion after its defilement by the Syrian-Greeks, and the final small jar of ritually pure oil which lasted eight whole days to keep the Temple *menorah* lit until new oil was produced

Chas v'shalom - *Heb.* Literally, "mercy and peace"; often appended to a mention or illustration of adversity as an expression of one's fervent wish that the feared negativity should be replaced with G-d's compassion and peace

Chassid [pl. Chassidim] - *Heb.* Literally, "pious one"; a Jew who goes beyond the letter of the law in his *Torah* observance and service of G-d and does everything with vitality and joy; one who adheres to the ways of *Chassidus* and studies its teachings; a member of the *Chassidic* community, or a follower of a *Chassidic Rebbe*

Chassidic - Of or relating to *Chassidus*

Chassidus - *Heb.* Literally, "piety"; Hasidism; the eighteenth-century movement founded in Eastern Europe by the *Baal Shem Tov* which revived Judaism at a physically and spiritually adverse time in history, with strong focuses on the importance of the mystical dimension alongside the practical in serving G-d, the power of joy, love of G-d and one's fellow, and our task to reveal the G-dly spark within all of creation; the teachings and ideology of the movement, which are based upon *Kabbalah*

Chayal - *Heb.* Soldier

Chazzan - *Heb.* Literally, "cantor"; one who leads the congregation in a prayer service

Cheshbon tzedek - *Heb.* Literally, "righteous [i.e. honest] introspection"

Cheshvan - *Heb.* The eighth Hebrew month of the Jewish (lunar) calendar (also called "Marcheshvan"); the month in which no holidays are celebrated, and Jews in Israel begin praying for rain

Chevron - *Heb.* Hebron, a city in southern Israel; one of the "four holy cities" of Israel in Jewish tradition (the other three of which are Jerusalem, Safed and Tiberias)

Chol Hamoed - *Heb.* Literally, the "weekday during the festival"; the semi-festive intermediate days of *Pesach* and *Sukkos*

Chumash - *Heb.* The *Five Books of Moses*, the first section of the Written *Torah*

Chuppah - *Heb.* Canopy beneath which a bride and groom are wed; the marriage ceremony

Daas - *Heb.* Literally, "knowledge"; consciousness; the third of the ten Divine creative energies or attributes (reflected within the human soul); the bridgelike third phase of intellect, at which concepts have developed from a flash of intuition and contemplation, and are now made applicable in one's emotions and actions

Daven - *Yid.* Pray

Devarim - *Heb.* Literally, "words" or "things"; the fifth of the *Five Books of Moses*

Din - *Heb.* Judgement; law or ruling

Dirah b'tachtonim - *Heb.* Literally, "a dwelling-place [for G-d] in the lower realms"; the essential Jewish concept (emphasized by *Chassidus*) that G-d desired to create an existence where His Omnipresence is concealed, in order for us to reveal the Divine essence in the material universe, by elevating it to serve G-d according to His will and thereby transform it into a place welcoming His presence

Dovid HaMelech - *Heb.* King David

Dugma chaya - *Heb.* A living example

Dvar Torah - *Heb.* Literally, a "word of *Torah*"; a *Torah* thought one presents

Emunah - *Heb.* Faith (in G-d)

Erev - *Heb.* Eve

Farbrengen - *Yid.* An assemblage of *Chassidim* addressed by a Rebbe, or informal gathering filled with singing and inspiring talk, strengthening resolve to *Torah*, *Mitzvos* and spiritual growth.

Gabbai - *Heb.* A warden, who assists in synagogue services or other matters to maintain their organization

Gan Eden - *Heb.* The Garden of Eden, from which Adam and Eve were banished after their sin of eating the forbidden fruit

Gemara - *Ara.* Literally, "study"; collectively, the recorded elucidative discussions and debates of the Sages on the *Mishnah*, which comprise the bulk of *Talmud* (see glossary below for "*Talmud*" and further elaboration)

Geulah - *Heb.* Redemption

Gezunt - *Yid.* Good health

Golah - *Heb.* Exile

Haggadah - *Heb.* Literally, "the [re]telling"; the volume which guides the *Pesach Seder*, primarily recounting the Exodus narrative and wonders G-d wrought for our People along the way

Halachah [pl. Halachos] - *Heb.* Literally, "the pathway"; Jewish law (in the general overarching sense as well as the term for a single law), guiding every aspect of life as a Jew

Hamantash - *Yid.* Literally, "Haman's pocket"; a triangular-shaped cookie with a tasty filling, symbolic of our enemy Haman's pockets from which he bribed the Persian monarch for permission to annihilate the Jews at the time of the *Purim* story

Hashem - *Heb.* Literally, "the Name"; G-d

Hatzlachah rabbah - *Heb.* "Much success"; a popular phrase meant as a sort of blessing, that one should have much success in their endeavor(s)

Havdalah - *Heb.* Literally, "separation"; the blessings recited over wine, (usually) a special candle and spices, after the Sabbath's conclusion, to signify the weekly transition from the holy dimension back to the mundane

Hoshana Rabbah - *Heb.* Literally, "the great salvation"; the seventh day of *Sukkos*, considered to be the day of finalization of *Tishrei's* Divine judgement, whose customary observances include remaining awake the entire preceding night to study *Torah*, processions in the synagogue called "*Hoshanos*," and beating willow switches on the floor to symbolically 'sweeten' Divine severities

Igros Kodesh - *Heb.* Literally, "holy letters"; a collection of letters by the seventh *Lubavitcher Rebbe*, Rabbi Menachem M. Schneerson, in correspondence to the countless requests that he received daily for blessing and advice on virtually every subject, and at his behest were published in 1987 as a series of twenty-three volumes

Im yirtzeh Hashem - *Heb.* If G-d is willing

Ka"h - *Yid.* This is an abbreviation of "*kein ayin hara* - no evil eye" (see glossary above for "*bli ayin hara*" and further elaboration)

Kabbalah - *Heb.* Literally, "received tradition"; Jewish mysticism (passed down from a reliable *Torah* source), the foundational text of which is the *Zohar*, authored in hiding by the twelfth-century sage Rabbi Shimon bar Yochai

Kaddish - *Ara.* Literally, "holy"; a brief prayer recited by a mourner or whoever is leading the prayer service, in the presence of a *minyan*

Keli - *Heb.* Vessel or receptacle; utensil

Kiddush - *Heb.* Literally, "sanctification"; the blessing(s) recited, typically over wine, to declare the holiness of a Sabbath or festival; the repast or refreshments served after the actual recital of *Kiddush*

Kislev - *Heb.* The ninth Hebrew month of the Jewish (lunar) calendar; the month in which *Chanukah* celebrations begin

Klal Yisrael - *Heb.* All of Israel; the collective Jewish People

Ko'ach [pl. Kochos] - *Heb.* Strength; power

Kohanim - *Heb.* Priests; descendants of Aharon, the first High Priest, entrusted with the precious service of the Holy Temple

Kol Nidrei - *Heb.* Literally, "all the vows"; the solemn prayer releasing one of their vows in the past year and commencing the *Yom Kippur* evening services

Kosher - *Heb.* Literally, "fit"; complying with the Divinely-endowed dietary laws set forth in *halachah*, fit for a Jew's consumption; fit to be used for ritual purposes

L'chaim - *Heb.* Literally, "to life"; a blessing, proclamation or toast, often made over alcohol or another beverage

Likutei Sichos - *Heb.* Literally, "collected talks"; the transcripted, edited and published collection of the *Lubavitcher Rebbe's* talks

Likutei Torah - *Heb.* Literally, "collected teaching"; a classic treasury of *Chassidic* discourses by the *Alter Rebbe*, collected and edited by his grandson and the third *Lubavitcher Rebbe*, Rabbi Menachem Mendel

Lubavitch - *Rus.* Literally, "City of Brotherly Love"; a village in White Russia, whose residents are called "*Lubavitchers*" (see glossary above for "*Chabad*" and further elaboration)

Maharash - *Heb.* The acronym by which the fourth *Rebbe* of *Chabad-Lubavitch*, Rabbi Shmuel, was known

Malachim - *Heb.* Angels

Mashpia - *Heb.* Literally, "source of influence"; a spiritual Jewish mentor

Mazal tov - *Heb.* Literally, "good fortune"; a popular expression often used in a context similar to "congratulations," and a blessing that one should continue to merit good fortune

Me'aras Hamachpelah - *Heb.* The Cave of Machpelah, located in *Chevron*, Israel; the burial site of Adam and Eve, Abraham and Sarah, Isaac and Rebecca, Jacob and Leah (but not our Matriarch Rachel).

Megillas Esther - *Heb.* Literally, the "Scroll of Esther"; the book read annually on *Purim*, describing the Persian minister Haman's scheme for Jewish genocide, its overturn by G-d's hidden hand through Queen Esther and the sage Mordechai, and the establishment of the *Purim* holiday in commemoration

Mei'chayil el chayil - *Heb.* Literally, "from strength to strength"; an expression taken from *Tehillim* 84:8, used to describe or encourage steady progression or increase in all good things

Mekabel - *Heb.* Literally, "receiver"; often contextualized as the counterpart to a *mashpia*

Melech Malchei Hamealachim HaKadosh Baruch Hu - *Heb.* The King of All Kings, the Holy One, Blessed Be He

Menachem avel - *Heb.* Comforting a mourner; the act of visiting the mourner to provide consolation and support

Menorah - *Heb.* Literally, "to illuminate," derived from the Hebrew word "*ner*," meaning a "lamp"; the eight-branched candelabra on which an additional flame is lit each night of *Chanukah*, commemorating the miracle of oil; the seven-branched gold candelabra kindled daily in the Holy Temple

Metodika - *Heb.* "Methods in Teaching"; a subject and course of study for Jewish educators-in-training

Middas hadin - *Heb.* The (Divine) attribute of judgement or severity

Minyan - *Heb.* A prayer quorum of ten Jewish adult males

Mishnah - *Heb.* Literally, "[to study and] review"; the first compilation, by Rabbi Yehudah HaNasi (approximately 200 C.E.), of the orally-transmitted laws of *Torah*; a single law from this masterwork, the basic statements of which are elucidated by the *Gemara* to form the *Talmud*

Mitzvah [pl. Mitzvos] - *Heb.* Literally, "commandment"; one of the six hundred and thirteen Divine commandments transmitted in the Torah; also stems from the Aramaic root "*tzavsa*," meaning "connection," since its performance binds you to G-d

Mizmor l'Dovid - *Heb.* Literally, "a song of David"; a reference to a chapter of Psalms opening with these words [note that while there are many Psalms beginning with "*Mizmor l'Dovid*," the individual cited by the author meant the twenty-third chapter]

Modeh Ani - *Heb.* Literally, "I give thanks" or "I acknowledge"; the brief prayer of gratitude to G-d for restoring the soul and a new day of life, recited upon awakening in the morning

Mohel - *Heb.* Ritual circumciser

Moshiach - *Heb.* Literally, "the anointed"; the Messiah, our long-awaited Jewish leader descended from King David, who will usher in the everlasting era of Redemption, universal peace and awareness of G-d

Motzoei - *Heb.* The "conclusion" or "departure" of

Nachas - *Heb.* Joy and satisfaction (often in the context of parents from their children)

Nechamah - *Heb.* Comfort or consolation

Neilah - *Heb.* Literally, "closing"; the fifth and final prayer of the *Yom Kippur* services, before the day's conclusion, when the heavenly gates are being 'closed,' explained by *Chasssidic* masters to be secluding us with G-d

Neshamah [pl. Neshamos] - *Heb.* Soul

Neshek - *Heb.* This is an acronym for "*neiros Shabbos kodesh* - the holy Sabbath candles"; in Hebrew, this word also literally means "weapon" (and our *Shabbos* candles are our potent weapons to overcome darkness in the world!).

Niggun [pl. Niggunim] - *Heb.* A melody (often wordless)

Nissan - *Heb.* The first Hebrew month of the Jewish (lunar) calendar; the month in which *Pesach* is celebrated

Ob"m - Acronym for "**o**f **b**lessed **m**emory"

Ohel - *Heb.* Literally, "tent"; a term used in reference to the burial site of the *Lubavitcher Rebbe* and his father-in-law, the Previous *Lubavitcher Rebbe*, open to any person seeking connection, blessing or guidance, located in the Montefiore Cemetery in Queens, New York

Ohr Hatorah - *Heb.* Literally, "the light of the *Torah*"; a compendium of *Chassidic* thought encompassing a vast array of subjects, by the third *Lubavitcher Rebbe*, Rabbi Menachem Mendel

Oneg - *Heb.* Literally, "delight" or "pleasure"; often refers to an informal Friday-night social gathering for enjoyment of the Sabbath

Parashah - *Heb.* Literally, "portion," "passage" or "section"; commonly used in reference to the weekly *Torah* portion from the *Five Books of Moses* to be read on the Sabbath

Pasuk [pl. Pesukim] - *Heb.* Verse

Pesach - *Heb.* Passover; the seven-day festival (eight outside of Israel) beginning on *Nissan* 15, in commemoration of our miraculous liberation from Egyptian bondage; the name of the special offering brought up in the Holy Temple on *Erev Pesach*

Pesukei D'Zimra - *Heb.* Literally, "verses of praise"; the selection of praises, primarily sourced from *Tehillim*, that constitute a significant section in the morning prayer service

Pirkei Avot - *Heb.* Literally, "chapters of the fathers" (also known as *Ethics of the Fathers*); another name for the tractate called "*Avot*" in the *Mishnah*, containing ethical teachings from the *Torah*'s perspective as taught by our Sages

Purim - *Heb.* Literally, "lots" (as in a lottery); the holiday celebrated amidst great joy with the reading of *Megillas Esther* and other distinct *Mitzvos* on *Adar* 14, in commemoration of our miraculous salvation from genocide at the hands of the Persian minister Haman

Rambam - *Heb.* Acronym for **Rabbi Moshe ben Maimon** (also known as Maimonides), a renowned Rabbinic scholar and prolific author, as well as philosopher and physician in the twelfth century, born in Spain

Rebbe [pl. Rebbeim] - *Heb.* Literally, "my master" (like "Rabbi"); acronym for "**Rosh Bnei Yisroel** - Head of the Children of Israel"; a *Chassidic* master who guides *Chassidim* (and often far beyond); frequently, the appellation is used to simply refer to the seventh *Lubavitcher Rebbe*, Rabbi Menachem M. Schneerson, of righteous memory

Rebbetzin - *Yid.* Wife of a Rabbi; the appellation is often used in reference to a specific individual (e.g. the *Rebbetzin*, i.e. Chaya Mushka, wife of the *Lubavitcher Rebbe*, Rabbi Menachem M. Schneerson)

Refuah sheleimah - *Heb.* Complete recovery

Rosh Chodesh - *Heb.* Literally, "head of the month"; the one- or two-day mini festival marking the beginning of each Hebrew month, wherein the moon is at minimum visibility and starts its cycle anew

Rosh Hashanah - *Heb.* Literally, "head of the year"; the serious yet joyful Jewish New Year (the first of the High Holidays) occurring on *Tishrei* 1-2 and initiating the Ten Days of Repentance; the anniversary of Adam and Eve's creation, when the universe was completed and is renewed, when we coronate G-d as our King, when we are Divinely judged for our conduct in the past year and our future for the coming year is decreed; also called "Yom Teruah - Day of Blasting [a ram's horn]," "Yom Hazikaron - Day of Remembrance," and "Yom Hadin - Day of Judgment"

Rosh Yeshiva - *Heb.* Literally, the "head of the [*Torah* or *Talmudic*] academy," i.e. the dean

Seder - *Heb.* Literally, "order"; the orderly service observed on the first night of *Pesach* (the first two nights outside of Israel), which includes recounting our exodus from Egypt, song-filled praise of G-d, a festive meal corresponding to the original *Pesach* offering, and much more

Sephardic - *Heb.* Of or relating to Spanish-rooted Jewry ("*Sepharad*" is Hebrew for "Spain") and their customs

Seudah - *Heb.* Meal

Shabbat Shalom - *Heb.* Literally, "a peaceful Sabbath"; a customary greeting and blessing exchanged between Jews shorty before and during the Sabbath

Shabbaton - *Heb.* An inspirational, celebratory and often educational program or gathering on *Shabbos*

Shabbos [pl. Shabbosos] - *Heb.* Literally, "rest" or "cessation [of work, creation]"; the Sabbath, established by G-d as a day of rest on the seventh day of the week

Shalom Aleichem - *Heb.* Literally, "peace unto you"; a typical form of greeting; a song traditionally sung on Friday night to acknowledge the angels who've escorted us home from the synagogue

Shelah - *Heb.* Acronym for "**Shnei Luchot Habrit** [The Two Tablets of the Covenant]" the title of a legal, ethical and esoteric masterwork by Rabbi Yeshayahu Halevi Horowitz (1565-1630); also a reference to the author himself

Shema - *Heb.* Literally, to "hear"; the Biblically-mandated daily declaration of faith and devotion to G-d, recited in the morning and evening, and before going to sleep at night

Shemos - *Heb.* Literally, "names"; Exodus, the second of the *Five Books of Moses*

Shevat - *Heb.* The eleventh Hebrew month of the Jewish (lunar) calendar; the month in which *Tu B'Shevat* is celebrated

Shidduchim - *Heb.* Matches, specifically for (potential) marriage partners

Shir Hamaalos - *Heb.* Literally, "a song of ascents;" a reference to the multiple psalms opening with these words, but often specifically the one hundred and twenty-sixth chapter as an introduction to the Grace After Meals on festive occasions

Shirah - *Heb.* Song (often of praise)

Shivah - *Heb.* Literally, "seven"; the seven-day period of mourning for an immediate relative, following their burial

Shlichus - *Heb.* "Mission," "agency" or "task"

Shloshim - *Heb.* Literally, "thirty"; the first thirty-day period of mourning following the funeral of an immediate relative's passing; often refers to the memorial gathering at the consummation of the first thirty days

Shlucha [pl. Shluchos] - *Heb.* A female emissary

Shluchim - *Heb.* Emissaries; this expression is frequently used in reference to a *Chabad-Lubavitch* Rabbi-and-wife team who further Jewish life and involvement

Shul - *Yid.* Synagogue

Sichah [pl. Sichos] - *Heb.* A talk; often used especially in reference to a talk given by the *Lubavitcher Rebbe*, of righteous memory

Sidrah - *Heb.* Literally, "order"; the week's order of the *Torah* portion to be read on *Shabbos*

Simchah [pl. Simchos] - *Heb.* Literally, "joy"; a joyous occasion

Simchas Torah - *Heb.* Literally, "the rejoicing of the *Torah*"; the festival occurring in the immediate wake of *Sukkos*, when the annual *Torah*-reading cycle is publicly concluded and begun again amidst great joy, singing, dancing, and chant-filled processions with the *Torah* scrolls

Sukkah - *Heb.* Literally, "booth"; the temporary structure in which we celebrate and dwell for the weeklong festival of *Sukkos*, reminiscent of our ancestors' actual nomadic habitations during their forty-year desert sojourn, or the fully-encompassing Clouds of Divine Glory with which G-d sheltered them from any harm

Sukkos - *Heb.* Literally, "booths"; the joyous seven-day (eight outside of Israel) autumn festival, also called "*Chag Ha'Asif* - Festival of the Ingathering," beginning on *Tishrei* 15, distinguished by the *mitzvos* of dwelling in a *Sukkah* and taking the Four Species (date-palm frond, citron, myrtle and willow)

Talmud - *Heb.* Literally, "study"; the primary compendium of Jewish law and thought, comprised of the *Mishnah* together with its corresponding *Gemara*, divided into tractates; the unspecified term usually refers to the edition of *Talmud* developed in the Babylonian *yeshivos* and revised at the end of the fifth century C.E., while there is also the *Jerusalem Talmud* compiled in Israel at the turn of the fourth century C.E.

Tammuz - *Heb.* The fourth Hebrew month of the (lunar) calendar; the month in which the Fast of *Tammuz* 17 is commemorated and begins the three-week period of mourning the siege and destruction of Jerusalem

Tanya - *Heb.* Literally, "we have learned"; the foundational masterwork of *Chabad Chassidic* philosophy, penned by its founder, Rabbi Schneur Zalman of Liadi, or *Baal HaTanya* ("Master of the *Tanya*"), based on the essential concept that serving G-d in this existence is a real and achievable goal, and exploring how we understand G-d, the human soul's anatomy and the purpose of creation

Tatty - *Yid.* Father; Daddy

Tefillah - *Heb.* Literally, "attachment" or "to judge"; prayer

Tefillin - *Heb.* Phylacteries; carefully-crafted, black leather cubes housing selected *Torah* passages on parchment scrolls, which are bound upon the arm and head by adult males

Tehillim - *The Book of Psalms*, authored by King David

Tishah B'Av - *Heb.* The ninth day of the Hebrew month of *Av*; the anniversary of the destruction of both the first and second Holy Temples in Jerusalem, marked by a day of day of fasting, mourning and repentance, but with an undercurrent of hope and promise, as it's traditionally taught to also be the birthday of the Messiah

Tishrei - *Heb.* The seventh Hebrew month of the Jewish (lunar) calendar; the month in which the High Holidays - primarily *Rosh Hashanah* and *Yom Kippur* - are celebrated

Torah - *Heb.* Literally, "teaching"; often used in specific reference to the *Five Books of Moses* or the Bible; the all-encompassing body of Jewish religious teachings and tradition, laws and observance; G-d's contraction of His infinite will and wisdom, the 'blueprint' with which He creates the universe, into the 613 commandments whose fulfillment fulfills the purpose of Creation: to reveal the Divine essence within all existence

Torah Or - *Heb.* Literally, "the *Torah* is light" (Proverbs 6:23); a classic collection of *Chassidic* discourses by the *Alter Rebbe*

Toras Chaim - *Heb.* Literally, "the *Torah* of life"; a two-volume compilation of *Chassidic* discourses by the second *Chabad Rebbe*, Rabbi Dovber Schneuri, on the Mosaic books of Genesis and Exodus

Tu B'Av - *Heb.* The fifteenth day of the Hebrew month of *Av*; a mini holiday (the greatest of the year, says the *Talmud*) and time of renewal, being the anniversary of multiple joyous events in Jewish history further accentuated by the earlier tragedies of the month; a day when the *Talmud* describes that historically, new marriages would be made between the young men and women of Jerusalem

Tu B'Shevat - *Heb.* The fifteenth day of the Hebrew month of *Shevat*; the mini holiday celebrated as the "new year for trees," around which time the trees in Israel first begin to bloom in the renewed fruit-bearing cycle, and it is customary to partake of different fruits, particularly the Seven Species for which the Land of Israel is praised in the *Torah*

Tzaddik [pl. Tzaddikim] - *Heb.* A [completely] righteous person; one who has eliminated his animal impulses and is filled with devotion to G-d

Tzaharayim - *Heb.* Midday

Tzarah - *Heb.* Affliction, difficulty, pain

Tzefat - *Heb.* Safed, a city in northern Israel; one of the "four holy cities" of Israel in Jewish tradition (the other three of which are Jerusalem, Hebron and Tiberias)

Tzohar - *Heb.* "Light," or "radiance"

Yahrtzeit - *Yid.* Anniversary of a passing

Yerushalayim - *Heb.* Jerusalem, the capital city of Israel situated in the Judaean Mountains; the most sacred city in the world and site of the Holy Temple; one of the "four holy cities" of Israel in Jewish tradition (the other three of which are Hebron, Safed and Tiberias)

Yeshivah [pl. Yeshivos] - *Heb.* Literally, "sitting"; an academy of *Torah* study

Yiddishkeit - *Yid.* Judaism; one's essential Jewishness

Yizkor - *Heb.* Literally, to "remember"; the special memorial prayer for the deceased - especially one's parents - recited on certain festival days, bringing merit to and elevating the soul

Yom Kippur - *Heb.* Literally, "the Day of Atonement"; the solemn fast day and holiest day of the year, occurring on *Tishrei* 10, when we connect to our pure soul-essence and G-d determines our judgment for the coming year

Z"l - *Heb.* This is an abbreviation of *"zecher livrachah* - [his] memory is for a blessing."

Zemiros - *Heb.* Literally, "hymns"; special, poetic Sabbath and festival melodies typically sung over the meal

Zt"l - *Heb.* This is an abbreviation of *"zecher tzaddik livracha* - [the] memory of a righteous person is for a blessing."

www.ingramcontent.com/pod-product-compliance
Lightning Source LLC
Chambersburg PA
CBHW021937290426
44108CB00012B/872